RED FLAGS

&ROSES

and everything in between

Susan Harrison

RED FLAGS AND ROSES
and everything in between

Editor: Eleonor Smith
Cover design and typesetting: Wade Hunkin

Set in Garamond 14/16

TR
publishing

Cassidy Summers, my courageous and beautiful god daughter for pushing me to climb the last hurdle.

This book is dedicated to you with thanks and gratitude.

CHAPTER 1
IT'S A BUZZ

I lounged in my newly acquired, gorgeous, spacious three-bedroom apartment overlooking the picturesque Kalk Bay Harbour with a spectacular, azure sea view encased with shades of soft pink, red, white, blue, orange and yellow. With large soft couches and high ceilings, it was elegant and welcoming.

I moved here eight months ago, after my separation from my husband of eleven years. There were no ugly fights, no ugly words, or hard feelings. We had spent eleven amazing years together. He was a fair bit younger than me. We embarked on a wonderful eleven-year journey that often felt like a lot longer, because we packed so much into it. Sadly, eventually, our road had run its course.

I was past chasing money, taking risks and felt we had both had enough. He was on the crest of a wave that had to be ridden and deserved to be surfed, in all its glory. Our lifestyles had changed, he loved to cycle, lived on adrenalin, took massive risks, raced motorcycles and dreamt, big. I still rode my Harley, which in the beginning, was a passion we both shared. He no longer loved a Harley, in fact, he hated them and all Harley riders were *persona non grata* in his book. He was eating special meals to be thinner for competitive cycling and was no longer the short, well-built man I had fallen in love with. He was racing competitively on race tracks on a motorbike. I was older now and not into cycling. (I had done my bit of being a spectator on the side, with a previous partner who raced motor cycles.) I was not about to sit watching motorbikes chase around a race track on Saturday afternoons either, when glorious sunshine beckoned, and beaches and mountain walks were calling. Eleven years earlier we had met on a Harley weekend away. He was my knight in shining armour and I fell hard. So did

1

he, and we were incredibly happy. He was everything I ever dreamed of and the Love of My Life. Today he still is, but I no longer own him, my love was way bigger than that.

We sat and had an open chat about it just before Christmas that year, and agreed our time was done. We had other lives to live and needed to do so, separately. Our big house we were renovating was to be his home going forward. He had the energy, drive and ambition to do so, whereas I was done with moving, as we dreamed bigger and better. I had for the better part of our relationship, moved on average every two years. We were both in the real estate industry and had bought and sold many homes that we had renovated. He did some developments as well, mostly commercial.

Right now, however, the recent euphoria of selfish indulgence had worn a little thin! I had seen all my single friends that I had neglected during my marriage. I had also done a solo three-week sojourn in an adorable cottage nestled at the foot of the mountains on a farm in the middle of nowhere. I had done countless Harley rides with magnificent sunsets, and spent many a night watching "romcom" movies that men never like, doing exactly as I pleased, and as I wanted.

I logged into my laptop and started to browse. Dating Buzz caught my eye among the assortment of dating sites that my friend Mr Google, coughed out

I liked the sound of it being a bit of a buzz. I was not looking for Mr Future, but rather Mr Part-time Fun, preferably a flight away to avoid any ideas of permanence, or love! I had experienced the great love of my life. I had a successful busy career that filled much of my time. I was happy alone, particularly because I did not have to cook, or to be domesticated. Cooking meals is something I have never understood! All those hours preparing a meal, only for it to disappear in thirty minutes, never mind the dishes that piled high and Lord oh Lord, those pots and pans! Woolworths has a great supply of ready-cooked meals, and a roast chicken lasts ages, when there is only one person in the house!

I set myself at best, an hour to complete the profile and questions. An hour goes by and I have not yet completed my profile. So many questions! I call myself "Joy of Living" describing myself as an independent, financially stable fun seeker and adventurer, who loves last-minute impromptu outings and escapes. That I love my Harley almost as much as my dog! Two wheels and shooting the breeze, my dog and independence – life does not get better than this! I realise that this is in fact, true. I ask myself, *What are you doing on here?* I even like to travel solo! I realise that my life is an adventure and that there just might be someone out there who is like me. I am, in essence, looking for an addition to my already full life that will make it even more complete. Besides, I have never done online dating and I am essentially up for new adventures!

The next one has me stumped for hours as I have to choose six pictures of myself that best describe me. I know from my career in real estate that a great picture sells a house. It occurs to me that I am selling myself! This makes me a little uncomfortable as I conjure up images of women on sidewalks, *ladies of the night*, and I have to stop and get my head around this picture that keeps crossing my vision. I berate myself and tell myself that everyone on here is doing it!

I find the perfect picture! It's one of my favourites. Beautiful. My hair is full, my smile wide and my pale blue eyes are striking. My best feature, so this is good! I am delighted and proceed to paste this as my first picture in my profile. But I stop as I realise this picture is two years old and then, to my horror, figure out that it's actually five years old! How is it possible that it was so long ago when it feels like it was yesterday? I try to convince myself that this picture is okay and that I have not changed much. Anti-wrinkle injections are after all a great "pick me up" for faces! I dash to the mirror and take a long hard look.

What looks back is not the person in the picture. The injections work, but not in all the lines and fine cracks, no matter how hard I try to kid myself. I sigh trundling back to my laptop, feeling less enthusiastic and a little weary. I sit down and decide it's enough for one night. I take my oversized pyjama-clad body, with very old slippers on my feet, down the passage and think, *Just as well this is not my profile pic!* I brush my teeth and get another look at myself and see that my hair has streaks of grey in it, despite my highlights. I decide to make a point of discussing this with my hairdresser. I begin to wonder how much more I am going to get to see about myself before this profile is loaded? I don't feel one bit excited and begin to think that this is way too much trouble!

I climb into my soft, warm, comfy bed that is big enough for four. I have never had an extra-length, king-size bed before! This is pure luxury! I have also never rented a fully furnished apartment before! I was fortunate to find this rental while my divorce was finalizing. Gabi, my miniature Yorkie, is often lost on here and it feels like hide-and-seek to find her. Mind you, that is when she is allowed up here. Currently it's quite a lot, but she is well trained and knows that "Go to bed" means her bed!

My mind wonders and I think about this "online dating" and I can't find sleep. Despite being so successful I have to admit I am feeling a little daunted by the whole idea. It's all good and well to be adventurous, but this is a big step when one has never done anything like this before. I also realise that I have not been with anyone else for over eleven years. I get myself out of bed and drag my feet across the floor removing my clothes, and look at myself in the mirror, again. This time I am less critical of myself, probably because only the bedside light is on and my glasses are on my bedside table.

Not bad, I think. No children, so no tummy that is doing its own thing! Good breasts, yes, they have had a little help. They look well rounded, full, and more importantly, whilst they do tend to be battling with gravity, as I said before, I have seen younger woman with breasts that are just like mine! My skin is still good, *Thank you Mom for insisting on suntan lotions and for passing on your good UK genes and skin to me.* My long legs are still a good feature, with well-shaped calves and thighs and my turquoise blue eyes are beautiful. I am feeling a lot better and decide to sleep naked to get into the swing of things and feel comfortable nude. I forget about my earlier doubts and fall asleep.

My day is busy with various appointments and social engagements so it's a few days before I am able to sit down and complete the online profile for the dating app, Dating Buzz. I can't remember who suggested it and why, but it must have come up somewhere in a conversation. I like that it is comprehensive as this means I get to know a lot about the person before I decide to talk to them, plus it means that it is not based purely, on looks.

I pick up where I left off, but I look at one particular profile to see what this person has to say, as it may give me some ideas on what I need to still do and complete, before this questionnaire is done.

He calls himself something like this "DeoGloria555" and I am a little baffled as to why anyone would choose this, other than to hint that there is a touch of Portuguese and I wonder if I am missing something with the 555? 007 may have been more like it!

He describes himself as follows: "Friendly, caring and don't judge other people." My critical mind stops right here as he has left out the word "I". This means he either does not have a good command of the English language, or he is in a hurry. "Openminded and willing to share my life with the right person. Straightforward and no hassels". Another alert button goes off as it is now clear that he also cannot spell, hassles! "Able to be a good friend and lover." He is a tad overweight and balding. His only picture tells me he is rather staid and ordinary, and that his emphasis on "friend" is his strong attraction, as its unlikely to be his looks! I have completely lost interest even if this is a test! I quickly go back to finishing my profile before I decide that this is not a good idea!

The dating site also asks questions, usually you choose from the answers they provide. They are things like height, weight, hair colour etc., pretty standard stuff; gender, where you live, and so on. There are also questions on daily diet, smoking, education, children or not, occupation and income.

I get to the section where I need to describe what I am looking for in a few sentences. The thought comes to mind, *Me!* and I laugh at this thought. I can't exactly say Mr Part-time, so I try a more subtle approach and say my successful career is demanding and fills my life. That I seek quality not quantity, fun, adventure and laughter. That I prefer someone who lives out of town and who also has a complete life.

I do a quick check on what I have completed so far and move on. I am inundated with questions, most of them are multiple choice. I realise during this process that I do not know myself that well, as I have to think about which answer I actually prefer. In some instances, I look at the possible answers at least two or three times. I realise however that this will allow for a more accurate match and it makes sense. I don't like wasting time and my attention to detail is limited, as I prefer to speed read and in so doing, miss out a lot! This dating site is teaching me to be less rushed. A good thing!

Another hour has flown by and now there is still more. What is your ideal holiday? A world cruise, an island resort, bush adventure, traveling the world, a log cabin in the woods, etc. What do I choose? I can't for the life of me imagine why you could only choose one on this particular pastime.

I rethink the choices I do like and the island resort dives off the page as I realise gravity has taken its toll and there are a few extra kilos from the wine at sunsets. It's not my fault there are so many damn good sunsets! Perhaps I could be more specific, so I tick traveling the world. Bush adventures can be amazing too, but being in the middle of nowhere with only wild animals, snakes, spiders, has less appeal.

Eventually I am finally done and check it all again. I do the odd bit of tweaking. I also realise that this entire process has taken up about 4 hours of my time. I know, I know, the pictures could have gone a lot faster! I don't do "selfies". I don't see myself as pretty or beautiful. I would at best be attractive. One has to post solo pictures and preferably not with other people! The big moment has arrived for me to enter into the new age of online dating! At this stage I am already a slow mover as this new form of dating has been around for almost three years.

I hold my breath, close my eyes, and press "done"!

CHAPTER 2
MY FIRST DATE - NO GO JOE!

Joe has sent a message. He is Cape Town-based and lives close to where I do. It is so strange that people are in our midst and we don't know that they exist! He is an architect, sixty, arty and rather bohemian. Dark hair, green eyes, a full mouth and a little taller than me. He strikes me as being rather introspective and quiet. We chat a little and agree to meet over the weekend for a coffee at a cute coffee shop where beachgoers hang out, so it's casual and not far from where I live.

Saturday arrives, and I am in a tizz! I have no idea what to wear and clothes are strewn all over the room. The soft top in pale blues and pinks looks great but it is long and my leggings that go well with it are in the wash. Grrr.... The Grecian dress is too cold, even though it has long sleeves. I settle on a pair of white jeans that are calf length, sneakers, and an off-the-shoulder top in a pale blue that matches my eyes. Not too much make-up, shades, and a small backpack complete the look and I jog to the car, as I am now running late.

He is at a table in the corner and reading something on his phone. I approach apprehensively and it occurs to me that I have no idea what to say or how to behave. This is a first "coffee meet" as I prefer to call it, the word "date" is just too serious when you hardly know the person. He stands up when I approach and kisses my cheek and says, "Thank you for coming." *Lovely manners*, I think.

We engage in small talk and the usual questions, where did you grow up, past relationships, interests, occupation, etc. His hair is shiny and it's not from the gel or leave-in-conditioner he uses! It's greasy. I get all uncomfortable looking at him! That head is so going nowhere near any of my white, crisp linen pillowcases! Stubble covers his chin with patches of grey, white and dark brown. His loose shirt does not hide the onset of a paunch. He is engaging enough, but I am already on a conveyor belt out of there and feel fake, as I am unable to say: *We're not a match*, and excuse myself, which I wish I had the guts to say but I had only just got there. I even feel a little cross. How can he possibly come out on a date with an unshaven face and dirty hair. Worse it hangs in thin greasy strands around his head.

He is very nice and attentive, leaning forward as I speak, looking directly into my eyes and asking all about my dog! That is a sure way to get to my heart. Right now, I have to force my legs to not move, as my feet want to shuffle and move me out of there, badly! I make more small talk and, as soon as I can, I tell him that I have to leave. I shake his hand as I go and he leans in to kiss my cheek again. I am mortified. What on earth must I do? I say, "Thanks, but it's not working for me," and wonder what he must think? That is hardly the right and polite thing to do, so I move as fast as my legs will take me, and don't look back. I leave, pleased with my honesty. I left soon and that said it all really!

As I get into my car I am a little breathless and stressed. That was awkward and uncomfortable, to say the least! *Looking presentable is surely rule number one in anyone's book!* I think to myself. Surely? I decide that I will have to spend more time engaging online before I venture out on a first date! How to manage this however, is another story! I don't have time for lengthy chats online, or even on WhatsApp for that matter! My career is demanding and my life is full, so I have limited time to waste engaging in lengthy chats. The site is great in that it does match you well if the other person has completed their online profile properly. A lot of people do not. My take on this is that they are not serious, and purely looking. Or, they have time to waste and are not intelligent enough to understand the importance of this information. I generally don't respond to anyone who has not taken the time, or trouble, to give the necessary information as I don't want to waste time with questions that could have been answered online. Even as a newcomer I see the importance of this! What I do know is that greasy unkempt Joe, is definitely not for me!

CHAPTER 3
MIGHTY MIKE

I am three weeks into the dating scene and have found it very interesting. More so, because I have seen some people I know on there, men who are popular, well-known members of the Harley Club that I belong to, and this came as a complete surprise to me! I would have imagined they would have met many women purely by being a member of the Club and riding a lot? There is a very sociable Harley Club in the centre of town and there are always women there! But perhaps it's a case of not fishing in your own pond, as when it comes to a break-up, it can be awkward!

I start browsing the site. Johannesburg-based, marketing manager, fifty-two, travels to Cape Town twice a month. Fit and healthy. He describes himself as, "Fun, fit and easy going with a good sense of humour." He has two boys and they are very important to him and take up a lot of his time. He is not looking for a long-term relationship as he would like to raise his boys first. This is his priority. He is tall, about 2 meters and his t-shirt hugs a well-defined, ripped torso that oozes sex appeal. It's hold your breath stuff and close your eyes! He has an open face, big grey eyes and smiles a lot, in all his pictures. He is clearly confident and uncomplicated. I send him a cheeky message and say, "Not your average girl, interested and curious? I think the T-shirt needs to be disposed of?"

He sends a smile mojo and a wink. I wait. It's his move now. He sends a message, "I like cheeky girls. I happen to be in Cape Town next Friday. Let's meet for a drink?"

I say, "Do you promise to at least bring that t-shirt along so I can see it for real?"

He laughs, "I will wear it for you!"

"Let's touch base next week closer to the time and decide on a venue and time," I say, and send him my cell number.

Friday is here and work is busy. I have appointments and errands to run. My day goes well until about 3 p.m. when I reverse my car out of a driveway and don't realise there is a deep trench on either side of the small bridge, that covers this. I can't see this either in my rearview mirrors and reverse my convertible right into the, left-hand trench. The bottom of the car is now resting on the bridge and the wheel is suspended in mid-air. I am mortified! I get back into my car, drive forward, and fortunately I am able to get my car back on the road. I do however have to get to the panel beater as there is a scraping sound and some bits and pieces have come loose from the undercarriage.

Sharief greets me and says, "Neyh man, wat het jy nou gedoen met die bregat kar van jou Miss S." It's slang Afrikaans for "What on earth have you done to this posh baby of yours," but a little bit more risqué, language wise. I shake my head and say well at least it's in one piece still! He laughs and says, "Let's get this baby up on the car lift and see what's going on underneath!" The car lift shows some quite severe damage but Sharief can do a temporary fix for the weekend and then it will have to be back. At that he pulls off a large loose piece and my eyes go wide and big! Ouch, that hurt. My car is my pride and joy. A gift to myself when I got divorced. It's a blue Mercedes-Benz 500 convertible with light tan interior and lots of power! I love this car so I feel like a part of me is being torn apart too. I am checking my watch, as I have a date with Mighty Mike this evening and I still have to drive miles to take my mentee to an interview in the townships. Needless to say, I run out of time to go home and change so have to wear my work clothes to my six o'clock date in Constantia. I get to the mall just ten minutes before six and rush into the nearest shoe shop and say, "I know you are about to close, what have you got in the way of super high black shoes partially closed?" I find a vaguely suitable pair but they are very high and I feel like I am on stilts. I say, "Hold these for two minutes," and dash into another shop but there is nothing there! So back I go with a minute to closing time and say "I will take these." I put on my stilts and walk to the car rather unsteadily. This is a good time to practice staying in the shoes, as I am only five minutes away and running late. The story of my life you have now gathered! I text Mike and say on way – traffic heavier than usual.

I slip into the familiar seat of my car and put the key in the keyhole. The engine roars to life and I get the thrill of the sound which is deep, gruff and so sexy! *So love this car.* I press my foot on the petrol and nothing happens. After a few more attempts I realise the shoes are so high that I can't get traction and the pedal does not move at all! Off come the shoes, I am on my way.

I get there a bit flustered instead of poised and calm. I berate myself and say, "Better planning Susan, this is not good!" I notice the big shoulders straight away. He is not hard to miss as there are only two other people at the bar. I am very aware of the stilts that take me across the floor and pray I don't look slightly off balance or a bit tipsy! I tap his shoulder and this open nice face looks at me. He smiles, a broad smile, and there is a dimple on the left. He smells nice and is better in real life than his pictures. I apologise for being late. He draws up a chair next to him and his hands gesture to sit on the seat. They are smaller than I would have imagined, as the rest of him is all muscle and he definitely works out often, and uses supplements. The contour and shape of his muscles say so, and I am not complaining! I am immediately at ease and we order drinks. I get adventurous and order a Vodka Martini.

In a way it feels like I just might be in a James Bond movie here, 007 and all.

He has a good sense of humour and soon I am laughing a lot and tell him all about the car and the shoes! At the back of my mind though is, *Are you nuts Susan, who does this at a first meeting.* Clearly, I do! I like him and tell him that I like him, and that I am not looking for a long-term relationship and that I am happy with a relationship that is part-time. I explain that work takes up a lot of my time and that I am very independent. The evening passes quickly and we agree to see one another when he is next in Cape Town and that he will let me know when that is. He walks me to my car and I show him the damage. He says, "You won't be driving my car anytime soon!" He hugs me goodbye and I feel lost in his broad shoulders. His body is taut and there is nothing soft about him other than his gentle nature. He entertains clients for his company when he is in Cape Town, so he is usually at a rugby event or some sporting event on a Saturday afternoon when he is down, and spends Fridays seeing his clients.

He is perfect for me and I feel excited on the way home. He sends me a text later and says thank you for a fun evening, and that he is looking forward to our next get together. He asks if I have a place in mind perhaps, as this is my neck of the woods, so to speak. I tell him I will give it some thought. I send him a hug mojo and he send me one in return. We chat a few times during the next two weeks and I come up with a surprise venue, but it is a sleepover, and half an hour from Cape Town, so we will get there on the Friday evening and leave the next morning so that he can be back to see his clients.

CHAPTER 4
MIGHTY MIKE
– HOT TUB HILARITY!

I fetch him from the airport, and we drive straight to the secret venue. It's a little place in the country called Bot River. I have booked a secluded chalet in a private nature reserve in the mountains. There are only four chalets, and each is far away from the other. Elevated and overlooking the fynbos and mountains, it is perfect for us. It is a two-bedroom chalet, as I am not about to jump into bed with Mighty Mike, even if he is irresistible! I am too nervous for starters and I don't know him well enough yet!

The *pièce de resistance* is the hot tub on a deck outside that overlooks the entire valley which has a wide open sky above. More intriguing is the big fireplace next to the hot tub that is used to build a fire and heat it. I love that this is how to heat it, and I can imagine how sitting in the hot tub, looking at a blazing fire, will be a truly unique experience. The chalet comes with loads of wood, and you are encouraged to get the fire going to heat the water, which takes a couple of hours or so. We do exactly that, leaving a huge fire to warm the water, and we head out for supper. I am so excited about the hot tub and can't wait to get back to jump in and open the bottle of champagne that is waiting for us in the fridge.

I had packed a full-piece swimsuit and a sarong. It's a chilly night, but this just adds to the ambience as steam rises from the hot tub, creating a hazy mist above the water. I bring a blanket outside, wrap it around me, and wait for the big reveal. It does not disappoint. I open the bottle, and we clink glasses. I step onto the side of the hot tub and put my foot into the water. It burns red hot. Oh my God, the water is boiling! I rush to the bathroom and put my foot under the cold tap.

Mike comes rushing in after me and says, "What's wrong?"

I can barely speak; my foot is so sore. I point at my red foot and say, "Hot, super, hot!"

He frowns and says, "You mean it's too hot to get in?" I think, *Of course it is, you idiot! Can't you tell I am on fire here?* He fetches some ice, and I bathe my foot in icy water for 10 minutes. I do not have the best-looking feet, I might add!

He joins me on the side of the bath and says, "You're a bit accident-prone, aren't you?"

I laugh till tears roll down my face and say, "Clearly, not a great start!" By now we are both laughing, and the evening turns into a night of fun with great seventies and eighties music from our era, as we discover we like the same kind of music. We console ourselves and say we can use the hot tub in the morning!

The morning dawns, and we're up early to get our hot tub time fitted in. This time I put my finger in, as the water still has steam rising from it and the fire is still smouldering. It's still hot, and I realise it will be impossible to sit in it before Mike leaves. I am not too upset, as I invited a girlfriend here for Saturday. I go for a long, relaxed walk. I do some yoga on the deck and read my book.

My friend Michelle arrives at 2 o'clock, and we catch up over coffee and stroll into the town for a late lunch, which means we essentially miss dinner by design. We have better things to do. When the sky turns orange and pink, we're in the hot tub, our glasses filled to the brim with a sparkling liquid that smells woody, with a tint of oak and lime in the mix. The bubbles in the hot tub dance around our bodies, and the warm water is the perfect temperature. Not a sound can be heard. Surrounded by trees, we watch the sinking sun in a cloudless sky that turns orange with streaks of yellow and red. Nothing moves, and the night is still. *Every hot tub does have a silver lining*, crosses my mind.

PILLOW TALK

I am scheduled for a trip to Johannesburg with my company, so Mike and I arranged to meet on Friday evening, and he will be staying over with me. We have been on a few dates by now, and the relationship has taken on a nice relaxed, even tempo; we don't ask too many questions; we just enjoy our time together. We both know that this is not a long-term thing. I work out that it is all of six months now, and we have seen one another on average, probably every three weeks or so. Effectively, we have spent only nine days together in total and have chatted regularly in between.

I arrive before Mike and am busy unpacking when there is a knock on the door and he comes in with a big suitcase and a shoulder bag. I am intrigued by the suitcase but don't say anything. I head for the bathroom and take a shower. When I step back into the room, the mystery unfolds before my eyes as he hauls out two large pillows and says, "I hate other pillows; my pillows come everywhere possible with me, even to Cape Town. I just have not brought them to your place yet." For some reason, this strikes me as a bit weird. I can't pinpoint why, but it continues to bother me all night. We get back from dinner, and the two hotel pillows on his side are now in the cupboard.

The next morning, I leave early for work as I am exhibiting property at a mall. The pillows won't leave my mind, and I try to focus on the job at hand. Once back in Cape Town, I forget about the incident, and life with Mike carries on comfortably for a bit longer. After a while, I find that I am not that excited anymore, and the pillows now stay with us whenever Mike spends the night. He trains a lot, and this often means that a Friday or Saturday afternoon is spent in the gym. But essentially, I am bored. I wait till he is next in town and tell him that this relationship has overextended itself timewise and that we both need to move on. He agrees, and all is good.

Two weeks later, he asks to see me. He tells me that he is a lot more invested than he realised and would like to take the relationship to the next level. I am mortified and have no idea what to say. My head goes into top gear, and I tell him that I don't feel the same anymore and that I don't want to be with someone who has young children; his sons are eleven and thirteen. I also don't want to be with a body-conscious individual who spends so much time preening and working on the perfect torso. It's too stressful and makes me feel like I need to be working out that often too. I can see that he is visibly upset. I am, however, a lot more tactful in my communication and emphasise my lack of fitness and my lack of body contouring and muscle. I can see he is not buying any of it!

I take home the thought that it could have happened the other way around and that dating is always going to be risky. What I never expected was to hurt someone else. I discover that I am better at being dumped than dumping someone. I would have felt better. I decide that I am going to be single for a while, as it makes things easier!

CHAPTER 5
YOU'VE GOT MAIL – URHAL
SCAM ALERT!

I decide to continue with my novel tonight and head to my desk, which nestles nicely in a corner of my lounge with a view of the mountains and the lake. It is nighttime, so the off-white wooden heavy blinds hide the view, but I can see it in my mind and feel inspired. My phone alerts me that I have mail.

It's a message from the dating site to say that Urhal, at 42, is a good match for me. In his short description, he says, "I come on this site with my total focus, to find my true love."

The site must be low on matches for me. It's not rocket science that older men are fishing in younger ponds! I feel a bit irritated. Apart from the fact that his narrative is far-fetched and a tad delusional. True love? It's time to be realistic after years of living! If you have not encountered an aspect of true love by this stage, my dear friend, then the chances of you finding it now, are really slim!

I decide to play along, deliberately making spelling mistakes. I say, "I too am looking for tru luv, like you, but I am older than you."

He replies, "You are so beautiful my dear, I like older woman."

I notice that he has only one picture, and it is photo-shopped! It's a picture of a handsome man on a ski slope. The white of the ski slope makes a nice backdrop for a tall, well-built man with sunshades and a ski suit as attire. I read his profile which says he works abroad and is a project manager. He works three months on site, and then has three weeks off. This appeals to my old self of part-time encounters and, for now, I am engaged but not feeling 100% comfortable. I sense a rat!

I reply with, "When will you next visit Cape Town? I would like to meet you when you next arrive here!"

He replies, "I am so happy to hear from a beautiful woman like you! I shall be there in a month."

"I must be honest," I lie. "I am a little larger than these pictures, about 20 kilos heavier and my hair is no longer blonde, but grey. I live in a caravan at the seaside and would like to find someone who can look after me. The caravan is very old and it leaks in winter. Are you much of a handy-man? I need a man who can help around the house and also someone who likes to cook, as I prefer to work in the garden and grow vegetables. Where was your picture taken? Will you be able to pick up some groceries for us when you arrive as I am a little low on cash next month? I would offer to fetch you from the airport, but my car has broken down and needs repairing. I am waiting for my son to send me some money to get it fixed. Your picture looks like an advert for a holiday resort with the snow in the background? We don't have snow in South Africa or ski slopes. Do you have any other pictures?" I hit send.

He reads it immediately and then, nothing. More of nothing! He is offline when I next look a few minutes later. I chuckle to myself and laugh; *I must remember to put this into a story some day! How to scare a scammer, in two seconds!*

CHAPTER 6
PERFECT PAUL

Since my encounter with Mike, I have not been vaguely interested in dating, and six months go by. I am sitting in a quaint and cosy coffee shop in Wynberg with a good friend when an old friend of mine walks in. She is an ex-beauty queen and everyone looks at her. Despite being in her late forties, she still turns heads and is looking gorgeous. She lives in the United Kingdom with her husband, a wealthy business tycoon, and her wardrobe is testimony to this. Her tall figure is clad with raw silk trousers, light yellow, that look brand new, and a matching top drapes across her significant chest. She wears a tan belt with matching shoes and large diamond earrings with a double string of pearls. Her auburn hair bounces on her shoulders, full and curly. Her dark blue eyes are surrounded by superlong black eyelashes and well-defined brows.

We once shared an apartment in our mid-twenties when we were cabin attendants with SAA. She has not changed one bit, and her fame and title did nothing to spoil her gentle, warm, friendly persona, and it feels like it was yesterday, we last saw one another. "Susan, Dahlin, how fabulous to see you! We have to catch up; I would love to see you." We exchange numbers and agree to meet later in the week for a coffee or glass of champagne.

We meet at the luxurious Hohenort Hotel in Constantia, where she is staying. Her husband is in England while she is here visiting her family and friends for ten days. She says that running so many homes is hard work and that they have a very demanding life. Despite the butlers, managers, and staff, she is busy. They have two homes in England. One in the heart of London and one in the country. There's a home in Switzerland and a home in the south of France. They also have a yacht moored in the Caribbean, but this is run solely by staff with a full crew, so this does not require much other than, I think to myself, *Mountains of money!*

We chat for ages, filling the evening with stories of our lives going back to our airline days. Although, when she lived in Knysna for some time with her first husband, we never got to see each other. I tell her all about my marriage to my younger husband, and she laughs and says, "Gosh, Susan, only you could pull that off!" When I try to tell her that he was very mature, an old soul with a really good sense of humour, she just rolls her eyes. A lot of people do that when they find out that my ex-husband was fifteen-and-a-half years younger than me. She says, "No wonder you look so good and so young."

I tell her, "Not having children helps a lot, plus this face requires maintenance and filler!"

She laughs, "Susan, you never did mince your words; always telling it like it is!"

I am modest. "Well, Sandy, I am luckier than most as I inherited my mother's good skin and genes of UK origin!"

Suddenly her face lights up, and she says, "Oh my goodness! I have the perfect man for you! Paul. He is the nicest man. Two years older than you, recently divorced, my husband's business partner, and he is single!"

"Sandy, he lives in the UK!"

"Yes, he does Susan, but he is retired; his two sons no longer live at home; one works, and the other is at university. Plus, he has a yacht in the Caribbean, and we see him when we are there."

"You do know that I get seasick?" Then I remind her of the disastrous trip we did together when I lay vomiting all day and had to get a dinghy to take me home while they continued to party and have a whale of a time.

"The Caribbean is a flat ocean with no waves!" This time it is I who rolls my eyes.

Two months have gone by since my catch-up with Sandy. My phone buzzes to tell me there is a message. It's from Sandy to say she has just seen Paul and told him all about me and has also shown him the selfies we took during our drinks evening together. She says, "I know you said no, but he insisted, and I have given him your number!"

She tells me he thinks I'm gorgeous; that I sound like a great woman, and he is keen to chat with me. I send her back a cross-face mojo and say, "You are impossible!" But then follow it with a smiley mojo too! I am secretly excited!

Two days later I get a message from Paul to say he would like to chat and would I mind if we communicated for a while. "Sure," I say, "let's do so by email."

He is quick to respond, "Sandy knows me well, and if she says you are amazing and that we are a good fit, then I am inclined to believe her! We have nothing to lose, and I make a really good friend!"

I send back a smiley face and say, "If you promise to visit SA, then I will think about it!"

He writes back, "I have always wanted to meet an African leopard." I laugh, thinking, *These Brits think we still live in the colonial era of yesteryear!*

I send a smiley mojo back and say, "Well, my next-door neighbour just happens to have a few in his backyard!"

By now I know that he is my height, medium build, blue eyes, and has short, blonde hair. No receding hairline in sight—I am always on the lookout for balding potential—a big no-no in my book! He has a good sense of humour and has done a lot of work with the Mankind Project, a worldwide organisation that has helped an enormous number of men. I too have attended Women for Afrika; I believe in the work they do and support this organisation in a big way.

We spend about five months emailing, and eventually, we chat on WhatsApp. He is softly spoken, with a great command of the English language, and has a good sense of humour. It is hard to imagine him as a top executive and CEO though, as he just does not fit the profile. He is a great dad to his sons and adores them. I gather from our conversations that Sandy's husband was the driver and deal maker, and Paul was the even-keeled, quiet thinker who listened and worked diligently in the background. Very much the yin and the yang of most business partnerships, and one I understood well as I was a top property broker and driven. I worked 24/7 and demanded high service levels of myself and the woman who partnered with me. I was the driver, intent on the sale, the sole mandate, and being first at all times. My partner was an empath, always listening and in touch with our clients' emotions and lives.

We made a brilliantly successful team and she often took me away from my driven self with her great sense of humour, and her ability to bring calm and order to our very demanding existence that I created.

I have booked a beautiful two-bedroom ground-floor apartment for his two-week-long stay in Kalk Bay, a picturesque, old-world little fishing suburb in the Southern Peninsula. The apartment is in Majestic Village, the same complex where I have lived since my divorce. It is close to home, as I am only one floor up.

The complex is a unique combination of seventy-two apartments, of which forty are housed in two large colonial buildings that date back to the early 19th century. It won an award for the best redevelopment design in 2007 and is exquisite, with a spa and pool. The area is surrounded by the old fishing harbour—still a working one—as well as shops, cafes, restaurants, and eateries.

I have arranged to meet him at the apartment that evening. I am nervous; he is a perfect match and the most exciting prospect since my divorce. I have also ensured that a bottle of French Champagne and some snacks will be in the apartment upon his arrival. His windows portray the hustle and bustle of the sidewalk in this quaint part of Cape Town. Blinds, of course, will shut this world out when desired.

He does not disappoint when I ring the bell. He is tanned, his blonde hair and blue-grey eyes striking against his beautiful skin tone. Just the right shade—not olive dark, but a golden tan that some Brits are lucky enough to develop due to Celtic heritage. His hug is warm and gentle. I like him immediately, and the chemistry is instant.

We will stroll down to a small Greek taverna called Olympia that has been around almost as long as the apartment block; it used to be a bakery in those days. I tell him we will go to Cape to Cuba for a drink as we have our little bit of Caribbean going on here! He loves it—the sand on the floor, the umbrellas, the vibrant colours, and the massive list of cocktails. It is like home from home for this Caribbean yachtsman.

It is autumn, the best time of year in Cape Town, as there is no wind, the ocean is flat, and it's almost warmer than summer when the wind cools the temperature. He tells me about his boat and how much he loves the lifestyle and the ocean. I casually ask, "How much time do you spend on the boat?" He says he will be doing a lot more sailing as both his boys are now out of home and, being retired, he would like to spend at least six months a year on the boat.

I ask him about the boat, and he says, "Let me show you."

He tells me all about how amazing the boat is. This is a massive catamaran with six berths, all ensuite. He has a crew of four that look after the boat. He is often at the helm because he enjoys sailing. I wonder whether that means steering? I picture him rushing about the boat hoisting the massive sails onto different posts, but then I remember that the crew, not the skipper, would do it.

It occurs to me that, other than watching the ocean and scenery, this is his joy—driving a boat, so to speak, rather than sailing! I dare not ask any questions! His gorgeous deep golden tan tells me he is in the sun a lot. However, sticky sun tan lotion all over, a sunhat all day, long sleeves and pants, somehow does not float this two-legged boat, as in "Moi", who has a sun allergy. This means I cannot expose my body to the sun. If I do, I start to itch at sunset and NOTHING will give relief! A side-effect of medication I have to take. It feels like there are minute crawling insects all over my body!

He tells me that the best sailing is an ocean with big waves, as this can be challenging and exciting. I understand, as I love corners and winding cliff paths on two wheels, but this is somehow hugely different, in my book, to a rolling boat that sways up and down and side to side! At the thought, I am feeling a little queasy and off-colour. I try to conceal a growing sense of foreboding as I begin to register that, as lovely as this man is, the yacht is a big deal breaker for me.

"How about you?" he asks.

I lie, "I have done very little sailing. In fact, none, but I have been on ocean liners twice and fared okay," which is true. "I managed to find my sea legs."

But this was on a cruise liner! I do, however, know, but do not share, that sailing is another ball game! I don't tell him about my trip on a rubber dinghy in Mozambique, where I vomited from the moment the boat stopped. On that occasion, on the advice of the skipper, I got into the water to stop the nausea and proceeded to feed the fish nonstop. It was the worst experience of my life! I was sick for two days. I lay curled up in a sleeping bag in the warm sun covered with a duvet and continued to shiver for three hours. I probably should have gone to hospital, but we were in the middle of nowhere. I was there to swim with the dolphins and do more spiritual awakening. Instead, I fed fish and felt like death!

I push the boat to the back of my mind, deciding that we have a week to spend together and that I am going to make the most of it. We talk for hours, and he tells me about his long-term marriage, his work, his home, his children, and his routine. He is fit and goes to the gym regularly. He looks after his retirement portfolio, and this includes some properties in the UK, but these are mostly commercial, so they are fairly easy to manage.

He is still very involved in the Mankind Project and does a fair amount of mentoring. This is what I love most about him. His dedication to helping troubled men find their inner peace, to heal themselves, and to let go of their demons. Broken beings who are products of less than desirable upbringings, often badly neglected as children, lacking love and care, and subjected to a harsh life.

We are kindred spirits on this front, as I took two young children, aged 9 months and 5 years, off the streets. They were fostered by the most amazing Xhosa woman, who to this day is part of my life, and although retired to the Eastern Cape, we stay in touch, and I see her every 6 months when she is in Cape Town to fetch her medication from the local hospital here.

The week flies by, and we have had a fantastic time. He is warm, gentle, affectionate, and thoughtful. We have remained in separate bedrooms at my insistence, as I realise that he would never consider Cape Town as a possible second home. I would never live in the UK, and the boat is the deal breaker for me! I tell him on our second date, and he listens and looks sad. He makes it clear that sailing is his life to a large extent and that this is more important than a relationship with me, and we both know that we are very settled in our respective countries too. Despite the chemistry and so many common denominators and similarities, we would be silly to engage in a relationship that has no possibility of succeeding in the long term. He is one of the nicest people I have ever met, and I too am sad—really, really sad.

This was one of the rare occasions in my life when I was strong enough to use logic, despite my heart brimming to overflow. The intensity of feeling meant neither one of us was prepared to simply take a short-term view and enjoy something physical for a week. It was, in real terms, just too risky. We were both already sad, and to enter into a lovemaking situation would simply make it worse. In fact, it would interfere with logic, which in this case, had to prevail!

It occurs to me that the big difference in dating when we're "40 plus" is that we rely more on reason than on emotions.

The heart-skipping beats and butterflies, are no longer main deciding factors. Seeking the fairytale is no longer the mindset. Rather, it's logic, shared characteristics and interests, and similar backgrounds. It takes guts and a fair amount of strength to see the wood for the trees and make a logical decision.

We all still want the ultimate "love connection" and the idea of happily ever after. I know that for me, when I first started on this dating journey, all I wanted was Mr Part-time. But I also believed that when I got older and my career maybe became less of a priority, I would want to settle down and join the "Couples" group, rather than the "Singles" group.

When it is time for him to leave, I am heartbroken. I have felt love for the first time since my divorce. It has been five years since I felt this way about anyone. We are both very upset, and he cries too. We have had the most incredible time together. We have been so intimate, but not sexually so, and this brought a lot more intensity into the encounter. Sex can often distract from all else, and it is the latter that leads to everlasting.

He has no desire to ever come back to South Africa, as he has a very jaundiced view of this country, as do many, and understandably so. I have no desire to ever visit the UK, so we know this is the last time we will see one another. I am reminded of the word "bittersweet" as I cry into his shoulder and feel the warmth of his body against mine. He feels so perfect! I inhale deeply, and his masculine aftershave caresses my nasal senses, and I cry even harder. I look a mess; my eyes are all puffy, and my skin is blotchy. I spent the night crying, so I am at my least attractive today.

He kisses my eyes, my forehead, and my nose. He looks deeply into my eyes and says, "Thank you for such a special time.

You are a remarkable woman." I can't speak; I am so choked up. I drag myself away from him, and he gets into the taxi that is taking him to the airport.

We had agreed it would not be a good idea for me to take him to the airport. I have hated airport and train station goodbyes since high school when I used to catch the train twice a year to see my mother, who lived in Zimbabwe. She never came to the platform.

I don't look back, as seeing the car pull away as the train did back then is too much for me.

I vow to myself that I am going to stay away from any form of dating from now on. I will be single. I have many girlfriends and the odd male friend as well. My career is demanding, and I certainly have enough outside interests. I am complete. Having a male presence in my life is, in my book, a bonus but not a necessity.

PERFECT PAUL

CHAPTER 7
MR CYCLE - IT'S A MATCH

I have had a four-year break since my last Dating Buzz subscription. I decide to go online and see if there are any new faces. It's a lot easier the second time around, as I can immediately spot the scammers, the unsuitable, and the weirdos! Well almost! I see some of the old faces, and this makes me realise that finding a partner on here is not necessarily a sure thing! In fact, according to women I have spoken to since I first joined the site, they have to meet a lot of frogs before they find a potential prince, and more often than not, he at some point turns into a partial frog and is no longer suitable!

I think that as we get older, we are more realistic; we know that finding a perfect match is highly unlikely, as we are too fussy, too specific, and, quite frankly, just not willing to settle for anything that is not at least 90% suitable. The truth is that many of us who have been single for a while are happy and do not need someone to complete us. We are no longer looking for Mr Right to ensure we live happily ever after. Which brings me to a topic that often crops up! A lot of friends and family are critical of dating sites and think I am desperate; that I can't live without a man. Nothing is further from the truth, as I am happy alone. I am comfortably off; I have many friends who fill my busy, interesting life. What I do, however, like is male company. Someone to dress up for, someone who may perhaps ignite my hormones, and if not, proves to be a good friend, interesting and fun, if nothing else.

It occurs to me that I should start a dating site called "Seeking Imperfection." This would take the pressure off everyone and make the whole process a little more relaxed! I could call myself "Just a bit of it all." My mind goes off on a tangent, but I force myself back to the matter at hand and scroll further. I see him on the second scroll. Cyclist, same age as me, widowed, businessman, looking for someone who is independent and who seeks to make a difference in life, whatever that may be!

He is tanned; clearly cycles a lot; quite slim and 1,95 meters tall. He has owl-like green eyes and is extremely pleasant-looking. He has short, light brown hair. He comes across as gentle and easy going. I send him a smile and, being an impatient person with no time to waste, I send a message at the same time, "Ever done the Tour de France? It looks like you could be a contender to win! Is it true that cyclists never drink their champagne after winning? If so, I would be happy to do it for you. I can never let anything good go to waste!"

As he is not online, I don't expect a reply and scroll a little longer, but nobody jumps out, and I am happy to wait for his response. I wait two weeks! I know he is not online, as I randomly check to see who is. So, I come to the conclusion that he is either dating someone already or he is offline for some other reason. This is often the case. He has not deleted or removed his profile, so this is a good sign.

Another week goes by, then suddenly an email pops up saying I have mail from Dating Buzz. I don't have time to check it, but the moment I can, I see that he has replied. "It's not often a girl is brave enough to make the first move! I like that about you! It tells me you are confident and someone who knows what she wants! I have been away on a cycling tour and only just got back, so my business needed some well-focused time. I am in the Southern Suburbs with offices at Westlake Business Park. Would you be keen to meet for a drink sometime?" He gives me his cell number in the same message.

I like his reply and say, "Yes, I will send you a WhatsApp soon."

Although impatient, I wait two days. I know that being too readily available to meet or respond too quickly can be seen as desperate! I send him a message after work and, not wanting to appear too keen, I say, "I could meet you next week on Tuesday."

We arrange to meet at Jakes in Steenberg Village, as it's close to where I work and live. The irony of this connection is that we both work in Westlake and have never met! What are the chances that your date works a few blocks away from your offices? I decide that online dating definitely has some advantages!

I wear jeans, a blue shirt that enhances my eyes, a warm jade puffer jacket with a multi-coloured scarf, and my boots. It's July and winter weather in Cape Town. Not my favourite time of year, but it is a time when my hair always looks thicker due to the moisture in the air. I deliberately arrive late in order to ensure he is already inside when I enter. I park my car, grab my umbrella, and dash inside as the raindrops pelt down onto the pavement. I am grateful for two things: an umbrella and a parking spot close to the entrance of the restaurant. The lighting is subdued, and there is a lovely seating arrangement with couches and chairs around a roaring fire. I recognise him standing near the fire, facing the flames, so that his profile is visible.

He walks over to greet me, leans over, and kisses my cheek. His pictures do not do him justice by a long shot! He says, "It was worth bracing the weather! Hi, Susan, I am Michael."

Michaelangelo indeed, this time in the flesh! Yes, please! We warm ourselves at the fire for a while and are both standing. He is a head taller than me, and I can see the finer details of his face. He has great teeth and a fabulous sense of humour. He has me in stitches, and we are both relaxed. A sense of humour goes very far in my book. He relays his cycling race stories and events. We decide to stay for supper as we definitely want to get to know each other better.

He has been widowed for four years. He dated a doctor for two years and has since been single for about four months. I tell him about my marriage and the dates I have had—Mighty Mike and the various encounters to date.

The one date I don't tell him about, the one who was actually a friend turned into a romantic encounter, comes to mind! Kevin was good-looking, wealthy, and had chased me for years.

Michael runs a family clothing business. He has no children from his marriage, and this is a big plus for me. He is not mad about dogs, though. I have to swallow hard and mention Molly, saying that she is not just any dog. She is human, and everybody falls in love with her! This is my first red flag, but I am convinced he will change his mind. He is an extreme sportsman, cycling every day, or should I say, he trains every day and rides most weekends.

I don't do any cardiac sport. I do a bit of hot yoga but don't see this as a sport really, as it's a very relaxed pastime and a very chilled one. It has its advantages, and one does build great strength, but it's not heart rate material unless one counts the heat in the room!

He had lived with his previous girlfriend and is currently staying with friends in Constantia. He has bought a townhouse in Hout Bay that he is busy renovating. I ask him how long he has been staying with them, and he says four months. This tells me he moved into their home when he split from his girlfriend. He says he will be with them for another two months and will then move into his townhouse. He says he would love to show it to me. As I am in property and always interested in renovations, having done many of my own, I love the idea!

I have finished off my second spritzer and am onto my third glass, and with another big sip, I venture, "I have something to ask you." He raises his eyebrows with a twinkle in his eye. I blurt out, "Is it true that cyclists shave their legs?" He pulls up his jeans, shows me his tanned calves, and is laughing! Indeed, it is. I want to dance with relief, but instead, before I can stop myself, I say, "Anywhere else?"

This time he splutters on his glass of wine and says, "Pardon?" and roars with laughter. I go blood red, as I realise it has many implications.

"Oh no! I mean, it just occurred to me that a back would get sweaty too."

He tells me there's nowhere else, but one must never rule out anything! It depends on the individual. *There must be an easier way to find out if he has a hairy back!* I think in frustration.

The rest of the evening flies, and we are the last to leave. I sling my arm through his and am relieved to see the rain has abated. He gives me a massive warm hug and says, "I am so glad we met, Susan! I hope to see you again soon." I drive off happily and sing love songs in the car.

He calls me the next day at lunchtime and asks me out to dinner at the weekend. I tell him that I am going away on a retreat for ten days just outside Hermanus and will not be back till Tuesday of the following week. I can sense the disappointment in his voice when he says, "I leave for a cycling trip next Monday and will be overnighting in Stanford." We chat for a while, and he says he is thinking about something and will call me about it later in the week. On Friday, he calls to say he has a plan! He will spend an extra day in Stanford and suggests that I join him there on Tuesday when I leave, detouring via Stanford on my way. I love the idea.

CHAPTER 8
MR CYCLE - STANFORD

The retreat is an amazing experience, and I get to do all sorts of things that I never would have dreamed of doing in my marriage. It's all alternative stuff, and I was a little dubious when I decided to book, but am so glad I did!

I am and have always been interested in doing many different things and firmly believe that we must experience as much as possible in one lifetime; that we should keep an open mind and remain adventurous. Had you asked me five years earlier if I would have been interested in something alternative like this, I would have said, "No!"

On the first night we are introduced to Bernie Prior, who teaches The Form Reality Practice, which takes you into Bliss. With a strong New Zealand drawl, a long, thin ponytail, and decidedly bohemian clothing, he tells us how we will experience bliss during a 6-step process. Half the time I don't really understand what he is saying, as words like energy, breathwork, sound work, inner bliss, export of energy, inner work, etc., are foreign to me, and make no sense.

I look across the room and catch the eye of a woman who is also new to this. She is well groomed, has a new branded Gucci tracksuit, perfect make-up, blow dried hair, and manicured nails. We both stick out like sore thumbs. I catch her eye, raise my eyebrows, and roll both eyes. She does the same; I have found a kindred spirit!

I am hugely sceptical and do not for one moment believe that I will discover Bliss or find myself in Bliss. I am more likely to do so after a few glasses of wine than with all this weird stuff and energy they are talking about! She is from Durban, Jewish, an attorney, and ten years younger than me. Very switched on, she is highly successful. We are on the same page and become firm friends over countless glasses of wine and late-night stories at the end of each day.

This morning starts early, and we all gather in the hall where we met Bernie the previous night. Our day is divided up into different things. Bliss is up first and has to be done in pairs. We will need one chair between two people. He explains that during this first process, one person will sit on the chair and the other will stand. The person seated receives, and the other person performs various hand movements to music, very slowly and deliberately. I sit to receive. My partner is a woman who has been doing retreats like this for a few years in various forms or another. She is part of the set here, with her wiry out-of-control hair that glints bright orange in the morning light, her blue shirt, and billowy psychedelic pants in a variety of bright colours. On her feet she has fur-lined boots that are well worn, and I imagine her living in a commune somewhere and eating plants her whole life. We are complete opposites, but both here for Bliss.

I try to relax into the seat, sitting bolt upright. The music is repetitive and gentle. I close my eyes and feel her movements as they cross my closed eyes and hover over various parts of my body. With eyes still closed, I am aware of a deepening darkness, and colourful spots start to dance in front of me. They move around, ebbing and flowing backwards and forwards. I am not perturbed by this and feel relaxed. It seems like this goes on for quite a long time. I find myself in what I can only describe as a vacuum. Nothing happens—no thoughts, no stories, no dialogue—and with this I experience the most relaxing place I have ever been in. I am in no-man's land; no worries, no pictures, no movement. Just this empty blissful space of nothingness.

I am so happy to be here and want to remain here indefinitely, but a voice is somewhere in the distance. It gets louder, and I am being asked to open my eyes when I am ready. I don't feel ready and remain in this state of calm and beauty until I become aware of movement around me, and this makes me open my eyes. My "forest friend" is at my feet, and she is looking at me with glazed eyes and a gentle smile on her face. I don't want to speak; I just sit in silence for what feels like the longest time. I am too scared to say, *This is the most incredible experience. Bliss is a place I want to be in, often.* My eyes well up as I feel such a deep sense of gratitude for this time in my life and the opportunity to experience such new and wonderful things. No words are exchanged between us. I simply get up off my chair, sit opposite her, and hug her for the longest time.

By the end of the ten days, I am a fully-fledged "forest being" and have not had meat for ten days. I have also stopped the wine and now drink spearmint, mint, ginger, and lemon with hot water. I am feeling fit from the yoga and more relaxed than I have ever felt in my life. No make-up for days, no hairdryer, no fancy clothes—just sheer comfort and simplicity. I don't want to go back to the real world and get caught up in the demands of daily life. I want to become a hippie living in a commune. My phone has hardly come anywhere with me, and I don't read any messages unless I have to.

On the morning of my departure, I send Michael a message to say I am running late and will only be there at 12, not 10. My usual punctuality has flown out the window. I am now on "slow" time, and I like it. He doesn't read my message, so I try calling, but there is no answer. I am in no hurry to leave, as I want to stay in this wonderful environment with all these incredible people who, in the past, were "weirdos" in my book. They are far removed from that and live a way more conscious life than I do. They are non-materialistic, very inclined to help others, and easy to be with. Life is simple and uncomplicated in their world.

The guest house is quaint and down a small road that ends in a *cul de sac*. I have booked my separate room. It's odd that he is not there when I arrive. I check my phone and see that he has called me five times. He has sent three messages as well. "I was worried about you, so I drove to Bodi Khia, but you are not here? Are you okay? Please call as soon as you get this message."

For some reason, I am not comfortable with the fact that he has driven all that way. I find it strange and a little too intense for my liking. But I push this to the back of my mind. Another red flag, but they only emerge later on.

I call and tell him that I am at the guest house. He says, "Why did you not answer my calls or messages? I could have saved myself this long trip."

I want to say, *You made the call to drive there, not me.* Instead, I say, "Gosh, I had my phone on silent; I kept it on silent while at the retreat, and when I left, I got straight into my car without checking it. I am so sorry." He calms down and says he will see me in about forty-five minutes. *Poor man, he will have wasted over an hour and a half driving.*

This gives me time to unpack, shower, blow-dry my hair, and put some makeup on! It strikes me how time-consuming this all is and how lucky men are, but then they do have to shave every day, so I figure being a woman is way better. It reminds me that I hate beards on men. I won't look at anyone with a beard; I mean, who wants to kiss a polar bear? Worse even than that is a dreaded moustache, "Yuck." As I shudder at the thought, I mess up my mascara application. This is not going well.

We meet in the garden at the guest house, and he looks so handsome. He is wearing a red jersey with a lawn green golf shirt that complements his colouring, beige slacks, and sneakers with cheeky multicoloured socks peeping out. He is in vogue and with it. I'm wearing black jeans today, short black boots, a striped white and pink shirt, and a pink zip-up jersey. My multi-coloured pink, black, grey, white, and dark maroon scarf is tightly wrapped around my neck. It's marginally cold, but the sun is shining and there is no sign of rain.

His face lights up when he sees me, and I am beaming from ear to ear. He gives me the best-ever hug, and I want to just stay in his embrace for the longest time, but move away and kiss him on both cheeks. The garden is magnificent with gorgeous rose beds. There are huge trees on the property; many have shed their leaves for winter and now stand majestically naked in the sunlight. The sound of water trickling from the large water feature amidst the roses permeates the crisp, fresh air.

We head back after our walk and enter the little "olde worlde bar" area. The day has gone quickly with the confusion earlier, so it's already five thirty. It's cosy inside, and heat emanates from a very old-fashioned coal heater from eras gone by! Old photos in well-worn frames adorn the walls, as well as oil paintings in ornate frames, some wood, some gilt-edged, and some needing a coat of paint. There is no one else in the bar this early, and while we stand in front of the heater, he kisses me. It's a long kiss that is gentle but gets more urgent and passionate. It makes my heart race and my head feel giddy. I want to dance in my boots right there, but that would be very odd indeed! When he finally pulls away, I am feeling light-headed and breathless. He says, "Susan, I have wanted to do that since I first laid eyes on you at Jakes. You are one hot, sexy lady!"

I roll my eyes, "Seriously gorgeous one? You say that to all girls! But It's okay, I accept graciously and compliments are always well-received. You are a great kisser and I need to sit down! It's rather hot in here and it's not the fire either!"

Dinner is at a delightful small, family-run restaurant that is actually located in the dining room of their home, and which extends onto a glass-enclosed patio. This gives the effect of bringing the outdoors inside. Being in the country, there are clear stars in the sky, as there is no reflection of city lights to detract from the night sky. I order their duck in orange sauce, and it's cooked to perfection. Michael orders the home-made chicken pie. We both skip dessert because he needs to stay trim for cycling. I see him, as dessert! But as this is officially our first date, there is not a chance of that. A fairly well-known rule when dating at 40 plus, is that one does not sleep with another person until at least the third date! A far cry from my youth in a small town where we waited until marriage. Life has changed a lot since then, and I find myself being grateful for this. I can't imagine waiting that long, and besides, nobody gets married at our age, why would you? But people do, of course!

The walk home is chilly so we walk briskly to stay warm. It's a refreshing short walk. More long lingering kisses on the way home. When we get inside, he says, "I respect you too much to say your place or mine, but I think it and my body thinks it!"

I seal his talk with a kiss and eventually drag myself away from him saying, "I really do hate being a good, decent girl, so know I will dream of you a lot tonight!" I'm barely seconds away from changing my mind, so I rush off.

He leaves early the next morning, and we talk almost every day. I meet the friends that he stays with, and they are great people. They are extremely close friends, and this is always a good sign in my book, as men who have no friends are a big red alert for me. I go to a barbeque at their house, and afterwards, he takes me to see the home he has bought in Hout Bay. It's not a very big townhouse with two bedrooms and a study. There is only one garage, and the garden is the size of my patio. I find myself hugely disappointed, as there is no place for a second vehicle other than to park behind the garage. Molly would not be happy. The cupboard space is also small, and my "wake-up woman" alert jumps up to the fore and stays there. I wax lyrical about it but don't mean a word I say. I mention that it's very much a bachelor pad, not really designed for entertainment, and has limited parking.

He says, "I cycle almost every day of my life, and I seldom entertain. I also don't eat out much on the weekends either, as I train super hard outside of my office hours." I can feel my interest wane somewhat. I am actually very disappointed.

More passionate kissing takes place during the visit, and we can't seem to get past a room without stopping. We are alone, and I put those thoughts to the back of my mind. This time we go a bit further than just kissing, but still keep our clothes on. My body is on fire, and his every touch is excruciatingly delicious. This is giddy stuff for me.

On the way home, I am sad, deeply sad. Reality kicks in as I start to realise that despite all the ticked boxes—good-looking; generous; kind; thoughtful; great sense of humour; well-off and comfortable; good physique; no hang-ups; no children; well-liked, and as sexy as all hell—this man is not going to be available on weekends.

Weekends are times for dining out, going for long lunches; walks in the forest or on the beach; entertaining at home;

going to the movies; the theatre; weekends away, and pottering around the house together. Instead, I see long solo weekends stretching ahead of me, and this is not what I am looking for. I may well not be looking for anyone permanent, but I do want to spend weekends with the person I choose to be with.

For some, this may seem a bit shortsighted as the relationship has not even started or got to first base, but age does help here. It's a pipe dream to expect him to change, and why should he? I can't compromise on this. Then I remember that he also does not like dogs. That pretty much is the deciding factor. There is just no point in investing any more time here. I think back to the missed five calls and three messages and also realise that he seems a little insecure in hindsight, and this would definitely not work for me. I don't like to waste time or energy on what feels like will be an unsuccessful outcome. This may seem like a negative stance, but those who know me well will tell you I am the eternal optimist, and if there was a chance of changing this outcome, I would be the first one to find it!

I send him a text the following day, "Let's meet for a coffee when you can." The weekend is ahead so we agree to meet on Monday, during the day – as both our offices are in Westlake it's easy, and I don't want to have a weak moment and not make this call.

We meet at a coffee shop close to my office at 4. He is dressed in office gear, and I crumble; he looks absolutely drop-dead gorgeous and tears well up in my eyes. I panic, cough loudly, and close my eyes tightly, trying to stop the tears. I manage to regain composure and say, "This is so hard."

I list all the things I love and like about him, and then I tell him that we are not a match. I state the already obvious reasons.

He smiles back at me sadly, saying that this reminds him of what his wife used to say, and he realises how lonely it must have been for her. He says that when one doesn't have children, one can become selfish, and that she was such a gentle, giving person that he never really understood. She never made a big thing of it; she had said it rather wistfully as an afterthought when, on the odd occasion, they had been away for a long weekend together. I mention that I am not good at compromise and that Molly is such a big part of my life. We are both sad but both realistic at the same time. I don't feel relieved, nor do I feel happy; I just feel empty and lost.

CHAPTER 9
MR "GENAU"

Tom and I are enjoying a cup of coffee as we sit and observe the lake and mountains on a perfect summer's afternoon from my lounge. The sliding door is wide open and a gentle soft breeze brushes my cheeks. He is taking a short break from the handyman tasks assigned to him for the day. Early seventies, with a shock of white hair and a dark tan, he poses a picture of health. His blue eyes shine brightly from his darkly tanned face. Character lines crinkle his face as he laughs. He is full of stories of the days when he owned a commercial fishing boat. He has a deep and respectful relationship with the ocean and its inhabitants.

We have only recently met, and he came recommended by my sister, who is a close friend of his partner. His face lights up after a while, and he says, "You must meet Meg; you will love her!" They are a new couple in the sense that they have been together for four very happy years. I am always delighted when I see that love is still possible as we get older. We arrange to meet at a local evening market.

Wednesday evening at the market is festive. A band is playing when I get there, and the place is humming. Within five minutes of meeting Meg, we are talking like women who have known one another for a lifetime. I love everything about her. She is bright, witty, smart, intelligent, and knowledgeable. Over dinner, which is the most delicious Thai food, Tom says, "I have a Swiss friend I would like you to meet."

Meg frowns, "Tom, she won't like Hein!"

"Tom, you are kind to think of me, but to be honest, I am happy alone." I explain. "My life is so full. I have been single for quite some time."

We have just sat down with another drink when who should happen to walk by but Mr Genau, as I later get to call him.

"Genau" is German for "exactly" or "yes," an affirmative response. He promptly joins us at our table and has his sister and brother with him, neither of whom speaks much English. I am surprised to find myself attracted to his look. He has grey, wild, wavy hair, green eyes, and very red cheeks and nose. I am not sure the latter floats my boat, but it somehow suits him. We chat a little, but he is busy conversing in Swiss with his family. He is medium-height has a firm body and is dressed nicely casually.

The band starts playing a great song, and I jump up. "I just have to dance," I announce, and head off to the dance floor. It's a Latin American song with great rhythm. When I next look up, he is watching me from the edge of the dance floor. He strikes across with purpose and takes my arm. He leads with confidence and knows his stuff as he propels me around the floor. I flow easily into his body movements, and we continue to dance to a few more songs. He is a very good dancer, and we move perfectly in sync. At the table, Tom casts a knowing look my way with a big grin on his face. I too am grinning and out of breath.

The evening is fun, and Hein and I dance often. When a man can dance and lead, it sparks my interest in a big way. Later in bed, I think about the night. It occurs to me that although he is typically Swiss (they don't have much finesse and are very direct), I do like him. He does not mince his words and is full of adventure. A man with a plan! He spends four months a year in South Africa at a property he owns not far from where I live. He is fit and walks every day, hikes too. He travels when in South Africa, as he always has friends or family, and they visit Namibia and the Garden Route. Both destinations are highly popular, as Namibia is desert country and the Garden Route is a coastline drive with lush greenery and vegetation. He knows both these exquisite "must-see sites" like the back of his hand. He works when it suits him in Switzerland, so he has a fair amount of independence and time off. His sons are grown up and off his hands. His home is in a small village outside of Zurich. He is an avid skier in the winter but spends most of the winter months in South Africa, which has summer.

I decide I like the idea of a continental boyfriend! Just up my old alley! Part-time!! I don't like South African winters, and the idea of spending three months in Europe appeals to me a lot. Switzerland is so central to all of Europe. The other most important thing, of course, is that I have chemistry with this man. I felt that all familiar heat between us as we danced. I felt my pulse quicken, my body temperature rise, and my breathing quicken ever so slightly that evening at the market. It was not because I was unfit, either!

He is off to Namibia for three weeks, and we have not exchanged telephone numbers, but I know I will see him again. I fall asleep dreaming of living partially in Europe and partially in South Africa.

The next morning my phone buzzes. It's a message from Tom, who tells me that Hein has told him that he likes me and was pleased we had met. A couple of weeks go by and life is busy. We head back to the market on a Wednesday evening, this time to celebrate a mutual friend's birthday. He is there and immediately gets up, coming over to sit on the bench next to me. He sits facing me with his legs on either side of the plank and says, "I am going to take you out!"

I laugh, "You are, are you? Well, it will be a little difficult because you don't have my number!"

"That is true, but I have you here now, so I will pick you up on Friday at six p.m. We will have a sundowner and then some dinner."

"So, you assume I am free? You are very sure of yourself," I say, smiling widely. "You are lucky because I just happen to be free." Never let them know that your entire week is free!

He fetches me promptly at 6 p.m. exactly a week later. He is in a microbus that he has hired, and with all the touring he does with family annually, it makes sense. No double bed mattress on the floor and surfboards on the roof! We drive to the other side of the peninsula so we can appreciate the perfect sunset over the Atlantic Ocean. He has brought a beautiful bottle of local good bubbly, and we are at Camps Bay Beach.

I have not ventured this side of the mountain for a long while and had forgotten how magical the sunsets are here. He is easy company and opens up. He was married for twenty years but had an affair with the manageress of a restaurant that he often frequented when selling his products outside of Zurich. He travelled a lot because of his business. She was a lot younger than him; he was flattered, and one thing led to another. When his wife got suspicious three years into his affair, she insisted on a divorce, left him, and moved back to South Africa. He took it badly and has never really been able to forgive himself for hurting his wife and children. He is open and honest about this, and I like this about him. Eventually, his daughter got a very good job offer from a large Swiss bank, and returned to Switzerland with her mother.

At this stage, sadly, his ex has a degenerative disease with only another year to live. They are now on good terms, and he takes care of all her needs and medical expenses. I like that he is a good man and is able to be honest about his mistakes and own them. He is very kind and caring towards her and sees her often. A man with good solid values and principles.

He married the younger woman, but it soon became apparent that she liked his money and loved spending it too. It took him five years to finally see through her motives, and he has since only dated one other woman. We go to a place I loved years earlier. I had not been back there in twenty years. Called The Round House, it's where, at 32, I got married to my first husband. A small private ceremony with just the minister, the photographer, and the manageress, who was also our witness. We later had a big wedding, but were quietly married for some months and never told a soul!

The restaurant is exactly as I remember it, but the food is different, and it is run by new people. We are at a table at the window, and the view is spectacular. The sky is orange and yellow, with clouds dotted along the skyline. The ocean is wide and vast in front of us, and the night is still, the waves small and gentle as they roll ashore. I had forgotten how special this place is, and I tell him about the role it played in my life.

The meal is superb, and I decline any further alcoholic beverage as two glasses of champagne is just about my limit, particularly on an empty stomach. He orders a double scotch on the rocks and adds very little water. He does not drink fast, nursing his drink until after supper and then insists we have a schnapps to end off the night.

As we leave the restaurant, he takes my hand and walks me to the edge of the parking lot that overlooks the beach and ocean. It is here he cups my face in his hands and kisses me. He is a good kisser and I am soon longing for more. He breaks away and looks at me. He has a direct look, open and strong. He says, "You are not going to be let out of my sight!"

He has more holiday commitments, so he is heading off to see the whales, and the trip is planned with Tom and Meg and his family. I hear nothing further from him, and this is a little unusual on the SA dating scene. Not even a note to say Namibia is beautiful or that he is still in one piece! He calls me a day before Valentine's Day and says, "Pack your bags; I have booked you to stay in Hermanus so that I can take you for a drink and lunch. I would like to spend the day with you."

I am now getting to understand that this man is a little out of sync with the real world and does not realize that planning in advance is a good idea. But I like the fun impromptu aspect, so I agree to join him. I drive to Hermanus to meet him. It is a very scenic, pretty drive, and I choose to go along the coastline for extra enjoyment, so it takes me a little longer to get there. This part of the coastline is particularly pristine, and the beach and road merge into one.

It feels like the ocean and sand are at my side, as I hear the waves roll and crash towards the shore before getting sucked back into the vast ocean that stretches into the skyline. There is no pavement—it's just my car, the ocean, and me. It's food for the soul, and I sing along with the romantic songs I am playing!

The hotel is beautiful—one of Hermanus's finest. He takes me for a beautiful five-course lunch at the well-known Benguela Cove estate, and it does not disappoint. Each course is paired with a different wine, and some of their finest wines are served. The service is world-class, and the decor is elegant, eclectic, and high-end, featuring rich hues of gold and yellow together with dark blue finishes. He takes me for a walk along the coast, and soon he is kissing me, and I am melting. We head back to the hotel and spend a leisurely afternoon making love. He is a good lover.

The next day we head out to the Hemel and Aarde Valley to join Tom and a few of his family and friends at Creation

Wine Estate. Described as a sleek high-altitude winery with mountain views, it nestles in one of the most picturesque valleys in the Western Cape, and the drive is truly breathtaking.

Tom proceeds to tell me that he gave Hein a lecture the other day. He found out that he had done very little with me and that, in his opinion, this was not enough for a woman like me! He said that Hein was very fortunate and needed to pull up his socks and had told him, in no uncertain terms, that he was to take me out and do something special with me on Valentine's Day. This amuses me no end, and I laugh. I tell Tom that I am happy with his lack of urgency, as my own life was busy and full. He also said that Hein would be leaving South Africa soon and that if he wanted to see more of me, he needed to make an effort. I had to admit, I did agree.

Later that evening, Hein drops me back at the hotel where I have left my car before he heads back to continue his travels with family and friends. He will be gone for a few days. He proceeds, however, to text me every morning and evening with a short message to say hello, and touch base. This is something new, and I wonder if Tom has anything to do with it. We go out on two more dates, and then he heads back to Switzerland, saying he may well be back in May and will touch base with me regularly to see how I am. On these dates he does not stay over the whole night and I am actually glad. I am private in many ways. He, on the other hand, does this because his friends and family are at his apartment, and he does not want to be seen sleeping out. I don't bother to tell him that they get the picture, loud and clear!

Just before he leaves to head back to Switzerland, he throws another one of his surprises at me by taking me on a beautiful drive up our West coast to see the wild flowers in the National Park. It is about an hour's drive, and we see some magnificent fauna and flora. Even when they are not in full bloom, the colours of the various flowers always manage to weave a perfect carpet among the greenery. One of my favourite pictures of us is a selfie taken on the rocks here. The wind is blowing as it always does, adding life to the scene. Everything on our bodies is out of place as the wind sweeps my hair, scarf and clothes, in all directions.

A month after his departure, I decide I am going to Barcelona for my birthday in April and ask him if he would like to join me. I have always wanted to see the work of Antoni Gaudi— the greatest exponent of Catalan Modernism. A pioneering figure of Art Nouveau and Modernism, his work has a highly individualised, sui generis style. His main work being the Church of the Sagrada. I also love Spanish clothing, a recent favourite of mine, when I discovered a small boutique called Desigual in the Constantia Village shopping centre. The fabrics, the use and mix of colour, and patterns, is truly unique, and I know instinctively that the city and its clothing, will not disappoint. He is agreeable and says that I should fly to Switzerland for a couple of days and, that as I am paying for an aircraft ticket, he will find us a lovely place in the city and show me around as he has been there a few times. I love this idea.

STEP BY STEP

It is the end of winter in Zurich, and I have packed warm clothes. It is a long time since I visited Switzerland. The last time—over seventeen years ago, was when I toured Europe with three friends on Harleys and we drove through the Alps of Switzerland and the countryside as well. I was forty then and had only had my motorbike license for three months! I think back and shudder a little as I recall my ignorance of packing and the use of the right equipment in the way of touring luggage and the like.

I had rented a bike, and one morning, when we departed from our overnight stay in Switzerland on a gravel parking lot, I could not understand why my bike was sliding around instead of driving, and then discovered that I had left the wheel lock, an antitheft lock, on! The front tyre was not moving, while the back tyre was straining at trying to push a non-turning wheel on the road! Luckily it was gravel and not tar, so the wheel just spun on the ground. I was ragged about that for months.

I also remember when we left Monaco in the heat of a wonderful summer morning wearing our bikini tops and jeans with boots. On that same day as we headed for Switzerland, there was snow on the mountain ranges as we drove along! A quick change of clothing ensued! I recall that often, and it never ceased to fascinate me how one can go from the height of summer to the cold chill of winter in a couple of hours.

The drive to Hein's home is picturesque and exactly as I recall the "Heidi" pictures of my youth. The Hansel and Gretel A-frame houses are dotted all along the slopes. There is melting ice, and the sun is shining high above the valley, and it is warm. One of my first observations is the lack of life along the road, as all restaurants, shops, and stores have their doors closed to keep out the cold and have central heating within. As a South African, this is not an easy adjustment for me, and I feel like I am driving through a lifeless country.

Soon we are at the house—yes, an A-frame! It is warm inside, and I have my own room. Something I insisted upon when I discussed the visit with Hein, and he was happy to oblige. His home is masculine and neat. It is a good size for one person and has three bedrooms, one of which is converted into a study. I unpack, shower in my ensuite, and change into fresh new clothes.

I hand him a gift of Biltong, which he loves. I chuckle to myself as I have yet to meet a man who has not fallen in love with South African Biltong! "They lock you up if they find this in your luggage!" he says. I tell him I know, but that my other home language, Afrikaans, is rarely spoken in Europe, which usually means they give up in the end, as it becomes too much work to find an interpreter.

We spend the day indoors and make love in the afternoon. I am thrilled with having my own room and space, as we have never spent a full night together. We drink champagne that I bought at duty-free. The day is cold outside despite the sun being out. A device on the floor catches my eye. Circular and electric, it says "Sweeper" on the top. I ask Hein what it is. So, he demonstrates what this device does by switching it on with a remote. It proceeds to move around the floor, and when it encounters a piece of furniture or a wall, it changes direction. I love it! At the best of times, housework is a waste of valuable time in my book, so I am eager to know more and also how effective it is. He says the only problem is if you have rugs, it cannot manoeuvre its way onto the rug. My enthusiasm wanes at this point, as I have lots of rugs at home. Darn!

This evening, we head out to his sister's house just down the road, for supper. We walk, and it's cold, and there is a slight drizzle. Call me spoilt, but walking in drizzle when there is a car does not float my boat. He walks briskly and I struggle to keep up. He is oblivious to my slower pace. Their home is a replica of his home, chalet-type, A-frame, warm dark colours, lots of natural wood, and it is warm inside. We leave our shoes outside, as do most Swiss and many Europeans, and I am grateful to be wearing black socks that match my pants. I don't often bother to color-code hidden socks, so I am relieved that I have done so.

They don't speak English, so Hein translates a lot. She is the same sister I met at the market on the evening Hein and I met, only this time I meet her husband as well. They show me their albums of photographs taken on Safari in South Africa, as well as Namibia and the Garden Route. They are magnificent pictures. She spends a lot of time doing this and has many albums from their various trips abroad. I am grateful to not have to sit through these. I can understand that with the amount of time spent indoors with snow, sleet, drizzle, rain and heavy clouds for the better part of a good few months, it makes sense to have hobbies one can do, inside! No wonder they do tapestry, needlepoint, and knitting here! A lot! These are hobbies we don't do much of in South Africa, where we have perfect, long, summer days and short winters. I really want to know more about Switzerland.

We discuss their respective children, and I learn something valuable. Swiss families encourage at least one son to learn a trade. They want their own people to build, plumb, plaster, build, and fix electrical issues. They are not keen to bring foreigners into Switzerland to do this work. These are respected professions. Switzerland is pretty much the perfect country and has one of the wealthiest currencies in the world. There is a lot to be learnt here. We could certainly take a leaf out of their book.

The food is traditional goulash and is delish. They promise a fondue for me before I go. Hein is fun and jovial and drinks a lot of beer. Never a favourite drink of mine, but is consumed in huge quantities by the Swiss, Dutch, and Germans alike! I feel fatigued after my long flight and also because I have such a full stomach! I ask if they mind if I move and sit on the couch in the lounge, which is in the same room just in a separate section. They don't mind at all, and I move across and get comfy. I fall asleep and wake up to gentle shaking about an hour later!

As soon as we get home, I head straight for bed. At this stage, any physical activity is simply not an option! I fall into a deep sleep, and the next morning I am grateful that Hein leaves me to wake up at my own pace. I always make a point of mentioning to any potential date that has promise, of my pet hate. I do not like to be woken in the morning, nor do I want your ever-amorous piece of anatomy up against my back before I am fully awake! I know that this is, for many men in their later years, a very proud moment as it's not always flexible, but I am clear on this: I am happy for you, but not happy for me! It's not as crass or cut and dried as this, but I have never loved the morning chemistry. This is where I call the shots like it or not!

That evening, I meet his children. They both speak fluent English as they had spent a fair amount of time in South Africa until the daughter Melanie, a CA, moved back to Switzerland in her late 20s to work for Credit Suisse. Her South African-born mother, who had returned to SA after the divorce, had also moved back to Switzerland.

Dinner is a home cooked meal at his daughter's house. I learn that she has just gotten married for a second time and has since quit her position after twenty years in the banking industry to become a train driver! This story fascinates me. It is such a contrast to her previous profession, and I am impressed by her bravery at forty to make a move that is so radical.

Melanie met her husband when she was doing the training course for driving trains. This is a six-month course and mostly computer-driven, which makes sense. They are often high-speed trains that are precision-driven and always on time. We could certainly take a leaf out of this Swiss book! She has been driving trains for two years and loves it. It is well-paid shift work, and she loves this aspect of the job, as would I. She is interesting, and we get along well. He has been a train driver his entire life and moved into a training position six years ago.

Hein's son is good-looking, charming, and has a good sense of humour. He is in between jobs and does not really know what he wants. He is not married and says I should find him a lovely, attractive woman in South Africa who would be happy to have a happy-go-lucky man around who prefers not to work! I mention to them both that I am very sorry to hear about their mother's illness. Melanie opens up and says that it is very difficult, as her mother needs a lot of help and care. She can get time off work to assist, but she does not like doing this and feels guilty. I tell her that family is more important and that, in time, she will long for a day that she could see her mum one last time and get time away from work. I am touched that Hein has introduced me to his family.

The next morning, we leave Zurich and fly to Barcelona and pick up a car from the airport. Our hotel is a high-rise building on the outskirts of the city centre and a fast twenty-minute walk to the city. We have a lovely, spacious room that overlooks the city. We are in the same room but have twin beds next to one another, and again, I am grateful to Hein for being considerate. We dress warmly and take a walk into the city. There is a lot of life, but it is still cold. A brisk walk, however, makes one hot, so I disrobe and walk with my jacket around my waist. I did not bring a backpack or a bag big enough for it. We have a coffee and head back to the hotel. I don't really like the big road, as it lacks character. Hein says we will stop off for a drink on our way home.

Halfway home I get extremely tired—this does happen sometimes, and I have to rest. He does not understand this at all, and I ask him if he would mind fetching the car, as I really cannot walk any further. It falls on deaf ears, and he insists that a drink and a short break will do the trick. I struggle back, and he dismisses my difficulty. I tell him I need to take a rest, and he kindly says he will head out for a walk before we go to dinner in order for me to do so. This is a man who hikes often and walks everywhere, even in South Africa. I am a girl who walks her dog short distances and who will do three walks for about five kms at a slow and steady pace three times a week, maximum. He tells me there is a really good restaurant close by, and we can walk there. I reluctantly agree, against my better judgment.

The restaurant is on the top floor of a hotel, and I don't mind the 20-minute walk. It is magnificent to be so high up and view the sea of lights across Spain and Barcelona. However, I really do not feel like walking home late at night after a relaxed evening, and would far rather be in an Uber. But Hein says it's close and we will soon be home. I am not happy, and we walk home with little conversation. It is clear to me that he does not understand how much this affects me and how important it is for me to be heard. I am happy to compromise, as we need to in all relationships. I will walk during the day, but at night, I want to drive to dinner and back, or Uber!

I get little sleep. Hein snores a lot, and loudly. I am not surprised as few people when they get older, do not snore, but this is on a different level. Eventually I fall into a deep sleep and wake up to him breathing loudly next to me, but now, coupled with the noise, is the smell of stale beer and old cheese. It takes all I can muster to stop the bile from rising up in my throat. I jump up and rush to brush my teeth and entice him to take a shower with me, at the same time giving him a toothbrush to use with toothpaste on it. Phew. Saved by paste and a brush! We still have four days together and I have no idea how to address this with three more mornings to go!

Thankfully, we take a drive to see Gaudi's architectural masterpieces in and around Barcelona. I am thrilled that we don't have to walk miles. During the course of the afternoon, we find ourselves at a café close to a pharmacy, so I rush in and buy some mouthwash. Fortunately, I have a large bag in which to hide my purchase until later! We park near the university, and Hein insists on walking around the hilly, picturesque area to get some nice viewpoints. I am wearing sneakers, so I am prepared and equipped with my hat and water.

Hein is in good spirits and we have a fun afternoon and laugh a lot. Although a drinker, Hein is good company and we stop often for him to have a beer or two. I don't mind as it's an opportunity to rest my legs. I am beginning to understand that the red face is indeed a warm alcohol spread across his nose and cheeks! I also know that this is the reason for the morning situation which I am now agitated about, as it's hampering my ability to fully enjoy our time together. I ask myself if I am being silly as surely a mature woman should have the courage to speak openly about this?

I have never been good with awkward situations, and at best, avoid confrontation or any form of negativity. It boils down to not really knowing how best to couch these things. Also, he is not local, but Swiss, and definitely different. It occurs to me that he is actually very direct himself, in fact most Swiss are, and it should be easy to discuss. Well, it's not for me, anyway!

We dine in the centre of Barcelona on the Las Ramblas, which is full of vibrant life and one of the most famous and iconic boulevards in Spain. It has medieval buildings and is lined with side cafes, bars, shops, restaurants and trees. We visit the indoor market that features great architecture, plenty of colour and items to buy, including fresh fish, herbs, meats, edible insects like grasshoppers, ants and more. Immigrants mean that there is a rich and diverse multicultural choice. There is an enormous amount of care and elaboration of display of produce, which in itself is a work of art.

I love this visit and feel very lucky to experience this creative and incredible produce market, which is like nothing else I have seen before, and I have been fortunate to travel extensively during my life. We also get to visit the Placa Catalunya, which is where the old and the new aspects of the city get to create social meeting points. This is something I have found in most of Europe, including eastern Europe a well. Tbilisi in Georgia has very beautiful combinations of old and new with spectacular Georgian architecture. I am reminded how each country and city have their very own style and character.

We get home quite late, so I put the mouthwash on the washbasin and tell him I got us something to use in the mornings and evenings, as we are drinking and eating so many different things, we need to help our constitution deal with the effects that may present as a result. The following morning, he is up before me, so thankfully, he has showered and brushed his teeth and used the mouthwash! I am secretly delighted that my little effort worked, but it has not resolved the problem! It has only made a small difference and a lot more is needed! A different diet altogether!

He tells me we are going somewhere special today - a small coastal town in the Southeast. I instantly fall in love with this adorable place and I don't want to leave. It's called Saint Antoni de Calonge. Hein's family had a holiday house here for years, but sadly it is now sold as the children are now adults, and no longer want to go on family holidays. The area we visit is quaint and small. There are a few restaurants and tapas bars with shops spread intermittently down winding cobbled streets that rise and fall with the hilly terrain. There are views all over of the ocean and the homes along the coastline. The weather is warm and we enjoy a light lunch at a small tapas bar cum restaurant, that was around when Hein had his holiday home here. The same person is still the owner and he is very excited to see Hein. He insists on pouring us a local Sangria that he makes, on the house. It is delicious, not too sweet and, as far as I can tell, is a mixture of orange, red wine, lemon, lemonade and spices. It's very drinkable and I have a few glasses. This makes me bold and adventurous and I tell Hein I want to find a spot for us to stay for a night here, tonight! He is not as spontaneous and says we have paid for our hotel room and it would be a waste of money. I try harder, telling him that I will pay, and we can just head down to the little local grocery store we passed to buy a toothbrush each. We can sleep naked! He says that he could not accept that I pay. He is firm, insisting that it's a bad idea. I am disappointed. It is becoming clear to me on this trip that we are not really suited.

Later that evening, when I lie in bed thinking about the day, I come to the conclusion that I am not suited to Hein. We are in fact very different. My romantic illusion of South African winters in Switzerland no longer has any appeal as I don't like Switzerland, plus the people are too straightforward for my liking. I don't like the lack of life in winter and although I realise summer will be very different, it's still a glaring "No" in my view. I have covered some of my other no-go views in here already, so there is no need to repeat them.

They say we are more difficult to please as we get older and I have to agree. Older and wiser, thankfully. I like communication that is sensitive and thoughtful. This is a bit of a contradiction in terms, as I have been known to be more than a little insensitive in my former years when I worked under a lot of pressure and spoke without thinking a lot. I am also not big on the walking everywhere and this remains a constant issue for me during our time in Barcelona. In fact, the following morning which is our last day, I just want to relax and take it easy. Hein is raring to go and we agree that he will go and walk the city once more, while I have a slow morning.

I fly home from Zurich when we get to Switzerland.

CHAPTER 10
MR GENAU – AU REVOIR

I nearly drop my phone when I get a message in August, four months since Barcelona. "Surprise, I am coming to South Africa in August and will arrive on the 3rd. I shall have no other family with me so we can spend some time together." At this point, I feel the blood drain from my face.

I am on holiday in Umhlanga with a friend, and she looks at me with concern. "Are you okay, Maatjie?" I roll my eyes. Maatjie is a South African word in Afrikaans for friend; directly translated, it is "Friendie," a term of endearment.

"You are never going to believe this, but Mr Genau is coming to SA next week and thinks we are still an item." I explain that I have had one message from him during the four months and it was insignificant enough for me to have forgotten its contents. What I do know is that I was somewhat relieved and assumed we were on the same page; a lovely encounter, but long-term is not on the cards. Short-term also flew out the window in Barcelona! Beer breath and mixed with old cheese is like waking up next to someone's smelly feet! Its debatable as to which would be worse!

Furthermore I have started seeing an old boyfriend I met in my thirties. Very casually, week-ends only, and not serious. He is away in the States visiting his daughter, and I decided on the spur of the moment to head to Umhlanga. Salt Rock, to be exact, to escape the dreadful August Cape winter. Who needs Zurich when beautiful affordable Kwa Zulu Natal is a two-hour flight away, and everyone speaks English! I often wonder why we feel the need to head out of SA in winter when we have summer all year round in other parts of our beautiful country.

I send back a message and say, "I am away in Natal and will only be back on the 15th of August. I am happy to meet for a coffee one morning as we need to chat."

"Okay great," he replies.

The holiday passes in a flash, as all good times do, and we meet in a small coffee shop on a small road in the heart of Muizenberg. I arrive a little early to compose myself. When I see him, the old chemistry flares up, and I give him a warm hug hello. I tell him that I have something I need to tell him, but it is not easy. He smiles and says, "You can tell me anything! I came back earlier than usual as it is my good friend's birthday, and I wish to surprise him! Tom! He does not know I am here, and I want you to help me arrange his birthday dinner."

At this point, I wish that we were in a bar so that I could down a shot of Tequila, but it's coffee only. I explain that I thought he had lost interest and that I had bumped into a friend shortly after he left, and that when I got back from Barcelona, this friend called me and asked me out. I tell him that we had been friends earlier in the year, but I told him that I was seeing you, even though it was early days and we had only just met. On my return from Barcelona, we saw one another for a few dinners, and things developed from there.

Hein registers no emotion or surprise at what I say, "I will see you still?"

I explain that this would not be right nor fair to Neil, who knows about him and would not feel comfortable. He continues to speak as though nothing I have said has sunk in and asks me to please help and come to the dinner. I agree, but say that I am also very busy with a deceased estate that is taking up a lot of my spare time. We part, and he gives me a warm hug. I know that he has not truly heard me.

I drive home and I am filled with guilt and loathing. *What is wrong with me? I should be more direct, stronger, and less concerned about hurting his feelings, as I know he has left feeling hopeful*

I wait a day and then send him a WhatsApp. I tell a white lie. I say that Neil, who has just returned from the States, is taking me away for ten days on a surprise holiday and that I will not be in town. That I am sorry and that I wish him luck with the birthday dinner. I feel worse after this, but sometimes the easier route is the less hurtful way.

I send him another message a month later when I know that he is back in Zurich. "Dear G" (short for Genau), my nickname for him. "I am sorry. Much as I like you and think you are amazing and fun to be with, when we were in Barcelona, I realised that I am not a match for you. We are very different. You love the outdoors and walking and hiking. At best I walk three times a week and don't ever want to walk to dinner and back.

"Beautiful as Zurich is, I don't see myself ever visiting there again, and I am too old to learn a new language. I respect the beauty of your country, but it's not a place I would visit again. I could never settle there. You are a man used to being alone, and you are, at best, only available for three months, maximum four months of the year in South Africa. Let's be good friends, as this would at least have a life expectancy!" I don't mention the morning after issue. It is silly in retrospect, but a deal breaker for me.

As I write and recount these stories, I think, *You are extremely difficult to please!* And the truth of the matter is, I am. I have been successful in my own right. I am independent, and I know what does and does not work for me. I am flawed in that I don't have the ability to discern suitability at the onset. This is one of my failings. But on the positive side, it means I get to go on many journeys and that each is worthwhile and teaches me something. I am also fortunate that as I have got older, I have got braver and learnt that life is too short not to take risks, too short not to put yourself out there just in case love beckons, and that making the first move means you meet a lot more people.

Don't wait for a man to start a conversation with you online. Be bold! You have Zero to lose! In most instances, men love this, and 7 out of 10 times you will get a response. Even if you get 1 out of 10, it is 1 more than 0! Personality counts a lot!

CHAPTER 11
DR MIRACLE

He touches my lower back and presses on my C1,2,3,4 and 5 vertebrae. I wince and he says, "I will be as gentle as I can." He then asks me to bend left and right, and on the right bend I feel pain in my right hip. He says, "Just as I thought." He asks me to turn my head left and then right and I find it difficult to turn my head a full angle to my left. My right is perfect.

"Please take a seat, Ms Harrison." Hot warm salty drops fall down the side of my cheeks and I have to hold my breath to stop crying. I hear his footsteps as he walks across the floor, my eyes are tightly closed.

When I open them, he says, "I can tell that you are in a lot of pain. I have not looked at your X-rays or scans yet, but I can tell what is wrong. We will look at them afterwards. Tell me when this started." I try to remember, but I'm not sure. In the beginning, I never registered pain as such. I simply recall being extremely tired and not planning any social engagements, as I honestly never knew how I would feel on any given day by nighttime. My life became a series of last-minute outings and visits with friends. Depending on my day, I would wake up at 7:30 and get to my office or appointments by 9 a.m. By 1p.m. I would need to lie down or rest—usually on the office couch for an hour or at home. I would then get up and carry on with my day's activities until around 7 p.m. most nights, bar Saturdays.

Once home, I would need to rest again, and my evening would continue until about midnight. My life as a highly successful estate agent was demanding, but hugely rewarding. I was passionate about what I did, was hugely respected, and well liked. I had an incredible Personal Assistant; my career was my life and dominated 80% of my headspace, my time, my physical space, and my thinking. With each successful deal came more wisdom, and I loved it. The adrenalin pumped often, and my body craved this high.

The real estate industry has no set routine. One never knows from one day to the next what each day will hold. The phone dictates how a day is filled up, and it rolls from there. I loved the unknown! Even to this day, I struggle with any form of routine. I have never enjoyed structure and easily get bored. The downside of this, is that my body never got any proper physical exercise other than my walk to the front door up thirty-five steps and walks with my dog, Molly. Furthermore, there were twenty-five more steps to my bedroom. The end result was back pain. High heels, groceries, briefcase, and a large handbag all played a role in putting huge strain on my back that had no core support. High heels, groceries, briefcase and a large handbag all played a role in putting huge strain on my back that had no core support. I was oblivious to this, completely unaware of the importance of a balanced life.

The question I asked myself for years afterwards is, *How is it possible that when one is so driven you don't register pain, but intense fatigue?* The first time it dawned on me was when I visited a Pilates studio above my offices. I spoke to the teacher who asked me what I needed and wanted and then I proceeded to cry for a full forty-five minutes. She told me that I was in pain and that my back had no support as my core was non-existent. I went to her classes for a while, but never really felt any better. However, I now knew that I was in pain, full blown, so I decided to see an orthopaedic surgeon on the advice of my GP who was now fully in the loop as to what was going down and how I was feeling.

Scans and X- rays followed with a diagnosis. "You have degenerative osteoarthritis and there is no way I can help you," he said. Crushing words, when you are hoping to see light at the end of the tunnel. Is that not what a specialist is for? To know, to have answers? At some point his words finally permeated the black vacuum that surrounded me. "I do, however, know a doctor who specialises in pain and can help you, and who will be able to alleviate some of the pain," he says. "As an orthopaedic surgeon, I can't help you, unfortunately."

Dr Miracle now sits before me. Grey-green eyes and brown hair. He is gentle and kind and tells me that he can help and that there are various treatments that we will explore, as we go along. "It is largely trial and error though, I must warn you. But more importantly, you need to see a good physiotherapist, as my treatment only solves half the problem!" He puts me in touch with Dr Grant, a sports science physiotherapy specialist, close to where I live.

He is still, to this day, a lifeline and confidant. These days, when I visit him for the odd check-up, it's like seeing an old friend. I jokingly say to him one day when I visit, "You are the second longest standing male relationship I have ever had!" He roars with laughter as he knows my life backwards. He says he loves my visits, that I am his most interesting and fun patient, and that I should write a book about my life!! "My longest relationship is with my dentist! Thirty years and counting; plus, the visits are becoming more frequent," I tell him. He is doubled over at this point, laughing loudly. He has, in the time I have visited him, had to undergo two shoulder ops and is younger than me. A reminder that the body wears down, even when the mind does not!

The first few appointments with Dr Miracle are short and to the point. I become increasingly aware of how handsome he is. He occasionally gives this quirky grin and he has a very dry sense of humour. I love this grin, and it was, in retrospect, what I loved most about him. He is part of an International Pain body and travels to conferences all over the world at least twice a year. I am an avid traveller too, and we discuss various countries; their pros and cons. He has visited many countries, as have I.

During one of my visits, I tell him about my month-long visit to a farm in Robertson, and my decision to leave the industry that was killing me. He asks me for the address, as he would like to take his two children there for a weekend. I learn that he is separated and in the throes of a very difficult divorce. It sounds awful and very messy. It is a second marriage, and there are young children aged eleven and thirteen. He has a lot on his plate, and life is not peachy by a long shot! When couples fight over money and a divorce, it takes forever; heed caution; it tells you a lot!

He suggests that I consider a pain block in the lower spine, as the medication is not really helping and I need respite. I agree and am relieved, as my energy levels are low and my life is now less frenetic but remains busy as I have bought a house that I am fixing up and will sell. This is my other great joy. On the day of the procedure, I will need to lie on my back, and he will insert a needle and run a current through the nerve that will kill it off, two thirds. It is known as a Radio Frequency Rhizotomy – it takes me ages to remember this!

This stops the pain messages; the pain is then hugely diminished and relief is found. On the morning of the procedure, I stop when I am putting on my underwear. I take off the cotton panties and put on a pair of skimpy pretty briefs with lace inserts as it occurs to me that my butt will be exposed! I laugh at myself and admit that I like this man more than I realise. In fact, a lot. Later, I do get to undress, but for all the wrong reasons, as there's no romance on this front! I am acutely aware of the doctor and patient protocol that has prevented me from thinking about how nice he is, how attractive, and how interesting!

He comes out to greet me before I walk into the small procedure room. He is wearing a green cotton operating top with matching pants. When I notice his well-defined bi-ceps, my body does a little dance and I stare! My eyes feel like they are glued to his arms! I finally manage to avert my eyes. He catches a glimpse of this and swiftly looks away. I pray he hasn't seen or sensed my feelings.

I am awake throughout the procedure but don't see anything or feel anything. He stops by to say hello while I'm resting in recovery and tells me how happy he is with the procedure. He tells me that my lower back is in fact not the worst region and that my neck is in worse shape, so I am lucky it has not manifested in any way. He asks me to schedule a follow-up appointment in six weeks' time and gives me some core exercises to do insisting that they be performed slowly and gently. He has ascertained very quickly that I am an A-type personality, and never do things slowly! I operate at full tilt on every level and don't have an "off" button. We laugh when he tells me three times, that I am only allowed to do five of each exercise to begin with. I roll my eyes and promise.

For the first time in six years, I wake up pain-free and can live a normal life again.

My follow-up appointment six weeks later, is a happy one. I write him a personal thank you note and tell him that he is "My Dr Miracle". I insist that he read the card while I am there and he blushes! He smiles and my heart melts. "You give me way too much credit!" I am just a specialist doing my job."

"It's not just any job, it's an incredible job! You improve and change people's lives in the most profound way," I say. "You give them their life back! You have given me respite that I never imagined possible! I had forgotten what a pain-free day looked like! I have energy, I can make arrangements and stick to them now. I can look forward to each day and know that I am going to have a full day without pain. I don't think you realise how incredible this is and how deeply grateful I am to you."

"You are so kind and it means a great deal to me that you have taken the time and trouble to write a note expressing how you feel," he says. "It makes what I do so worthwhile. Thank you."

He tells me that his life is still in turmoil and that he is looking for a home to buy for himself but just needs to wait out another six months before he can do so. Living in the apartment on the property where his wife and children reside, is counterproductive and stressful. He will be taking the children to a cottage in Robertson in a few weeks and is very excited. He needs the break and loves farm life. I give him my WhatsApp number and tell him to let me know how it goes and if he enjoys it.

I'm at my desk when my phone pings. I look down – a message, from Dr Miracle! I allow it to sit for a good hour. I am on an all-time adrenal high as I'm working on a big sale. Selling property has, in real terms, never been about the money for me, but more about the challenge and the ability to close a sale, that drives me.

He has rented a cottage at the dam and sent me some pictures of it that I only ever saw from a distance. It is super rustic with the toilet and shower outside! I am impressed by his ability to rough it as I never saw him as the kind of person who could do without the basics. Life is full of surprises! I tell him this, and he sends back a laughing mojo and says, "There is a lot about me that you don't know!"

"Clearly, I see Dr Miracle!"

"I have been called many things in my life but never Dr Miracle. I love that you are so different, Susan. You have such a fascinating and interesting life, and the fact that you ride a Harley is a complete enigma to me!" he says.

I'm smiling, "I am the eternal adventurer and am never going to be your average individual."

Since the WhatsApp chat we have not spoken again. Six months go by and it is time for my check- up. I am 100% fine. He looks healthy and fit and I notice that he is a lot more upbeat. A broad grin crosses his face and his eyes crinkle in unison. The appointment goes well and we chat for ages about his recent overseas trip to South America and he updates me on the newest pain techniques.

"I am fortunately never going to need any further medical intervention and they should simply take a leaf out of your book Dr Miracle, you're the best pain technique I know," I say earnestly.

"You put me on a pedestal where I do not belong Ms Harrison!"

Forty-five minutes go by, and I know that we are way past patient-doctor time and are now on 'Susan' and 'Dr Miracle' chat time. My mind is racing, and I have just had the most outrageous thought! I argue with myself, *You are not getting younger, and life is passing you by! You know he likes you, but you are a patient, so he cannot ask you out! I know! My mind continues, Plus, he has made it clear that he has no intention of ever dating again in his life, and you are clear that you have had the great love of your life and are happy solo!* My throat is dry, and I feel nervous! My tongue feels like it's glued to the top of my palate. I cringe at the thought of him saying no, but then console myself with the knowledge that since the pain block can last up to three years, this will be my last session for some time. My palms are sweating; I can feel my heart beating ten to the dozen, and I swear my red-hot ears are on fire!

Before it's too late I blurt out, "Dr Miracle it occurred to me that you travel solo, and so do I. I have an idea! When you attend your next conference, let me come along? I can tour and do my own thing during the day, and then we can have the odd dinner at night? We are both single, and neither of us wants to be in a relationship again."

I hold my breath and can't believe I have done it! I am secretly super pleased with myself. This is a big moment, as I have never had the guts to ask anyone out before. I have taken a step outside of my comfort zone and it feels exhilarating and so liberating! I am on a high and it doesn't matter what he says now. I am just so pleased with myself!

He looks at me with eyebrows raised and then says, "Susan dear, doctor-patient protocol does not allow me to go out with you." But his eyes are smiling and that gorgeous grin spreads across his face.

With a cheeky laugh, I point across the room to another doctor's room and say, "Your partner across the way, just so you know, is my new doctor!" I jump up and almost run from his rooms but glance back just before I exit and say, "What's his name, because I will need to see him on my next visit; who knows how long from now?"

An email flashes on my screen later that night. "Name the top ten places you would like to visit?" Underneath he has listed his choices!

I mail him back, adding a smiling mojo, "Any place you go, I will go too!" *Bali, South of France, Saint Tropez, Amalphi Coast Italy, and New York* come to mind, but I've learnt from experience to remain open to new opportunities, as countries I least expected to like, let alone love, over the years have turned out to be some of my favourite places! We arrange to meet on a Sunday morning in Kalk Bay at a lovely bistro.

The bistro is cosy and filled with books. The small tables mean that we sit in close proximity to each other. He is casually dressed and looks relaxed and happy. He is leaving on Tuesday for an overseas conference. We chat easily and laugh about the various things we discover about one another during our time as Dr and Patient. I tell him about my underwear indecision and he tells me he noticed me looking at his arms and that whatever panties I wore would not have made any difference! He shares with me how he wanted to keep talking when I visited, but that he was strongly bound by his patient protocol and is still dealing with the dreadful process of his very challenging divorce.

At the end of breakfast, he leans forward slowly and kisses me ever so gently on my lips, and says, "Thank you, brave woman. I have had a great time and not been in stimulating female company in a long, long time. You are different and I like it," he whispers in my ear.

"You are gorgeous Dr M and I like you a lot." I say.

The following evening, I am on my way home from the office at six when my phone pings. Dr Miracle sends me a text, "I am coming to see you before I leave and will be there at six thirty." I am ten minutes away from home, so I dash off and quickly freshen up. He is at the door with a beautiful bunch of pink and white roses in one hand and a bottle of champagne in the other.

"Such a brave girl deserves to be spoilt. Let's celebrate our freedom and have a fun evening. Besides, how could I refuse such a gorgeous and special human being? You were brave enough to ask me out, so the least I can do is oblige!" he says.

He leaves at midnight, and we are both smitten and starry-eyed. We are a perfect fit. I am happy and giddy. I feel carefree and content. His good night kiss is long and lingering. I feel safe and warm in his arms, rest my head against his broad chest, and deeply inhale the masculine smell that lingers on his body. Later that night, when I lie in bed, I tell myself that life is never going to stop me from doing what I want, and I will never be afraid to speak my truth. I feel blessed and lucky, and I fall into a deep, long, and happy sleep. I am pain-free, I am "in love," and I am beyond content. Life is perfect.

CHAPTER 12
MORE DR MIRACLE

He is overseas for ten days, and we arrange to get together as soon as he is back. He sees his children every other weekend, and it will be his weekend when he returns, so we agree to wait till the following weekend.

We go to dinner at a lovely restaurant in the centre of town that I have never been to before. It's called The Bombay Cycle Club and it's at the top of Kloof Street. I am reminded of places I have visited in Bali. It's a mix of India, Indonesia, and Thailand all in one. It is described on the website as a wonderful wacky, bohemian, love den at the top of a hill where even the most jaded palate will be kept amused. A place where you are encouraged to let your hair down and stay way past your bedtime. It strikes me as being out of character with the person I imagined this Dishy Dr to be.

He says that he is a loner and that his closest friend is a fellow doctor with whom he studied, and she lives in Australia. He has no other friends, as all the ones he had during his marriage were the friends of his future ex-wife. At this point, I should have been on high alert! This is usually a red flag in my book, but my starry-eyed vision was decidedly cloudy, and I wasn't seeing clearly!

The evening is full of promise and does not disappoint. We are both smitten and happy. I feel like my face is in a constant state of grin, and my facial muscles actually ache after a while. The night does not end too late, as we both have commitments the next day, even though it is a weekend. He is also not able to stay the night as he is still living in the apartment. The children are taking a lot of strain now, and he is worried about both of them. I feel a faint tinge of concern as I am not interested in two troubled teenagers and even further disinterested in a messy, ugly divorce that seems to be a war zone that does not abate. However, I push this to the back of my mind.

A few days later, he calls me to say that his Best Friend in Australia is unexpectedly coming to South Africa as her parents are ill. She has suggested that we meet at a game farm in Gauteng for a weekend.

It's a two-hour flight and a two-hour drive to the farm. His friend is already at the lodge. She is petite and blonde, not easy to read, and cool. I don't feel comfortable in her presence. Dr Miracle and BF, as I call her—the name still eludes me—have a lot of catching up to do and chat nonstop. Soon after we arrive there, we go for a walk, and I trail behind, aware that if I were to stop, they would not miss me. I feel a little put out and try to hide it. I know they have a lot to talk about.

The rest of the weekend is a blur, as they are inseparable and I often find myself on the periphery. I don't feel important or validated in any way and wish I had stayed at home. Dr M is oblivious and I don't mention how I am feeling. I am quiet and withdrawn on the way home and when he asks what is wrong, I tell him that I am just very tired; that I had a very stressful week and it just caught up with me. He does not ask about my week. Later on, he tells me more about the drama of his divorce and how angry he is. How he will fight to the death. He will not give her a cent more than she is entitled to. I am still not getting the picture at this point! Whoever does?

I don't hear from him for quite some time after that weekend, and I wonder if the BF has perhaps put him off, and he has had second thoughts. It does not really matter though, as I am relieved that I managed to see the wood for the trees. He is very engrossed in his unpleasant situation and is not in the right space for a relationship by a long shot. Six months go by, and out of the blue he calls and says, "Let's do coffee; I have news."

We meet in Constantia Village at Tessa's, a trendy place that is open and spacious. He is glowing and declares, "I have the best news ever! I have bought a house in Kenilworth, and I want you to see it! I am going to need to renovate it to make it more suitable for myself and the children. Will you come and have a look?" I forget the reasons we had not been in touch and get caught up in the excitement. I have spent the better part of my life renovating homes and love it.

The house is in a small complex that I know well. I had been to cocktail parties at the main house there with my previous husband. At the time, it was owned by the CEO of a well-known bank in Cape Town. They had subdivided the land and four Georgian houses were built. The house is in perfect condition as far as I can see, but he soon explains what he sees, and I get caught up in the picture and excitement of it all. It's not going to be cheap, and he does not mind.

It would be unusual for anyone who is fighting a divorce so vehemently over money to spend a lot, so I gather that the situation has improved and that a settlement of sorts has been reached. He engages an interior decorator who is bubbly and outgoing. She is not pretty, but she has personality, plus she is brilliant and "gets" exactly what he wants as it fits with her personal style of interior. She works hand in glove with the architect. I am headed overseas for about four months on a trip to the UK and Malta, where I want to look at property investment opportunities, as I am concerned about South Africa in the long term.

We have a few meetings with her, and it becomes apparent that she does not like me one bit. I pick up that she is smitten with my Dr Miracle, and I notice that he is oblivious. She can hardly contain herself in his presence, and it occurs to me that she is way better suited to him than I am. They are both "suburbia," as I call it. They both hail from the Southern Suburbs and have mixed in similar circles. Her husband has died, and she is quite well off. She has loads of friends, is one of twins, and comes from a large, very close family. I don't say anything to Dr M and soon I am overseas. He sends me pictures of the progress, and we talk fairly often. During this time there is a big hic-up on the home front, and Ms Décor is on hand. She is a shoulder he can lean on, and she goes beyond the scope of ordinary friendship to support him. I am acutely aware of this, but at the same time I know that he is unaware of how she feels and, presumably, not interested.

I arrive home just before Christmas, and he proudly shows me around. The house is gorgeous "coffee book table" stuff. It's rich in colours of blue and maroon. The ceilings are high, and a strong Georgian theme runs throughout. The kitchen, in traditional white and black, opens out onto a huge family room and dining room, all in one. Massive conservatory doors and windows open to the perfectly manicured small outside garden that is beautifully landscaped. The outside comes inside, and it's spectacular. The master bedroom is massive too, and the dressing room houses all his clothes, and there is a separate shoe cupboard! It occurs to me that he has not mentioned anything about making space for a woman's clothing! In fairness, there is enough room for two people, but I feel uneasy, and my red flag signals. He is having a party later in the week, in fact the day before Christmas, and Ms Décor has invited all her friends and family, as he does not have any.

The evening is a huge success, and the room is full of "suburbia" people, and even people I know. I befriend a gay couple who I absolutely adore and spend the better part of the evening talking with them and a woman I worked with, who was the nastiest person alive, resulting in me leaving a job. She has no idea who I am, and I spend time talking to her and her lovely husband, whom I knew long before she did. I get some joy out of the moment, knowing full well how much she hurt me, but I have passed that and can converse without any pain and revel in my own bravery and ability to move on. When Ms Décor arrives, I do not recognise her and mistake her for her twin sister. She has lost a lot of weight and looks amazing!! "How can you not know who I am, Susan?" I apologise and quickly move off; no point in telling her she is so much thinner that nobody would recognise her! It occurs to me once more that her friends and family are the perfect fit for Dr M and that my eclectic mix of single, married, and gay friends are a far cry from this. At this point, I know that we are not a fit. He gives a speech. I expect certain things in a speech and find the content empty and emotionless. Little gratitude; a lot about his search; the detail; the renovation process without much mention of her, in fact hardly any.

He asks me to join him at dinner the following evening, as he is hosting the Chairman of the International Pain Association. It goes well. He tells me that he has never done this in his marriage, and I wonder why not, but do not ask. They are a very interesting, lovely couple, and we talk about Bali, where I have just spent two months. He is a strong humanitarian and, like me, has enormous respect and admiration for the Hindu people who are the majority in Bali. Their lives are focused on their fellow human beings; they have a strong sense of community and family. They spend each day in deep gratitude, and material possessions are not important.

The following day is Christmas, and we spend it together in his new home with the children. During the lunch, I suggest that we say a form of grace. I make the fatal mistake of asking each person to share what they are grateful for. His son has to think about this, so his daughter decides she wants to share her gratitude before him, and I ask her to wait, as he is thinking. He is younger than her and often overlooked by his father; the daughter is clearly his favourite.

Later that night, when I speak to Dr Miracle on the phone, he tells me that his daughter is most unhappy. She felt slighted and hated me, and there was no way she would accept me as her stepmother. He is decidedly upset and has no idea how to deal with this. I tell him that it's okay, that it's normal, and that she's had a really tough time and it will blow over, and the more time we spend together, the better it will get. I had successfully parented two stepchildren, so I know how to deal with this and find common ground with her. I know that she is a sweet girl, but traumatized. I do not hear from him again after this call. I am devastated, and feel very sad. I had spent four months overseas and had thought about him often and was looking forward to being with him again.

When new year comes and goes without a word from him, I know that it is over. In my head, I know it is for the best, as we are not a fit. I have learnt over the last couple of years that often what we want is not right for us and that logic has to prevail. Love, or infatuation, is just not enough.

Three months later, I learn that Dr Miracle has married The Decorator! Right after his divorce came through and that he sold the house, and they bought an even larger property for twice the price, in Constantia! Mr and Mrs Suburbia.

I am reminded of the words, 'here today, gone tomorrow'!

CHAPTER 13
MR VANISHED, MR GONE!

Dark olive skin, shaved head, piercing brown eyes, and a body that you only ever get to dream about! He has a kind face with a gentle glow to it, a beautiful full smile, and "Colgate advert" teeth. A fair bit younger than me, but I never let this bother me! His description centres around humanity and helping others. He is widowed and very family-orientated. "My daughters are now grown up, and I am in a position to look for that someone special now." I "like" his profile, although I do suspect that a muscular guy like him probably does spend an inordinate amount of time in the gym, so we would certainly not be a match on that basis! But he is really good eye candy that is definitely worth meeting in the flesh! My profile is clear on the age front—that I am older than him.

Two days later, 31 March, there is a reply from him, and we exchange some information online before we convert to WhatsApp. I have established that he has built RDP houses for the poor in South Africa for the better part of twenty years; that this was not a lucrative position, but he was more interested in assisting those less fortunate than himself. This speaks volumes in my book of life and values, and I am very interested to learn more.

During my travels, as I mentioned previously, I was fortunate to visit Bali with its beautiful, gracious nation, that changed my life for the better. Each day starts with giving thanks and gratitude before you do anything else. This permeates throughout the day. "Matur Suksma" is the Balinese word for "thanks very much." It is second nature to each sentence. There is no emphasis on money. Everyone has a scooter, which makes up 95% of the population's form of transport. Life is simple and revolves around the community, family, and gratitude. You look out for your neighbours, and most families all live together. Grandparents, parents, and children all live in communion together. There is no showing of opulence when a person is wealthy, and they smile all day.

You rarely see a miserable Balinese. It's not in their DNA. I am reminded of a phrase I saw recently that stayed with me: "If you want to find happiness, find gratitude," and this resonates with my own belief system. It's a sure way to be happy when you may be feeling a bit off-colour! It will change your mood and thinking fast!

I message him on WhatsApp, "Thank you for your number! Would you be able to chat later this eve, perhaps? It would be great to meet for a coffee? I gather your days are busy, so perhaps at the weekend? I am flexible and work when I want to."

His WhatsApp profile has a picture of him holding a baby, and I gather that this is his grandchild. I say, "adorable pic" in my message to him.

His response is somewhat later that evening, and he explains that he has two phones, "One for work and one for home, lol. I get home later than most as I do a cardio workout, plus I drive around all over the country for work."

He now works for himself as a project manager and consultant on massive RDP housing projects. These housing projects are hugely pressurised as many houses have to be built in a short space of time. We're talking numbers of over 400! He explains that he is on a housing project up the coast and will be spending the weekend helping his daughter, who is preparing for her wedding in March. From this, I gather that he has a very close and cohesive relationship with her. The other daughter is older, married, and working independently and successfully in her chosen profession.

He explains that he has deadlines, and I know from my days in real estate that there is no time for administration until the day is over, as one is out and about all the time, and in his case, out all day on site, managing and organising. He explains that the picture is of himself and his grandchild. He has lost two grandchildren, so she is extra special to him. I am very sad when I read this, as he is not only a widow but has also had to bear the loss of two grandchildren.

I immediately send a voice note from the beach and explain that I am not so fit and have just come from the physio as I have overdone it. I also tell him that I prefer to speak on a voice note than to type, as it is easier. While I am talking, Molly suddenly runs off at the sight of another dog on the beach, so I have to excuse myself, and I call him back a bit later.

I thank him for being so gracious and for explaining in depth what he does. "I am completely impressed with the work you do, and I look forward to meeting you. I also know about being busy from my past career in real estate, plus my best friend died in January, so I have been very busy, but I try and keep the balance. I am sorry to learn of your loss. That is tragic."

He sends me a voice note, "I also have a second business that assists people who don't have ownership of their homes and need the documentation, so assist them in obtaining this. It has always been my passion to work with the poorest of the poor." He explains that 42 of the current housing project owners of homes he is busy building cannot read or write and they are also elderly. He loves what he does, as he has always wanted to help the poor. He tells a story of the domestic worker who worked for him and cleaned the toilet with shampoo, and his children found it very funny. He explains that she did not have a toilet where she lived; she only had an outside toilet, and gently explains how tragic this is.

He explains that a lot of his funding comes from the government, and he has to load the applications as they can't do this themselves. At one point in his life, he was also a government bookkeeper. As a qualified accountant, he allocated funds for projects but explains that he really wanted to be part of the project, rather than fund it.

He took a big step by leaving the comfort of "dead sure" employment with retirement. He took the plunge. Soon after this, his wife passed away, and the family had to rely on his income with no backup of her income. He managed and also looked after his girls on his own. The eldest is now a qualified attorney. He often took his children along to work so that they could see what shacks look like and explained to them that when he says he does not have enough money for what they want, they need to focus on being grateful for what they have and realise how lucky they are. I find this very noble, and he becomes a "hero parent" in my eyes. He says that it does not make massive profits, but he does what he is passionate about—making those less fortunate happy and helping them.

I am very taken with this message, and it sits with me for quite some time. I now know that what I want is to meet this man very much. It's not about wanting to date him anymore or seeing him as a potential boyfriend, but rather to sit and listen to this noble individual who is so intent on giving to humanity. It resonates deeply with my own mantra: "If we can make a difference to humanity in our lifetime, we have achieved our purpose."

I send him some exquisite pictures of a sunset drive I do with my brother along the Atlantic coastline from Muizenberg to Camps Bay. It is a warm, light, and sunny day on the Muizenberg to Cape Point side of the ride. The sea is a gorgeous blue, and the water twinkles as the last of the sun's rays dance on the big, vast, endless ocean. Soon we are turning towards the other side of the coastline, heading west, past Cape Point. Black, dark, angry clouds greet us. The sea is churning up big, rolling, grey waves. The darkness and waves move towards us, and the light of earlier has become so dark now that we have to turn our headlights on.

I have not witnessed anything like it in my time of living along this southern coastline, and we stop to watch this movement of nature at its finest. It's a fascinating transition from one side to another that happens in less than five minutes of driving. I am mesmerised as the massive black clouds in the distance ebb and flow towards us in warlike unison. A warrior dance at sea. There is a lovely picture of Molly and me in the car on that day that has remained a favourite of mine.

I get this message from him, "The beauty of the Cape and its coastal areas are the reason why I will never leave the Cape. Growing up in Observatory was nice. We were all friends, and everybody tried to help each other. Those days, many of us were poor, but we survived. I went to a good school in the city where 80% of the kids came from rich families, so that was hard. These children looked down on those of us who were poor, as we did not have fancy stationery, school bags, etc. I was raised in a tough school of life, but I would not change a thing. I think that you and I are very different, but I am sure we will share some values, etc. That's what makes this world an interesting place. My life is simple. I have a small family and few friends, but those I do have, I love dearly. I am not a lover of the TV set, and I mostly watch Richard Attenborough on "Life on Our Planet." I have to head off to a meeting now. Aaarrgh!"

Our communication is frequent and lengthy. Sometimes it is a voice note, and other times it is texting. I am not bothered that we have not met, as I am so busy with winding up my late friend's estate, so I have little time, and it's a welcome distraction. I am semi-retired and run a small rental portfolio from properties I own, so I can dictate my hours to a large degree. It is a lovely distraction to speak to a man who really gets me thinking about how much value we place on the material and how little value it actually has.

I send him a message telling him that I am off to a forest dance that weekend and looking forward to it. I had recently been to a beach one, and I loved it. This one is in the woods, though, so it will be a different experience. It's a disco set up, but nothing like you would imagine! There are three DJs set up individually at their own stations, and they each play a completely different genre of music! Each person who attends this event is given a set of headphones, and you then simply tune into the DJs whose music resonates with you. It is amazing fun, and people do their own thing, oblivious to those around them. It somehow also frees the spirit, and you don't really worry about who is doing what. I tell him about this event, and he responds by saying he loves dancing but has two left feet.

"I love nature; it's been a recent discovery of mine with the garden project I embarked upon with no knowledge of plants, fauna, or flora," I say. "Watching flowers grow each day is a miracle in itself. Small, tiny plants start to root and grow. Flowers bloom on the smallest of plants, and in some instances, they weigh down the leaves and stalks of the young plants. Thick succulents, severely trimmed of their thick leaves due to being so neglected and eaten by bugs and worms, start to grow within three weeks. Thick young leaves emerge in the shortest space of time, and I gaze in wonder at this incredible display of nature at its best. It is here that I encounter a closeness with our universe and the creator of all things beautiful."

"We have loadshedding again," he replies. In South Africa, this has become a regular phenomenon, as our previous president abused billions of rands and the government is basically bankrupt! "The meeting was just for feedback on the Alsbury project, where we are doing 400 houses; they will complete 20 to 30 houses by the end of the month," he says. This communication is such an eye-opener for me. I was in real estate for thirty years and sold top-end houses to the wealthy and fortunate.

I reply and say, "I have a roof over my head. I have food to eat. I can pay all my bills. I have income that is secure and ongoing into my old age, with a small rental portfolio of my own that provides me with a monthly income. I have a car and a motorbike plus a pedal boat. I have a bed to sleep in, clothes, and all that I need. I have always been deeply grateful in my life, but you open my eyes to a way more profound and deeper sense of gratitude, and I am so thankful. These people, who are the poorest of the poor, are finally given homes after years of empty promises."

"Our ANC governing party held such promise when our beloved Madiba was President in 1994, but now this political party rapes and steals from their own people. The country is on a downward spiral. When Madiba was in power, he converted years of unfair distribution to helping the poor and the disadvantaged, who make up a good 90% of our nation.

"The country prospered until his reign ended in 2005. Unfortunately, the following presidents raped the country as billions of rands landed up in the hands of others for whom it was not intended. A tragic situation that today, in 2022, results in zero money in the government coffers to right the wrongs of the past.

"This is often the case when there have been decades of disadvantage, as those who vote for the ruling parties continue to remain uneducated with lowered education standards plus a massive 45% unemployment rate. The end result is more poverty and a rise in crime. A never-ending cycle."

This man, despite all of the above, continues to make a difference in a corrupt world. I am reminded of the elderly man who walks on a beach picking up one starfish at a time and tossing it back into the ocean despite the hundreds washed up on the shore. A young boy walks by and taps him on the shoulder, "Sir, why are you bothering? There are just so many." The elderly man picks up another, tosses it back into the ocean, and says, "Because I made a difference to that one!" This is what this wonderful human being is doing— making a difference to humanity slowly but surely. That is my mantra: If you seek a purpose, make this your purpose. Make a difference for one, as each opportunity counts, and very soon you will have made a difference to many!

"These are castles for those people," I say.

Later, he responds, "I am a Sagittarius, and I do things on impulse, and sometimes it's not my best choice. I have to try and think before I do things! I love music, and without it, the world will be a sad place. I link so many songs to memories. I am off to the gym, and you must have a fabulous day, and I am sure Molly will, for her every day is a good day with you as her mom."

"Thanks for the lovely message. I am an impulsive Aries and get on well with Sagittarian males."

For eleven years I had a fantastic relationship with a Sagittarian man, whom I still adore and have respect for today. A wonderful human being who was a fair bit younger than me, and it was the happiest relationship of my life. I don't share this with him, but I do so for the purposes of my story. I have already shared my time in Bali with him and through our communication with one another. I relive that experience as he reminds me time and time again of the beautiful people who give thanks daily for all that they have.

The next day he tells me that he is ill and, in response to my get-well messages, says, "I am not one of the many who are near death when I have a cough!" This makes me laugh. He gives me a rundown on his usual training programme and I get tired just reading it! He does, however, have the body that is worth every effort as it is almost perfect!

"You will not find me talking about gym as I am not a gym freak," he writes.

He tells me that he will be downscaling from his home that is too big now and also selling off his little seaside home in Onrus, a gorgeous small seaside village that is a two-hour drive from Cape Town. This resort is right on the beach! The latter is in a caravan park with mobile homes on it, so it's not "high investment stuff." I know this place well, and it is one of the loveliest spots I have seen in my time. The only drawback to these kinds of investments—as a keen real estate enthusiast—are the people who sometimes spend holidays there. Not always the kind of people you want to be in such close proximity to. However, if you have less, you reduce your expenses and free yourself, so there is definitely some advantage in that. As a property investor, this rings true and resonates with me.

He says, "I have so little in real terms, but I carry such riches in the work that I do."

I respond to his message with a voice note, laughing about the cough explanation, and tell him how well I know the place where he is selling and how much I love it. He elaborates and tells me that he has promised it to a woman whose mother lives on the same site and that she would like to buy it; that she has been staying there rent-free, just paying the levy. This highlights his ever-giving spirit. I know instinctively that he is selling it to her for below-market value. The profit is not monetary in this sense, but one that enriches the soul. I learn from this man daily, and I am grateful for the encounter that reminds me so much of "messed up"' western societies where we chase money and live poorer, less rich lives as a result and are oblivious.

I share with him that I like the freedom these days of deciding on the spur of the moment where to go, having also sold a farmhouse I once owned in the Karoo town of Calitzdorp, as well as a small holiday apartment in Hermanus many years ago.

Whilst it's wonderful to own these places that are home from home, they do at the end of the day own us as there is the upkeep, maintenance, and cleaning that is needed on a regular basis. As a seasoned property professional and developer with my ex-husband, these were also investment properties and served us well over time. To be tied to the same place can limit one's sense of adventure, so this is another reason for selling after a few good years of fun and enjoyment. Women ultimately like to nest, and it is this too that drives me as I make a home from home when buying these properties.

Later on in our communication, we share more details about our lives. He explains that during Covid his daughter and son-in-law came to live with him as they had both lost their jobs. It is in this voice note that he shares the death of his two grandchildren during this time, which is tragic. The daughter carried full term in both cases, but after giving birth, both the little boy and girl died within days of being born. I am deeply affected by this tragedy, and it hovers around me for days. I find it hard to come to terms with this very sad story

I wake up daily in deep gratitude for how incredible my life has been. I look at my own hardships, which have their own tragic attachment, but I have never lost a child—only a mother, a sister when I was ten, and a father at seventeen. I find a sense of comfort as a result of his experiences. To lose a child that has a life to live is incomprehensible to me and, I would imagine, to most people. In the journey of dating, I learn so much and am so grateful. I realise how different all our lives are and how different people respond to what happens to them.

This man, despite all the difficulties and tragedies he is exposed to daily in his life and through his work, remains a deeply humble and giving human being who places zero value on material possessions and things. I am reminded of how little value these things have and how important it is to live life to the full. To remain grateful daily, to give to those less fortunate, and to find value in what money cannot buy. This man is a great teacher. I tell him as much, and he shares an Afrikaans idiom with me, "Elke Huis het sy Kruis," which means "every home has its own cross to bear."

Later on, I share with him that I am taking my goddaughter to dinner to celebrate her securing a job overseas and that we will spend the night together. She has to sleep in my large queen-size bed with me, as her room is let because she no longer lives at home. We have turned it into an income producer for her on Airbnb, which she now manages, and she can then save it. Molly is also on the bed with us at this point and is perplexed at the setup.

He is frustrated today. He has a lot of completed homes ready to hand over to the new owners, but they had either not arrived or fulfilled certain requirements in order for the homes to be handed over. Only sixty out of the 169 applicants have completed the necessary steps. This is the frustrating story of dealing with a community that is so challenged on every level. At this point I have to admire him for continuing to do the work he does, as I would be very disappointed had it been me. He clearly has a very determined nature and staying power. A lot more than me!

We finally agree to meet the following weekend—on the Sunday, just after 2 p.m. It's a favourite spot of mine, set under gigantic trees and beautiful greenery. The historical Cape Dutch building stands majestically proud amongst the trees. The large, beige-coloured umbrella-shaded patio is very tranquil and complements the beautiful African blue sky. I am wearing a long, flowing casual dress, as it's hot. I arrive at exactly the same time he does. He is taller than I expected and very good-looking. He is easy to converse with, and the lunch lasts two hours.

We talk about the people for whom he builds these homes. They are an interesting, colourful mix of individuals and stem from the days when Dutch sailors landed in the Cape and then slept with the local women. This resulted in a mixed nation of people called "Coloureds," who are an ethnic group in South Africa that live in the Western Cape. They are part and parcel of the country's "disadvantaged" community under the then National Party, which ruled the country and gave the White population control, albeit being one of the smallest populations in the country.

We don't talk much about me, but I put this down to nervousness and know that many people simply rattle on about themselves as it's easy communication. I am happy to be a listener. I share less of myself, and often this is a blessing later on. What he does share with me at this lunch is that both his daughters are very possessive of him and that they would not welcome someone else in his life. He puts this down to being 100% available to them while they were growing up. I sense that he did this to try and make up for the loss of his wife. He did meet someone many years ago, but it did not work because the children were his priority.

We continue to chat about how very busy we both are. He is away and has lots of family commitments. I suggest cooking him a thank-you dinner for the lunch he bought me. He says he will let me know and that we must take Molly for a nice walk on the beach as well. He shares the Nightbirde video with me, and I tell him that I watched it too and that it was just the most encouraging and uplifting message ever. I send him a voice note on the 24 February 2023 and mention I am free on the Saturday and that if he is available, we can meet at the beach and I will bring Molly, and we can then have a meal and that it would be my treat.

He does not reply to my message. "Have I offended you in anyway?" My message is delivered but not read, and I never hear from him again. This floors me initially, for I know he is a lovely man who has some incredible values and principles, plus he is well mannered.

I rack my brains, and it occurs to me that perhaps his daughters have listened to our messages and even read them, and they have decided that our chatting to one another is not a good idea? Perhaps he has met someone else? Based on the chats we had, he is way too busy, so this is highly unlikely. Maybe he got ill? Maybe he died? Or he has decided I am not a match for him but does not know how to tell me? Either way, I will never know, and then his profile disappears off the dating site as well. A mystery indeed!

I look back on this encounter and I am grateful. Life always teaches us, and I am reminded that material possessions are not important in the greater scheme of things. That what we own does not define us; that there are millions of people who are much worse off than I am; that helping those less privileged is one of the most rewarding things we can do in life. He grounds me to the real values in life, and I am so thankful for this encounter.

CHAPTER 14
MUSIC TO MY (Y)EARS

He sends me a voice note, "This man will find you, and if there is no beach, he will create a beach." He chuckles, and it's a soft yet deep, throaty, melodious light laugh. I like his sense of humour and that he is willing to move mountains, yet we have not met! Our first phone call to one another earlier connects us in a deep way. He is a romantic, funny, and kind. He is gently spoken, and the sound of his voice is soothing. We message a lot and agree to meet the next day, and he is driving 100 kilometres to do so! He writes well, and as he is also a songwriter, this is engaging and a joy to read. This man practices what he preaches, and I like it! On the Friday morning, he confirms that he will be staying in a small coastal area that is close to a cosy restaurant that I had booked for an early dinner to enable us to catch the sunset.

I am attracted to his handsome, kind, and gentle face, his blue eyes, and his full, sexy mouth. He is not very tall though, and I wonder if this will turn out to be a deal breaker for me or not. I recently met someone who was slightly shorter than me—which I can live with—but he was smaller boned than me as well! I had visions of crushing him at any God-given moment, so this has made me very aware of build, which previously was not that important.

En route to our "date," he sends me some pictures from his Airbnb, and the views are spectacular. The blue sky and mountains in the distance are picturesque. He certainly chose a perfect spot. He sends me another voice note while driving, saying that he has not dated anyone from the site and feels extremely fortunate that he clicked on my profile with his one free click. At this point, I do not realise that he is, in fact, not a paying member. This is something I am usually very aware of, as "free click" will often indicate a scammer or person who can't afford to subscribe, and neither one of these are ever people I continue to speak to, but I am oblivious to this for now. I also discover he is an anti-vaxxer. This is also another red flag for me, as more often than not, these people are anti a lot! He tells me he is young at heart and a livewire.

He informs me that the guest house needs some work and is not as nice as it used to be. We agree to meet at the guest house and then drive together from there to the restaurant that has always had rave reviews. We meet at the entrance, and he is way nicer looking than his pics and yes, he is short but just my height. He is also smaller than me physically, so this is a little disappointing, but I lose sight of that as he is lovely, with a warm glow about him that resonates with his inner being. He says, "I am pleasantly surprised, my gosh, you are so lovely, such Hazy Blue eyes!"

We jump in my car, as it is outside the garage where he has parked his vehicle, inside. The drive is short, and soon the thatch roof restaurant with white wash walls comes into view. It is a refurbished, old fisherman cottage and very well known. It nestles at the foot of a small beach, and the sun is just setting. I have not been there in years and am looking forward to a dinner and, perhaps, a trip down memory lane.

Over dinner, I learn that he is Afrikaans-speaking but has a really beautiful English accent. That he played music professionally in his younger days and toured the world on cruise liners as a member of the resident band. He has toured most of South Africa and supported some pretty impressive local and overseas bands. He is gentle, very artistic, and in touch with his feminine side. I like this about him, although it does set off the odd warning bell! However, if one is going to be truly creative, then one is always more alternative.

He runs and owns a very successful tour company but has been adversely affected by Covid. We get a lovely table, and I feel fortunate, as it is very full, so I am very glad I booked. I am starving and eagerly look at the menu, and Mike sits back. He does not look at the menu and says he is not really hungry. I tell him that it's my treat as he has driven a long way to meet me. "It's the least I can do," I say. He protests, but I insist.

He is an interesting man and calls me "Hazy Blue." He tells me that I am beautiful and that he is so pleased we have met. He moved to the West Coast two years ago from The Garden Route, which he says was not a nice place to live. I find it strange, for it is one of the most visited spots outside of Cape Town in South Africa for overseas tourists, and this would bode well for his business. He is very pleased he made the move and sold a bigger property and bought a small seaside cottage. I am in a fragile state, having lost my very best friend two months earlier. He is kind and caring, and this appeals to my vulnerable state.

During dinner, I burst into tears as I recount the journey with my best friend, who died of cancer in January. At this point, I am exhausted from the work I am doing as a co-executor with one very rude, unkind, and nasty beneficiary who lives abroad. I am trying so hard to honour my friend whom I loved dearly, and the amount of courage and strength it requires to keep my executor hat on and say nothing to this unkindness and ungrateful behaviour takes all the strength I can muster. It carves deep piercing, wounds into my already broken bleeding heart, and each day is a struggle of grief and work that has to be done, no matter what. I am not embarrassed by these moments of immense sadness and hurt, for they tell me just how much I loved her and how important carrying out the task of executorship that honours her is to me. I do, however, find it unusual to share this with someone I have just met. The gentle nature of this very kind and caring man moves me and opens up this very vulnerable place I find myself in.

At the end of the evening, he puts me under no pressure and gives me the sweetest good-night hug. He strokes my hair and tells me that he is in no rush. He leaves me a good-night voice note, which I play once I am in bed. "Hazy Blue, I want to see you again! Let's meet for lunch, as I would also like to introduce you to my son. I send a voice note in the morning thanking him and suggest we meet at a hotel in a lush, pretty valley not far from where I live and that I would like to introduce him to my child, Molly, who has four legs. I warn him that she is beyond adorable and that everyone falls in love with her. He tells me that he loves dogs, and this is a big plus for me.

I arrive a little earlier to walk Molly around the park, where the trees are green and lush. I chat to Molly and tell her that we are meeting Mike's son and that she too is family, and that is why we are here. We sit outside under the shade of massive oaks that rise high up into the sky, their branches creating shady spots, which at the same time let the sunlight in, and it's warm and fresh outside. Over lunch, before his son arrives, who is joining us for a short while, Mike tells me he has written a song about me and that he can't stop thinking about me. He says I am the one! I feel uncomfortable and find this kind of "love" unrealistic and tell him he is infatuated. He says that I have no idea how much he can do for me and how happy he will make me. He loves to cook and has no problem with my dislike of cooking. He even sews and paints too. He is good with his hands and can fix most things in my house. He will take all my woes away, and all I will ever have to do is just relax and have fun. I smile as this is so kind and loving. I say nothing about the work involved in the running of a small private rental portfolio, of which the admin takes up most of my time, as does the Airbnb side. I have people who manage my maintenance for me, and that is at least off my hands, so these skills he is offering will not be needed. The cooking, however, appeals to me a lot! I dare not tell him that I do not do the dishes either!

His son is model material and a lovely young man. Mike does not eat, and so only his son and I eat. He insists on paying. I have a sense that he is not in a position to really do so. He tells me he has arranged to stay another night and that he would love to see me later. This takes me by surprise, but I don't tell him that, as I don't want to hurt him or make him think that I do not appreciate it. I also have no plans for the evening. He has to take his son back to Table View, so we agree to meet later. He calls me at six to say he is on his way to the Airbnb he booked and that we can meet later. I have invited him to my home and said we could have a small braai.

At seven thirty, he tells me that he has found an Airbnb but that it is in a terrible area and that he is now looking for something else. I explain that I am not in a position to offer him a space as my Airbnbs are all let, and that I know he will appreciate that I cannot invite him to my home to sleep over as I do not know him well enough. By eight thirty it is clear, he won't find accommodation, and I encourage him to head home before it is too late, which he does. I feel awful and spend the night tossing and turning and wondering if I should have succumbed and let him stay over. I do, however, know that my current fragile state means I need time to prepare for this kind of thing and that this has all been very sudden.

Once home, he and I spend more time chatting and messaging, and he sends me a song he recorded. It's a very well-written song, and it has some deep emotion as it's about a place where he used to live here in SA. It refers to this town setting him free, for he is headed to Croatia to live and set up a business. He plays a classical guitar and is clearly a talented musician with a very good voice. He refers to being given a second chance and talks about life being a gamble. This is all relevant to this move overseas. He also sends me two pictures he took of us, and they are lovely. He really has the most handsome face that is gentle and warm.

He calls me, "My Little Mouse, you have totally and utterly invaded my heart." It is said with such deep sincerity, and I feel sad as I know the feeling is not reciprocal, but I am determined not to make any call on this special individual for two reasons. My emotional state leaves a lot to be desired, and he happens to be one of the nicest human beings I have met in a long time.

He is very artistic and sends me some of his paintings and his pottery in his home. The colours are vibrant and strong. From the pictures, I sense that his home is quite messy, as he writes music too, so it appears as though the lounge is a mix of all three pastimes, and I don't see anywhere to sit! His voice notes are always gentle, quiet, and relaxing. This calms my fragile state, and I am drawn to him because of it.

"I will come and take care of you, my Hazy Blue; you are so fragile and in need of care and rest," he says, and tells me he will come and look after me that weekend. As I have a free apartment that is not let, I tell him he can stay in the flat. "Men who call themselves partners are just lazy bastards," he says. "I will cook; I will clean up; fix anything that needs fixing; and let you rest; just be with you."

I am comfortable, as I know he is a man who will not push for any kind of physical encounter or anything that I am not comfortable with. He is also upbeat because, with the opening up overseas from Covid, bookings are coming in, and he is positive and happy.

He is very reassuring and upfront with how he feels and does not hide his emotions and feelings. I feel special and loved despite the short time we have known one another. He reassures me often that he is different from other men, and I tell him that I know that he is.

While he is on route, I am very busy as we are about to put my friend's house on the market. We have finally cleared out a mountain of stuff and rearranged the furniture, and it has been a huge job. I send him pictures and feel deeply satisfied, albeit exhausted. It has been a week of sorting, clearing, moving things, cleaning, gardening, and fixing.

We meet at five at my home. He settles into the suite, which has its own entrance, and we agree to have an early evening and to get some food from a local restaurant not far away, as he loves curry. I insist on paying as he has driven a long way again, and it's an hour and a half at least, and then he will be driving back as well. He fetches dinner, and we have a lovely, quiet evening.

I am tired, so we watch a movie together and snuggle up on the couch holding hands, and I nestle in his shoulder for part of the evening, and I only just fit. I move my body a little lower than his on the couch. He understands that I am nowhere near ready. He kisses me ever so gently and sweetly. I weep from deep, long sadness, and I am overwhelmed. He kisses my tears away and tells me that he loves my deep emotions and understands the pain I am in. That he is patient and will wait, as we, after all, have the rest of our lives to live together.

We fall asleep in the same bed, and he is the perfect gentleman. He leaves once I am asleep and moves to the suite, where he has unpacked and made himself comfortable.

In the morning, I feel well rested, and he brings me coffee in bed. He has quietly waited till I wake up and comes in wearing just his t-shirt and nothing else. This is not a come-on, as he told me that he loves walking around with no underwear, and I was intrigued when he told me this. He certainly is, by all accounts, a man comfortable in his own skin! He also prances around, and I am taken back to my airline days when all the male crew members who worked in the cabin were gay. They called, walking down the aisle, "mincing," and this comes to mind, and I have to stifle a laugh. They would mimic passengers once everyone had disembarked and were an endless source of entertainment.

I know that this kind man is NOT gay, but I do find his feminine side now a little too much for my female comfort. He waves his hands about too, and this is also another trigger, as the "boys," as we called them, would hang their wrists limply and flap their arms about during the process of the "mince" walk. I try to keep a straight face.

We head out for a walk, and I suggest the small island that is part of the estate that I live on. There are unlikely to be many people and definitely no one, I would know. I am now terrified of bumping into someone I know in case they see me with my friend who "dance minces"—a new description I just invented. Molly looks like she is mincing too now as my mind runs amok and I tell myself to teach her how to walk and not mince!

He makes a lovely lunch at home for us, and again, I sense there is a need to do so in order to preserve funds. I don't mind as he has driven all the way here, so that is a cost, and I try not to be small-minded. I berate myself for being so pedantic, but then I remember that I have worked very hard to create an independent life for myself and that mentoring is an additional cost, which means my funds are limited too. Although I have enough by more than average standards, I grew up poor, and I am always nervous about not having enough money to live on in my old age. I cannot begin to imagine supporting another person on my limited budget! I am generous by nature, so if I were wealthy, this would not matter to me, but I am not. I have enough for Shahkira, Molly, my schnauzer, and my goddaughter if she needs help, but not for anyone else. However, I do feel mean, as I don't like to be money conscious, but I have to be.

This thinking comes from my gut as I have gathered by now that he is struggling financially, but not telling me.

I know from my dating experience that a non-negotiable criterion for me is that the person I want to have a relationship with must be three things: he must be more intelligent than me and more successful than me, and if he is those two things, he will invariably be wealthier than I am. Does this matter? I am semi-retired and creative when it comes to income and have ways of creating additional income when needed, but it is for unforeseen expenses they never warn you about when you are young! Brace yourself now, girls, as you read this, if you are still young!

As you age teeth are a constant cost and every year these repairs, caps and cleaning make a huge dent in my income. Thank goodness for face lifts, anti-wrinkle injections and fillers! Never mind physiotherapy which is in fact, even more costly. Yoicks, why is all this awful thinking now coming to the fore! Just as well we don't have to give a medical history on sites and a list of current medication!

My mind is on a roll and next up is, medication! Chronic, vitamins, supplements and allergy pills. There are other medications, too! Hormone replacement therapy and hormone vaginal inserts to keep the vagina moist—they don't tell you it dries up as you get older! Anti-inflammatories, painkillers, the odd sleeping tablet, "happy pills," and special toothpaste for gums!

I am now getting depressed as I type this, and a change of thought is a must. I have not even tallied these annual costs, and now I am too scared to! It will make me severely depressed, and I may even take myself off the dating site, roll myself up in a heap, and forget about living! For about five seconds, and then the old vibrant, never-say-die me will be back!

After lunch, he tells me that he is going home. That he senses this is not working and that I am not into him. I simply reply, saying I am not in a good space, and again, I want to kick myself for not just being upfront and saying that he is right. I don't want to hurt him, as he put so much effort and energy into this encounter. He was "in love" and had met the woman of his dreams, and he knew we would have a fantastic future together. He leaves and looks so sad and forlorn. The house is silent when he goes, and all I can think of is how relieved I am that he has left. I will write to him in the week and apologise for hurting him and for not being able to be honest and upfront.

At the end of the week, before I send my message, I decide to look at his Facebook profile to see if he is okay. I have compiled a message that I am comfortable with and that took some time to compose as I wanted to be sensitive and kind. I am surprised to see a picture of him with a girl dated the 14th of March, which is the same day he left my house in the afternoon. The caption reads, "Exciting dinner and great company." Three days later, he updates his cover photo with a picture of the two of them. A day later they are having a family evening! Another post of the two lovebirds looking at one another adoringly!

I am relieved but at the same time taken aback that this man who professed to love me and know we were destined to have a future has moved on, exactly 5 hours later! He was talking to her while he was seeing me that weekend. I learn something new in the game of dating: that it is possible to move your "undying love and allegiance to another" in less than an afternoon! I delete the message. I am pleased to see that they are still very much an item three months later and are living in the same town, in all likelihood together. Wonders never cease!

This event, however, makes me question myself, and I wonder if I am truly stupid or just naïve. I don't believe in love at first sight; at best one can feel what you think is love at first sight, but one is fully conscious of the fact that real love takes more time—at least a year together, when you have passed the bulk of the honeymoon stage. I never use the word "love" in the early stages. I say things like, "I really like you a lot," "I love spending time with you," "I am so glad we met," and "I have a good feeling about this," which is how I voice a stronger feeling than just "like."

I am always apprehensive when someone I meet says they "love me" early on, and when this happens, I try not to judge, as they may genuinely feel that way and may not have felt this way before or have felt this way only once or twice in their lives. The question, however, is: how is it possible to "love" someone you have only just met? When I look back on the people I did love in my life, I do find that I pretty much felt that way from day one, but just never said so.

This is getting confusing in my head as I continue to write, and it boils down to there is no "correct" formula and that we have to allow each individual to be who they are, and the freedom of expression to do so; whether it is too soon or not, is debatable. I at least have a conclusion of sorts! On the flip side, it is always an ego boost when someone does say this, no matter how old you are. We all want to feel seen, cherished, beautiful, loved, and appreciated. So, it's okay; as long as it doesn't cause any harm and you feel good, embrace it!

CHAPTER 15
THE MERCENERY - BARTO

By far the best body on the Zoosk website for a senior! He is a slalom water skier and leans his well-defined, muscled body almost on the water. His brown, tanned skin glistens in the sunlight; short, wet, greased hair lies tight against his scalp; chiselled features and green-blue eyes peer out from under his perfectly defined eyebrows. He is eye candy in its finest form. One cannot help but notice his profile, as each picture of him is better than the last. There is a picture of him riding horseback, and my mind conjures up images of cowboys and Indians chasing across vast fields in battle in a remote part of America. There is an old antique Jeep picture he has amongst his profile pictures, with Monty, his very old dog and long-time companion, sitting on the passenger seat, and another has him on the couch with Monty. The last two pictures give him serious points. He is definitely worth some time and effort!

He lives in the Garden Route and is looking for a lifetime partner. He is of Swiss origin, and South Africa has been his base for the past eleven years. I "like" his profile, and a few days later he "likes" mine and suggests our dogs meet sometime? I thought this was clever and cute. I did not have the heart to tell him that my dainty, gorgeous, highly-pedigreed miniature Schnauzer would have no interest in a tired-looking scruffy dog called Monty! He is retired, so he is able to travel readily and easily. We chat online for about three weeks. We voice call, and our conversations are brief. His accent is very strong, and he is forthright and rather negative at times, but this is often a cultural thing, so I don't take too much notice, as he is a nice human being and shared some stories with me that interest me. He has had a fascinating, very private life on the work front and does not elaborate much but has travelled extensively.

I visit my good friend Michelle later in the week, she too has been on dating sites and we chat over a glass of wine. I tell her about Barto. Her hand flies to her mouth, and she clasps her hands over her mouth, with a startled look in her eyes. She takes a quick sip of wine and says, "I know him." She describes a bald man, and I say no, he has short hair. I pull out my phone and show her his picture, and she says, "Oh my word, he has grown his hair!" She says he is a lovely man but that they never got to really spend any time together, although she was in Plettenberg Bay and he was literally down the road. She explains that she made it clear she was available to meet him, but he seemed not to get this, and after three weeks in Plettenberg Bay she only gets to see him once, so she gave up on him. She, however, says he is worth pursuing and seems like a nice man.

One evening he asks me if there is a guest house close to where I live, as he is coming to Cape Town soon and would like to meet me. It has to be dog-friendly for Monty, who apparently does not like to travel. I am not sure if this means it has to be a fancy spot or not! I send him a few options, and he replies saying that he will be down on Friday, and could we meet somewhere close by that is dog-friendly for coffee? I suggest a pet-friendly outdoor place in St. James where dogs are welcome. I am walking towards the entrance and see his dog before I see him—still scruffy, shuffling along, and clearly very old. Before he even says hello, he says, "You sent me a very bad link, and I drove around and around looking for this place, as well as the guest house!"

"Hi Barto," I say, "It is so nice to finally meet you," and ignore his rude statement, but it makes him less appealing, none the less. We chat avidly, and he shares his life story with me, filling me in about his career, which has seen him in various parts of the world. He was part of the military in Switzerland and Canada, so this explains his dry humour and perhaps his cold front. However, every now and again, he shows a very sensitive, vulnerable side. This endears me to him.

After two hours, I say that I need to go home, and he says he does too. I jokingly say, "I am sure you have other girls to meet," and he just grins! I then feel very awkward as he has not said anything about seeing me later or the next day, and I awkwardly stand a little distance from him and say good-bye when we get outside. I am a warm person, so under different circumstances I would have given him a hug. I say, "Enjoy the rest of your time and chat soon." Once home, I feed Molly and take her for a walk and then catch up on some work I need to do.

Two hours go by, and there is no word from him. I figure he must be having a good time and is probably meeting more than a couple of women. I send him a text and say, "Thank you for meeting today and for driving such a long way. I hope you are having a good time. I am unsure how long you will be in town, but if you like, we can meet up again before you go?"

He replies immediately with a voice note, "I am on my way back to Knysna, as it seemed like you did not like me, and I see no point in staying!"

I am completely floored and call him straight away. "But you were meeting other women, so I did not want to make a fool of myself!"

"I was just joking with you; I would never do that. It's not my style, and you should have known that." I don't reply to him and say that *The site is full of men who profess to be something they are not*, I just think it. That in most instances, everyone is always talking to more than one person to start with, as well.

I apologise and tell him that I feel terrible as it has been a big misunderstanding.

He says, "Well, I can't turn around now." I tell him that I would not expect him to, but that I would make it up to him and visit the garden route soon.

Five weeks later, I find a gorgeous pet-friendly Airbnb. It's nestled at the foot of a hill and has lovely views of the lagoon. Upon arrival, it is even better than I expected. It's tastefully furnished and has everything I need. A comfy couch that Molly promptly claims for herself, so I have to prize her off and tell her "No", in such a way that she understands it is out of bounds. The wooden deck is my favourite place and where I enjoy sitting most. I have a good friend in Plettenberg Bay, so I intend seeing her and Peter, her husband. I have come up for a break and to unwind a bit, so I have some good books to read and also a decent pair of walking shoes, as Molly and I love to walk. We arrange to meet two days later.

He asks where I am in Knysna, and I explain that it is just above the main road. He says, "That is not a good area, you know; the township is just at the top of the hill, and they have a lot of break-ins. You should have booked somewhere else." I decide not to say anything in return but think to myself, *He's not the most positive person, and it's not very tactful to be so blatant and forthright when I have driven six hours to be here, only to be told on my arrival that I am not in a safe area.*

I walk Molly later in the afternoon, and it's a stunning walk. The area is so untouched and has a mix of house styles. Some new, some very old, and others refurbished. It feels like my old home town, Paarl, where I grew up. There are few pavements, and the roads have virtually no traffic. There are lovely big trees on the roads and many colourful, pretty, well-manicured gardens. I feel safe, and Molly loves it.

The best thing about the position is that it is in the town and a stone's throw from the main road, but high enough to be away from the noise. The road is not visible. Knysna main road is a slow and lengthy ride, and to be smack bang in the middle is first prize, as the road is always clogged with traffic as it also serves the N2, so it is always congested at all hours of the day.

To my delight, Leisure Isle, one of the oldest residential establishments, is less than 7 minutes away by car, and its breath-taking, with flat, calm water surrounding the residential island. There are nature trails and big trees, so there is a lot of shade. I love it there. Barto and I have arranged to meet there and have a fabulous walk, albeit slow, as Monty has come along. He is half blind and deaf, so he is compromised, but he stays close and manages well. Molly sniffs at every opportunity, and she and Monty ignore one another. They have watering spots for the dogs, and walkways line the nature reserve.

There are numerous information placards that tell you about the plants, fauna, and flora. There are some whisps of clouds that now and again get thicker and longer against a backdrop of vivid blue sky, and this provides some shade as well. The rainfall here is high, and it's overcast more often than not. The vegetation is thick, dense, very green, and lush as a result. It's the next best place to live apart from Cape Town, I decide.

Coffee is at a little gem of a tea house hidden amongst a forest of trees and greenery. It's like coming to a shack in the middle of yesteryear. There are books to read if you wish;

you can sit outside under the trees or on the veranda, which is shaded. We have to sit under the trees as they do not allow dogs on the veranda, and we are happy with this. Monty immediately falls asleep, and Molly follows suit soon after.

Barto tells me about the guest house he owned with his Swiss girlfriend for ten years here in Knysna. They split up, and he sold the guest house. He elaborates and says that where the guest house was is not a great area in Knysna anymore, as it is unsafe and crime is on the increase. He, in fact, does not have many positive things to say about anything, and I wonder if he is always so negative. I don't like this side of his character one bit, but try to ignore it as nobody is perfect and he is perfect-looking, with a body that would knock the socks off most young men.

He tells me that he did other work once he left the military but does not say what. I gather, however, that it is highly confidential, and that can only mean one thing. This kind of work is not for the faint-hearted. Only the best would have been elected to carry out these missions. This would explain his rock-hard torso, his strong arms, and his high level of fitness. He trains six days a week at the gym. He water skis twice a week and is the best skier in the area, winning all the competitions. It's rather exciting to be with a man who's lived such a dangerous life and who now works on the planning and strategic side.

After our walk, I visit my friend in Plett for the afternoon and read a bit at the guest house as well. Barto and I meet for an early dinner at his favourite Italian restaurant. He is a creature of habit and has coffee there most mornings, so he is part of the furniture. He knows the owner well, and when we get there, they are full. Mario is a tall Italian man, and has a large belly with an apron sitting mid-height as it covers the protruding stomach. He gives Barto, who towers over him by at least a head, a big bear hug. He barks off some commands in Italian, and a table is brought outside on the small veranda. They make seating available for us.

Barto ignores the menu and says I must choose whatever I like. He always eats the same dish, and I see military precision at play in every sense. Yep, he has the same breakfast whenever he eats here, and he has the same drinks as well. I can't imagine being so unadventurous. He is engaging, however, and well-read and can hold an intelligent conversation. His command of the English language is not great, but he manages well. He is the perfect gentleman and walks me to the car, opens my door, and drives me home. He gives me a goodnight hug, and we agree to see one another on the Sunday evening as he skis on Saturdays. This works for me, and I have a great day relaxing.

I go back to Leisure Isle, and we do the same walk but find a little beach, and Molly has the best swim ever. We meet a lot of residents walking their dogs, and I notice a number of very old folk, some with walking sticks, others in wheel chairs, with their children. It is something I do not see in Cape Town, and I am rather touched by it. It seems like the families here are a lot more cohesive and that Saturdays are family days.

Molly and I find a fabulous restaurant with two swinging couches, and there are only two tables for us. I settle on the large swinging couch, cover the back with my sarong, and lie back for a while. They have fabulous fish in a phyllo pastry that is open-roasted, and I order a glass of wine, which is most unusual. By the time I finish my meal, it's just Molly and me left in the restaurant. South American music drifts across the empty spaces, and it's a song I recognise. The beat is electric and has a great rhythm. I stroll over and ask them if they would mind turning it up, as there is only Molly and me. On my way back to my seat, I swing my hips and step to the beat. Before I know it, I am dancing solo and loving every minute. The staff come out and clap and love what they see. I manage to convince one of them to dance with me and watch her in awe.

The African women can dance in this country, and my dance is lost in the rhythmic sway of her voluptuous body that moves so gracefully. Her body knows this beat well—music is the root of all African culture, and children are dancing soon after they walk. I watch her, and my heart fills with joy. My eyes well up. She is happiness personified, and her faultless footwork and arm movements are a perfect union. I stop and watch her, mesmerized. I would give my eye teeth to dance like that. I have loved this time here and assure them that I will be back, and they say I have to come back! They will make sure there is good music.

Barto's house is clinical and precision-built. It has very little warmth despite the lovely fire glowing red and orange in the lounge. He proudly tells me that he did all the alterations himself and did all the work too—apart from the bricklaying. I know instinctively that nobody would be good enough for him and that this is the main reason he did the work solo. It's the sort of home you feel uncomfortable in. It has no personality, and it strikes me that the owner and the house are alike. It occurs to me that he is super serious; that he never laughs.

One of the things I do like about him is his consistency. He will send a lovely good-night message every night and a greeting every morning. I lack consistency, so I find this appealing. It makes me feel special. He has cooked a very nice risotto meal, and we eat at the kitchen counter on high bar chairs. Not an intimate or inviting way to do so. I notice that the table looks like it has never been used, and I realise that it has not! A little bit of OCD going on here. I am a neat and tidy person myself, so I like this about him, but it strikes me that he is a neat, tidy and clean freak! There is no trace of this house actually being lived in. Its sterile. I sigh, what a shame, as he is so gorgeous.

We listen to some great music, and Molly settles down happily in front of the fire. Monty moves from the floor to the couch intermittently, and Barto spends the evening moving the dog back and forth. I like his company, and we land up sitting close together, and I lean my head on his shoulder. It's comfortable, and I feel relaxed. Not long after this, we kiss, and like his body, his kisses are purposeful. Not gentle and lingering to start with, and I am a little disappointed. Gentle kisses are a great lead-up to a hot, heated connection, but sadly most men don't get it. They are "not with" the linger longer, teasing technique that makes one swoon and long for something more. They dive right in and wonder why women are not turned on.

Men are visionaries of a different kind; the physical form is enough for them. I go with the flow because I have been around a long time. I move into a position where I am in control and proceed to try and teach him the art of gentle persuasion. He cannot get his head around the gentle lips approach. I move away when he gets more heated, as I don't want to have sex. I need a personal connection before that happens and have to like him more as a person, and we have to seem like a compatible union. I don't see this picture emerging anytime in the future, to be honest.

It is past eleven, so I prize myself free, and Molly and I leave. She is more than ready, as 10 p.m. at home is "let's move to the bedroom" time, where we both settle in for the night. When we're at home during winter in Cape Town, she heads straight to her bed close to a wall heater, and I put my hot blanket on. Sometimes she is allowed to sleep with me. However, I do allow her to snuggle every morning. Like me, she is a late riser, and she only gets out of bed when I put my tackies on, as she knows it means walk time. She has her basket, toys, and blankets at the guest house and heads straight for bed. She is snoring by the time I get into bed. Her snores are baby soft and adorable, and it's often my bedtime sleep music. If I take too long to go to bed, I am usually party to a bark session of woofs, grunts, and little growls as she sleeps, playing and defending herself amongst the pack in her dreams.

In the morning there is a lovely message from him, "Thank you for a lovely evening, for coming to my home, and for the lovely bottle of wine. Drive carefully. I shall see you in Cape Town in the not-too-distant future." I smile. I love this about him; he is always consistent. He never misses a night or day of messaging.

By January, my life has turned around in a big way. I have my brother visiting, and his stay seems to be indefinite, which is not good news. We have not had a good relationship in the last twenty years since my mother passed away and have lived apart from the age of seventeen when my father died. He is full of trauma and pain. It is hard to be around him, and up until the previous year, we had not spoken for five years. The history is a long and painful one for both of us.

As mentioned before, my best friend succumbed to cancer after a four-year battle, and I am a co-executor. Both her children live overseas, and it's been a difficult job from the word go. Her funeral is a beautiful farewell at a mansion overlooking the ocean in St. James that once belonged to a count and countess. It is grand, gracious, classy, lavish, beautiful, and magnificent. It is a fitting place for my friend who spoke the Queen's English, who mixed in the top-end circles of Cape Town, and who always wore the best labels. She was always well groomed, and her red lipstick was her trademark. She had porcelain white skin that had never seen the sun, dark blue eyes, and platinum blond hair that was always perfectly in place.

She was loved by all who knew her. Behind her classy demeanour lay the most generous, loving, and loyal friend you could ever wish for. She was strong and formidable and lived a full life till the end. She died with grace and dignity. I felt blessed to have walked a close journey with her from the onset. On our final visit to the oncologist, we went for a superb lunch in Cape Town to celebrate the last predicted six months of her life. We laughed, we cried, and we loved every minute she had left. She went overseas two weeks after her diagnoses and came back almost half unconscious as her oxygen levels were so low from the cancer in her lungs. We did an incredible trip on the Rovos rail a month before she died. Our friendship took on a higher and deeper level.

Here are the words of a song by Faith Hill called "There You'll Be."

When I think back on these times and the dreams we left behind

I'll be glad 'because I was blessed to get to have you in life

When I look back on these days, I look and see your face

You were right there for me

In my dreams, I'll always see you soar above the sky.

These words aptly describe our friendship: "I will keep a part of her wherever I go, and everywhere I am, there she will be."

This time period saw me stretched to capacity. Emotionally, physically, and mentally. I moved into "work mode," and all feelings and emotions took a back seat. I worked day and night. I would sleep at four in the afternoon just to escape myself. I would wake and be back in auto mode. My beautiful young Shakira, who is fifteen and whom I mentor, was the only person who got any attention, and then it was a stretch for me to do so. She is a joy and delight and brings light to my days, which remain blank and emotionless.

I hear from Barto every morning and explain my situation. He is consistent and keeps sending a morning and good night message. After two months, he comes to Cape Town for a weekend and stays at my home in the second bedroom. I am no fun; I am tired and exhausted and just want to sleep. I can't pull myself out of my hole even though I invite friends who are German over for supper. Barto is inappropriate at dinner and strong in his views and opinions. He is incapable of putting his point across without seeming rude or derogatory.

The evening does not progress well. I thought that, as they were German and Swiss, it would be a good mix. Ursula pulls me aside and shakes her head; she says, "He is not for you, Susan."

I have to admit that I agree with her. He is kind, attentive, and caring towards me, and I feel even worse because now I know. I tell him later that day and say I am just too depleted. That I am unable to be in any relationship. He does not take it well, and I can see he is very upset. He says he understands, packs up, and leaves. I am so relieved, and a weight is lifted off my shoulders. I decide to forget about dating and meeting anyone. I phone Michelle and fill her in. We have a giggle, and she says, "I have not met a single man whom I like after numerous coffee dates, and I am also no longer looking for the moment, either." I tell her she is too fussy, that men are intimidated by her elegance and smart brain—never mind that she is drop-dead gorgeous, vibrant, and outgoing. That it is going to take a spectacular man to match her, and they are like hens' teeth!

CHAPTER 16
IT'S A MATCH! - REALLY?

"**H**i, my name is Miguel. I very much like your profile. I am French speaking so my English not so good. I come to Cape Town in two weeks to buy house. I would like meet you for coffee, perhaps?"

Your English is shocking! I have decided to test the applicant's ability to match me, so I carry on for the sake of curiosity only!

"Gosh, I happen to know a lot about property, as this was my profession for many years, so I can assist you in making the right purchase. Do you know what area you would like to be in? Are you a resident of South Africa?"

"I please to find you, I have work permit. I am engineer. I in South Africa but Mozambique now. On project. You are very beautiful and I think you a lot. I look Noordhoek. For beach and mountain, I like."

"How much time will you spend there? Will it be a permanent home or a part-time home?" I ask.

"It will be permanent but for me, six months South Africa and six months France."

I am tempted to block him right there and then, but for the purpose intended, I read on! He is very good-looking, but there are only two photographs, so I ask him to send me a picture of him at work in Mozambique. I am sceptical at the best of times, and this time is no exception, and the RED ALERT is screaming with flashing lights!

As I love France and have travelled there extensively, I am able to read on. I put my fantasy hat on, and my mind conjures up images of being with this perfect match as we spend six months in South Africa and six months in France. It's the perfect situation! I will have eternal summers. What a dream situation!

I don't like our wet, rainy Cape Town winters. It is often stormy in winter too, and the rain lashes about angrily and with force and purpose. The days are cold, and heating is necessary to stay warm. As we only experience two months of really cold weather, there is no central heating like in Europe and other countries, so one has to wear loads of layers. We are actually very spoilt in that we have sunny skies and warm weather for a good nine months of the year, and it's only the winter mornings that can be cold, which is typical of Cape Town, where I live. I am also close to the ocean and on the water at home, so the temperature is generally a little lower than elsewhere and on the southern side of the ocean, which is always colder than the west-facing ocean.

People leave Europe to come and live in sunny South Africa! Despite living in one of the best weather places in the world, I still yearn for a cultural city in Europe steeped in history and tradition. We have a coastal region known as Kwa Zulu Natal, where it is warm all year round, so a two-hour flight locally would take me to perfect warm weather, but it is Europe I seek! France is one of my favourite countries. In fact, I intend to holiday there in the next year or so. I did French at university, so I have a vague understanding of the language and, with time, would be able to speak it. Not fluently, but certainly enough to be understood.

A few hours later, my phone beeps, and I have a message from the French dream man. It is a picture of him on a big building site; his face is not that clear. Most of his face is covered by the white protective hat they all wear on site. However, it looks authentic, so I tell him to send me his mobile number, as I would prefer to chat with him on WhatsApp. I get a reply immediately with a South African WhatsApp cell number, and he says, "Bonjour Madam, Miguel here."

"Thank you very much. Let me know when you can speak and we can call each other." I reply.

"Oji, I am busy now. I speak later. I will message soon. You are perfect for me. I want to spend time with you and we can look for house together. I want you must like it"

I ask him, "How long have you been single?"

"I break up with girlfriend just other day and it is not nice now as we fight a lot. She not nice me."

Okay! Scammer it is. I decide to play along as I am certain I know what is coming but want to test my intuition. I have heard horror stories of how women are scammed, so I play along to see how it happens. "I am so sorry," I say.

"She take lot money from me, we have one bank account." At this point I know that his English is limited not because he is French and has little command of the English language but uneducated too!

My fantasy dream of Europe in summer is now a nightmare in the making. I laugh despite the scary reality of how these things happen.

"I will try come Cape Town this week as I want meet you very soon."

"Lovely," I say.

I leave the conversation and get on with my day. Much later, there are a number of messages from him to say he is unable to work because he is thinking of me. Can I be free for the weekend and we can find him a house sooner? He is ready to buy. More messages come through about flight times and arrivals, and would I meet him in Noordhoek?

After five unanswered messages from me, as I am busy, he asks, "Are you speak other men because you no answer? I speak only you and I want us to be together, forever. You are so beautiful and I love you. Please can we be together and I will see you this weekend."

I send a message to the scam artist, "I am speaking to only you and nobody else. I am busy so not always at my phone. I like you too, and yes, I would like for us to be together forever. Please tell me when you will be here. I am waiting." I even say, "Je t'aime," to make it seem like I am completely in the dark and that I am firmly on his page. I want him to feel comfortable. I then wait half an hour and call the number from my phone on my cell, not on WhatsApp

I got the phone number for this very reason. The person who answers the phone is French, but definitely not from France. I say, "I called the wrong number, and who am I speaking to now?"

He replies it is Miguel. I say, "Oh, Miguel, it is Susan."

"I not speak now, Susan, I at work I call you later," and he is gone in a flash! This French person is either Congolese or Nigerian at a guess!

Then I get this message, "I sorry my Darling, I cannot speak when work. I call you later. I have a big problem to talk to you. I am very worry. I have big problem."

Later I get a message that his girlfriend has frozen their joint account and taken all the money from it, and he cannot come to Cape Town because the funds are not available.

"I am sorry. Maybe you have credit card?" I ask.

"I no card and now I need help?"

I ask, "What help do you need, Miguel?"

"My Darling I so sad because I love you now and we cannot be together unless you can help me? I need some money in my account to buy the ticket to see you. I can fix problem with girlfriend of before, but it will not be time for when we meet."

I say, "I will send you the money, but you must promise me to pay it back because I don't have much money."

"I will pay you more my Darling so you are safe to lend me the money. I am a true gentleman and I can't wait to see you and be with you. I think of you all the time. You make my heart racing and I am happy. I am looking long time for someone like you. I smile all day because of you. I will see you Friday at five pm. We can meet at the Café Roux? You know this one?"

I don't reply but block him on WhatsApp and also on the site. But not before I check his profile and pictures again online. On closer scrutiny, I can see that they are fake. The one picture is actually very different from the other. I am also aware that scammers, generally, are engineers. His profile, however, is well worded, and his command of the English language on the profile is good. The well-written profile and subsequent communication were very different. The introduction on his profile reads as follows: "I am French and working on a project in South Africa and would like to settle in this beautiful country. I seek friendship and hopefully love at some point."

Women, at the best of times, are romantics and generally operate in their emotional headspace. It's in our DNA to do so, and it takes a seasoned woman who has learnt to think outside of her emotions to see the wood for the trees way quicker than most of us.

A few days later, I am scrolling through the site, and I see that his profile has been removed. In fact, a few have, and this alerts me to the level of scamming that is actually taking place. It is unlikely that in a list of twenty, five of them have miraculously found love and gone off the site. In my experience, people tend to stay on the site even when they are dating seriously. The reason is that to recreate a profile is time-consuming. One can unsubscribe but remain visible or invisible. The site that I use does not give this option, which I find rather frustrating, but it's a sign of the times. In the early days it was possible, but it would appear that over time, the sites became aware of the advantages of not allowing this, as it would then seem like a lot more people were available than actually were.

"Hi Susan, we are excited for you to meet Jan! Are you curious yet? Your compatibility with this match is on fire! Check out their profile now and ignite the flame inside your heart! Does his profile spark your interest? Tell him! You can break the ice with a wink or 'like' his photo to let him know you are interested. Want more? Write a message and tell him about yourself, or start a chat about the things you have in common."

"Did you know...? We at Singles know what makes a happy, lasting relationship. Our powerful match engine runs day and night to find you great matches out of the thousands of new single members who join us daily. Today we have selected Jan especially for you."

This amuses me, and I take a look at his profile. I am a match based on the fact that we are both "tidy." He drinks socially, he believes in liberal parenting, and social activity is important to him.

In relationships, the following are important: Faithfulness, honesty, and reliability. Personal: Punctuality. Goals: Increasing my knowledge.

I chuckle to myself as I scroll up to see what he does. Scientist. Really? I am gregarious; ride a Harley Davidson;

have a degree. I am far cry from your average individual, but I am no intellectual!

I am spontaneous, light, have zero interest in science or math, and am always doing something new or stimulating that I have not done in the past. Last year it was creating a large public space garden in our estate with the residents, and zero knowledge of gardening—to writing this book now.

I picture him lecturing at a university wearing a suit and tie. He is telling the crowd about new scientific discoveries, and I arrive on my Harley Davidson and interrupt his speech as my motorbike is very noisy and I have had to park nearer the front of the hall as the parking is full. I am in full leathers, and my hair is flat on my head. "Helmet hair," it's very unflattering to say the least. My leathers are old, worn, and tell a history all of their own, which I am sure this crowd would not be interested in hearing about. Twenty-four years of travel fun, road trips, parties, and friendships supreme. Whilst the concept is far-fetched, I believe it tells you that we are definitely not a match! We are in fact a mismatch! It also looks like he could be another one of those scammers as well! Only one photograph. No introduction. But I am not looking. I just did this for the sake of this book, as it's very interesting, and I have never fully read the "Did you know?" part.

But in fairness, I have met wonderful people on the sites in the past, and more often than not, it's a decision I make as to who I believe could be a match—not the site, but they try hard and work with algorithms. The reality is that some sites are better at it than others, but they take longer to complete, like the first site in my first chapter called "It's a Buzz." This was by far the best and most comprehensive match questionnaire, and it came up with better matches. The drawback to this was that few people completed it, unfortunately, so it was not as successful as it could have been. What it did tell me though is that information from the other person was incomplete; that this person was too busy and perhaps not interested enough to do a proper job at finding a mate. Maybe a bit judgemental on my part. I would tell myself, *If you are not interested enough to actually answer all the questions, how interested could you possibly be in meeting the right person?*

One had to be more forgiving with newcomers though, as they often took time to realise the importance of this and then proceeded to complete all the questions. I have been known to simply pass someone by on the basis that they had not completed enough information—in fact, very little! But here is the thing! I have met the best matches on the last site—some ten years later, which is "Singles," and the quality of choice has been much better, although the match criteria is not as good. There is no right formula. Maybe you just have to be more experienced!

Then I see another email—I have not looked at any of them—and see that Gregory sent a wink! The site has an introduction of its own before I log on to see more. "Small gesture = BIG THRILL. Mark has set you a big smile. Someone has caught your eye," and it then proceeds to make it more alluring by adding, "a blushing smile in a cafe from your table to their table, a turn of the head on the street, perhaps a wink of the eye, online is just as easy. Mark has taken the first step and sent you a big smile, so why not send him a reply?

"MK likes your photo. Take a chance and show him that you are interested. Look at his profile and see how much you have in common." The email introduction, which appears in the dating site app on the email, says, "We thought you two would make a good match—and MK seems to feel the same. Will you take the next step and like his profile or photos as well, or send him a personal message? You have nothing to lose: MK already expressed his interest and is looking forward to hearing from you!"

And then, "Did you know? Members who send winks or compliments are two times more likely to receive a personal message! Could it be LOVE? Leonardo is anticipating your reply! Wahoo, Leonardo has reached out to you. He is thinking of you and looking forward to your reply. Don't disappoint him; write back now! Every love story at Singles starts with two matches wanting to know more about each other. Leonardo has taken the first step by contacting you. Are you going to take the next step?"

I log onto his profile. He has messaged me to say, "I like your profile photo! Looking forward to getting to know you." This is a standard computerised message that occurs when someone likes your profile!

He sends a message of his own a few days later, "Good morning."

Then, without me asking him any questions, he says, "I am fine thanks, hope that you had good day."

A few more days pass and then another message from him, "Please give me your number and I will send you a what's app message. I find your profile very interesting and would like to talk more".

This has been an interesting exercise in that I ignored his messages based on a few things: His first message just bored me to death. So standard! One has to add some spice in my book and write something a little more catchy, funny, or unique! The second message—when he answers a question that I have not asked—definitely makes him suspect, as this strikes me as being a bit odd and I conjure up images of an ugly Scammer on the other end, and it's a big NO GO for me.

The request for my number is another alert button, as I never give out my number to anybody, I have not messaged a few times in order to get a sense of connection. I never engage in lengthy messaging online, but there are a few basics that one has to find out before exchanging numbers. Perhaps someone should write a guideline on questions to pose when dating online. I ignore the messages and move on! I am done with this process!

CHAPTER 17
LARGER THAN LIFE KOBUS

"Farmer, businessman, adventurer, and more!"

He is much older than me. and not really my kind of look, but his narrative appeals to me, and I send him a message, "Jy het baie om te se, maar is dit alles waar? (You have a lot to say, but is it all true?) Or is it just in your head?"

He replies, "Seeing is believing, so get on an aeroplane and I will show you," and he sends me his phone number. I save the number and call him on my way home from work. He is a larger-than-life man with a deep, strong, throaty voice. He is active and interesting. He has a massive game farm in Kwa Zulu Natal that is his pride and joy. He has negotiated the lease of masses of pieces of land from the surrounding Zulu chiefs. The farmhouse is akin to a lodge with thatched roof, face brick walls, dark wood, leather furniture, and animal memorabilia. It's rich and massive in every sense. Large, like his presence. I know this from photos he sends me. He has a farm manager, whereas he resides in Pretoria. He is of solid Afrikaner stock, i.e., origin, and grew up on a farm in the Lowveld. He is your typical South African male. All man, strong, opinionated, funny, smart, and clever.

He entertains me for hours on the phone, and we chat fairly often. He was an ambassador in Italy at a young age and joined the Navy. He speaks fluent Italian and loves opera. He also loves classical music and is a man of culture and good breeding. He is a gentleman with a rough side and calls a spade a shovel. He speaks his mind and has strong views and opinions. At one point in his life, he farmed with cattle and was the chief supplier of the entire Woolworth dairy side. He dreamed big, and he lived big. He took massive risks, and they paid off. The ones that did not, he overcame. His face is full of character. He has a large, wide nose and the broadest grin. He is balding; the balance of hair on his head is unruly, curly, and grey. It is never the same on any given day. He tells the best stories, and I adore him from day one.

I don't get to fly to meet him, as I know that we are not going to be in an intimate relationship. We are both very strong characters, and I can see us butting heads. He is a man who dictates and others follow. I seldom follow and mostly lead! We stay in touch on and off for many years. He gets involved with a woman who is much younger than me, and I know straight away that she likes the spoils, the money, and the lifestyle. As long as she is happy, I am happy for him.

He has four daughters, in their thirties and forties, all of whom are massively successful. The eldest was headhunted and lives abroad. She is a C.A. a Dr., and is incredibly smart and clever. The second daughter runs her own successful ad agency that serves the pharmaceutical industry, and the third daughter is a vet. The youngest daughter, who is only thirteen—her mother was a long-term girlfriend after his divorce—is a top student, a top athlete, and sings like a dream. He lives, eats, and breathes success through every pore. He fascinates me, and I love our conversations, which get to be fewer and fewer over the years, but we remain in touch.

MALTA

Five years later, I travel overseas to Malta and Bali. It is during this time that I visit him in Greece on his boat. He is single, and I am single, and he suggests I fly and join him for a few days on the Island of Paxos. I tell him that I will touch base with him when I am there in July and that we can see what both our schedules are doing. I am going to Malta as I have heard it is a good country to invest in property, that they have had a four-year growth, and that it is a rapidly expanding market. I am concerned—as are most South Africans who own more than one property—that I am at risk in the future as the political situation in this country leaves a lot to be desired, with corruption rife and billions being stolen by the government. The country has no future, and the prospects are bleak. Our currency has nothing to hold it up in real terms. I plan a month in Malta and ten days in Italy.

Malta disappoints in a big way. It is barren, and there are no trees. The land is arid. There is a boom, and there are building cranes wherever you go. I counted eight in just one small area. What this means is that wherever you are, there is the clattering of boards, banging, chiselling of stones, large trucks coming and going, building sand, road delays, and dust everywhere. Buildings are being knocked down, and blocks of flats are going up everywhere.

They have one of the world's best banking systems and house the largest gaming business in the world—a Swedish-based company that has moved to Malta for tax purposes. There are a multitude of English-teaching schools, and their hospitals and medical facilities are in a growth phase too.

I am staying with a wonderful woman and her daughter in their apartment. Malta is also a popular expat retirement destination. It is totally crime-free and you can walk around at any time of day or night safely. They do not steal and the police are on the button. It's affordable, and the seaside is pretty. There are numerous marinas housing boats, and it's big boat country.

Some of the expats are the kind that sit outside the bar at 11 a.m. He is wearing a white vest with a see-through diamond pattern and slinging back a beer. She has greasy hair that has not seen a comb in days and her cigarette tilts between two long fingernails that are chipped and broken. They are already fighting and the day has not even started. He is muttering under his breath and she is pointing her finger in his face. In fairness though, I do realise that I am not staying in the top suburbs of Malta.

The weather is great, but it lacks greenery. There are only a handful of bushes, no trees, and there is one brown sandy beach. There are loads of boulder beaches, as I call them. Huge rocks with cement inlays to make a small space to lie on. Cooking hot, grey sand stuck together in the hot sun does not appeal to me. I can see myself sitting up to go for a swim with the towel sticking to my back from all the sweat. These and others are the deciding factors for me, as I would like to be able to spend some time staying in one of my investments in the future. I know that no matter how good the financial return is, in the end it's the landscape that kills it for me.

I send Kobus a message. I have been in Malta for exactly seven days. He is in Corfu and will be setting sail for Paxos, his favourite island, in the next few days. He is just waiting for some new sail ropes, as the ones they delivered were too small. He invites me to join him for a week. I am super excited and share my news with my host, who has now become a friend. She is thrilled and urges me to go soonest. I try booking my ticket online, but struggle with a site called "edreams" that I have never used before. The main problem is the payment. I can book everything up to the payment point, and then it just plays up. I try for three hours, and eventually I give up. The ticket is cheap and costs around R1,500. I decide to have a bath and go out for an early dinner. It's a beautiful night. The sun only sets at about 10 p.m., so it's broad daylight when I head down to the waterfront. I find a quirky restaurant that serves mostly seafood and order their pan-fried fish of the day and a beer with lemonade. This is the best thirst quencher in the heat. It amuses me because I never drink beer at home yet here; I do so all the time!

Rhythmic music wafts from an open area across the way at a restaurant. People are dancing and gliding around graciously. They are doing a Salsa, and I watch wistfully, as I have always wanted to learn to Salsa. It is one of the sexiest dances around. The closest I have ever come to ballroom dancing of any kind is a "Sokkie" which is a dance that is wholly South African and danced by predominantly Afrikaans university students in small towns. It is a great two-step of a different kind and fabulous fun, particularly if the man can dance and leads well. My best friend's brother at school—we grew up in a small town called Paarl—was a fantastic dancer, and I loved it when we danced together. He was quick and nimble, and we flew around the dance floor. I felt like a bird as he moved me around, my feet barely touching the ground, my body swaying to the rhythm of his body, swinging me around on the corners often in a two-step foot movement.

I was held captive by these beautiful dancers as they changed from a Salsa to a Waltz. Soon a Tango followed and then the Cha-Cha. For a moment, I did not mind the barren land. Effortlessly, they moved around—young and old. I vow that before I die, I want to attend ballroom lessons.

Later that night, success at last! Finally, my payment goes through. I am all set, and the flight leaves at 1 p.m. I get to the airport early and have already checked in online, so I am in no rush to go through the gates and wait for the boarding call. The line is long. Eventually I am at the check-in counter. I am informed that I have missed my flight as I was booked on an earlier flight. I can't believe what I hear and say, "But I have to be on this flight as my friend is fetching me later this evening." She tells me that the flight is full. They can offer me a later flight that evening at midnight, which gets me to Corfu at 6 a.m. the next morning.

I stand motionless in disbelief, and feel my heart sink to the floor. How did this happen? My mind races; *How am I going to tell Kobus that I am not on the flight? That I won't be there later that evening and that we cannot sail to Paxos because I will not be there on time!* I kick my mind into action mode and rush to the information desk and ask who else flies to Corfu. I am relieved to hear that I can catch a 5 o'clock flight and I head to the opposition airline.

Good news is that they have a seat! I ask how much it is, and the cost one way is R 3500. I do a double take and shake my head. I see my holiday allowance fast exiting my wallet, and it's not a good feeling. I decline the ticket and consider going back to the apartment, but I can't face telling my host that I made such a foolish mistake. I go back to the information desk. There is one other flight that leaves at midnight, and this ticket is more affordable at R1000. I figure out that the ticket, when I booked the payment, finally defaulted to a previous booking I had made, and I did not pick this up.

I call Kobus and tell a white lie; I say that they overbooked the flight and have offered me a refund and a special fare to travel on their later flight. I am reminded of Mighty Mike in a fleeting instant, and his words resonate in my ears: *"Accident Prone, I would say!"* To my relief, he says that it will be fine, as we only leave at about 8 a.m. and the airport is close to the port. I find a few empty chairs and make myself comfortable. I lie down on four chairs that are in a line and stuck together. I use my backpack as a headrest, put my eye shades on, and decide to try and sleep as I won't be getting to bed until after midnight. I set my alarm and say grace to the universe for being in a safe country where I can rest assured, I won't wake up minus a wallet and fleeced of all my belongings.

The flight is half-full, so I manage a row of seats to myself and tell the cabin attendant before take-off not to wake me until we are descending and that I do not want to eat but would like a bottle of water or two. I am grateful to see no children in my immediate vicinity, but I put my earplugs in, just in case

CORFU

The warm Corfu air greets me as I disembark. My body ignites from the warmth; the sun rays dance on my face, and a soft red, warm glow from the rising sun stretches across the tarmac in front of me. The tar shimmers and glistens in the morning's sunshine.

It's hard not to miss Kobus, and he waves to me as I come through the gates. He is tall and a big man, plus his voice booms! It's a poignant moment as we have talked on the phone on and off for five years and are now meeting face-to-face for the first time! His voice is loud, "My magtig, kannie glo jy is hier nie! Wat het jou so lank gevat!" In English, this means: "I can't believe you are here; what has taken you so long!" He takes my bags and gives me the biggest bear hug. I immediately feel completely at home, and we talk like two people who have been friends for a lifetime. I notice he seems a little off balance, and he says, "I woke up this morning feeling lightheaded, and I am feeling oddly unsteady on my feet." He says that it's unlikely we will set sail today until whatever is wrong with him settles. There is no smell of alcohol coming from him, as I conjure images of a recluse alcoholic. I feel a little uneasy. However, he chats away.

The roads are empty due to the early hour of the flight, and later I am grateful. He weaves on the road and says, "Sho, I am still feeling off-balance." My eyes are glued to the road; they have become slits. I am too scared to keep them open. I ask if he would like me to drive, but he says he's fine.

I stifle a squeak in my throat that says, "But you are not!" My fingers are gripping the door handle, my fingertips are white, and my hand is a tight ball. My other hand is gripping the seat in order to grab the hand brake, my lifesaving device in the event of a car heading towards us. I keep glancing back to where it sits in order to be 100% certain that I can reach it in a split second. We pass a parked car on the driver's side, and the sideview mirror clips the parked car's mirror, but Kobus does not notice.

We get to a roundabout, and there are no cars in sight. I feel less anxious until the car rounds the circle and Kobus ramps the centre island, and we are now half on the road and half on the centre island. I hold my breath, and I close my eyes, hoping to see us back on the road when I open them. I prize my eyes open, looking through my lashes to obscure any full view, and find we are on the road again and a car is approaching. We are over the centre white line, and the car hoots loudly. Kobus turns the steering quickly, and our car veers onto the road again. He seems unfazed, and it occurs to me that he is oblivious to the poor state of his driving.

In a squeaky voice I don't recognise, I ask, "How far is it still?"

He says, "Just two more blocks." I sit quietly and wish the road to end as soon as possible. I am sweating, and my forehead is scrunched up like a road of its own. All furrowed and dented. My teeth are clenched and my jaw aches. He is still weaving on the road, but fortunately, there are no more cars. We hit another curb as we turn into the marina where the boat is moored. He stops the car ahead of the boat, his sense of distance clearly off, and gets out. I look in disbelief as the car is smack bang in the middle of the road, which means no other cars can get past. He stumbles onto the boat and says he must lie down, and I should ask the staff to show me around.

There is a female Italian chef and a South African deckhand. I am surprised to see a woman deckhand, as this is usually a job done by men. Lilly, the chef, is fair, pretty, and young, while Angela, the deckhand, is close to forty, darkly tanned with weathered rough hands, short finger nails, and strong arms. She looks like she could do with a bath, but this, I soon learn, is because she spends an inordinate amount of time outside on the deck, and the salt air clings to her face, hair, and body.

The boat is spacious and immaculate. The lounge is inside, while the outside decks feature two tables on either side for dining. The master cabin is large with a dressing room and ensuite. My cabin is on the opposite side of the master cabin and also has an ensuite. I have cupboards and a porthole plus a skylight that is above the middle of the double bed which fills the entire cabin. The roof is sitting height, so opening the skylight is easy. By boat standards, this is luxurious, and I feel very indulged, grateful, and spoilt, but I do feel claustrophobic and find the short distance between the bedcover and the roof intimidating.

The entire boat is covered with beautiful wood inlays and the brass is highly polished. I can tell that Kobus is a man who likes perfection and feel sorry for the deckhand who would have to do the polishing. I feel comfortable and my seas legs are strongly intact and I am not in the least bit nauseous. I am told to use the shower facilities at the port, as the water is expensive and so is electricity, and this makes complete sense to me. I know that there is also a mooring fee for being in the marina.

There are a handful of shops and not much activity at the marina. I soon find out that although there is a cáfe-deli with basic necessities, it is pricey and goods are much cheaper in town. Not much else apart from a booking office and a small travel agency. Lacking atmosphere and with minimal basic décor, it leaves much to be desired.

I feel way better after the shower and head back to the boat. I sleep for three hours; the boat's gentle rocking motion is a wonderful "sleeping tablet." I wake at midday when the sun is beating down and the cabin feels hot. I venture out onto the deck, and Kobus is sitting at the table. He is eating breakfast and invites me to join him. I am hungry, and we sit on the deck with the sun shining down on us. The water around us is glistening and slowly dancing to a beat of its own as it moves and sways. He tells me that he has owned the boat for 13 years and sailed it from America to Greece. I am hugely impressed, as the thought of this journey makes me green, and I feel a little sick, as it seems to me like a terrifying experience. There are big waves in those waters! I had experienced them off the coast of Cape Town and vowed I would never do it again. He explains that there were more crew, that there are four crew berths, and that he did the crossing with an experienced yacht captain and another deckhand.

When I ask how he is feeling, he says a bit better, and it seems it is a minor kidney issue that plays up now and again. I know how bad a bladder infection makes one feel, so I can understand exactly why he was all over the place in the car. He says we will set sail in the morning.

We spend the afternoon playing scrabble, and I do not fare too well as I have not played in a long time. He has loads of games on the boat and plenty of reading material, and I find one about Corfu and read up all about it. There is quite a big community of English-speaking people who have opted to live in Corfu, and most of them lead a very simple, uncomplicated life. They live off the land, make clothes, bags, and shoes, and teach yoga, meditation, and the like. Corfu has the highest number of British expats. We do not visit Corfu itself, as Kobus is still unsteady on his feet. I feel a little disappointed but decide that on my return I could spend a few days on the island before returning to Malta.

PAXOS

The next morning, we set sail for Paxos. The boat rolls back and forth and up and down, despite a flat ocean, and my stomach tells me that I need to make a plan fast! The sails flap and billow in the light, firm breeze and pull us across the ocean. Kobus tells me to move to the front of the boat and look straight ahead. This helps, and I watch the horizon. The ocean meets the sky in the middle, and I see the perfect painting before my eyes. Soon I see land ahead. A small dot that gets bigger and bigger. Soon, I see trees, and then an inlet into the marina becomes visible. It looks like a huge river, and boats are entering and exiting. It's a narrow canal, and I feel my body tense, and my neck muscles strain as I move my head forward to see how the boats are actually managing to pass one another without touching. A big passenger boat eases its way into the narrow space, and I hold my breath as a big yacht heads towards the narrow outlet, while the large boat is easing its way into the inlet too! They seem to scrape past each other!

Soon we too are scraping past other boats that are leaving. It seems like despite the space on either side of the boats, they like to stick to the centre of the canal. We weave in and out of the canal, which then opens up into a larger "pond" marina. It widens considerably, and all along the side where we are moving, I see a multitude of restaurants, shops, delis, and eateries, and the sidewalk is bustling with people and activity. I love what I see and can't wait for us to moor so that I can go ashore and explore. The challenge, however, is to find a free and empty mooring. We have to go around, and it's only on our second trip down the canal that we find a mooring. The sun is already high in the sky. Docking is a bit of a process, and I am thankful that all I get asked to do is throw mooring ropes to the deckhand who has hopped ashore.

It's a truly beautiful island, and it's classy. It reminds me of Camps Bay back home, and I keep expecting to see a familiar South African face somewhere. People are beautifully dressed. An array of colours adorns the big sidewalk in the form of brightly dressed people, coloured tablecloths, and items for sale in shops. Everyone is glowing with anything from a light tan skin tone to a dark brown. Various exotic perfumes and smells fill the air, and opulence breathes through the spaces. Beach hats, sun dresses, chinos, slipslops, shorts, and flowing garments are the order of the day.

The island itself is tiny. I hire a scooter for the day and explore the whole island easily. It amazes me how much the greenery and scenery change from one end to the other. What catches my eye mostly, however, are the ancient olive trees and olive orchards.

The trees grow skew and curled. Each one is unique and beautiful. The trunks intertwine and seem to be held in a forever embrace, as there are a few trunks on many of the older trees that form one big tree. I have a love affair of a different kind during my time here, in beautiful Paxos.

I come back and spend hours sitting under these magnificent trees. I sit and write reams. The bark is varied shades of grey. There are lines that tell stories in each trunk, and it feels like wizened old furrows are beckoning and inviting me to touch and feel each one. The bark is a mixture of thin, thick, straight, skew, and uneven surfaces. Each one unique, each one with its own narrative. I feel embraced and adored whenever I sit amongst my tree "lovers". I feel caressed and loved as the fallen leaves under my feet make crunching sounds as I walk. The shade is cool and comforting under these trees in the full summer. The heat is intense and more so once you leave the shady covering of leaves and branches.

I laugh and smile at the strangeness of love amongst olive trees. I fall in love with Greek olive trees. Not with a man, or a person, but trees.

We spend many nights having supper on the boat, as Kobus feels that, as he has paid for a chef, he must use her. I look at the activity and food in restaurants within our view and long to be sitting there! As wonderful as yachts and boats are, it is boring to sit and look down on the action. I realise that never again will I look at yachts in the same way, from the quayside. It looks so amazing to be on a boat, but it's way more fun to be on the sidewalk, feeling the energy, heat, and movement of people around you.

I know that people think I am daft and that being on the boat is so much better, but for me, being in the hustle and bustle of the sidewalk is way more interesting. I long to see all the different restaurants inside and sample all the different delights. Kobus is a great conversationalist, and we talk about everything, and I learn a lot from him. In usual male fashion there is flirting, but I ignore the "come-on," and we agree that being friends is way better than being lovers, as that is when things always get complicated. We stay moored and mostly venture out for breakfast and the odd coffee. When he takes a nap in the afternoons, I get on my scooter and tour around.

All too soon, I head back to Malta. I am so grateful for the time I spent on the boat and to Kobus for giving me such an amazing opportunity. I am mostly grateful for finding such a beautiful island. I have been to a number of Greek Islands, and this is by far my favourite, but it may be because I am "in love" with trees! I get where the name "tree hugger" comes from now!

PAXOS SOLO

I head back to Paxos a few days later and find a lovely Airbnb in the middle of the island. I love the position as I can get to Lakka in the south, which is a large open bay, and the north port, Gaios, in the east of the island, which is the port where we were moored. Both are exquisite. Gaios is where all the action is, and Lakka has only one large restaurant and a handful of other shops. The best bathing is at Lakka, where you can wander in and walk into the water as it is shallow and warm. There are always a few boats moored in the bay, and people are on small rubber ducks going backwards and forwards constantly during the day. The architecture is Venetian. I spend days amongst the olive trees and find a favourite morning spot to have coffee, and soon the owner knows me, and we strike up a broken conversation each morning.

Lunch is always at a different spot, and there are many on the island. On my first day back, I ride my scooter into Gaios and park it in a familiar place with a landmark high table and chairs ahead of me. It's a site I have seen before. I spend three hours roaming the port before deciding to head home. I find the place but cannot find the scooter anywhere.

After an hour, I head to the police station to advise them that I have lost my scooter. A lanky young policeman looks at me with a bored look on his face. He does not get up off the counter where his arms are resting. He speaks little English but eventually understands I have lost my scooter. He raises both hands and says he can't help me. He is the only one there and cannot leave the station. There are no other police on duty. He is completely disinterested in my plight and cannot send anyone to walk with me or call anyone else to help me search. I burst into tears, but he just shrugs his shoulders.

I beg him to help me, and eventually he calls a taxi over and tells them to take me home and that I must come back the next morning to look for my scooter. I thank him but am unable to give an address to the taxi driver. I am, however, on one of the three big roads that runs through the island. I show him to just go straight, and we find our way with hand signals. I have no idea how I am going to get a taxi back from my apartment, but luck is at my door, as the man who lives in the house next to the apartment actually drives a taxi and is just getting home when I arrive, so I arrange a lift for 9:30a.m. I carry my small round watermelon, loaf of bread, and milk with me to the front door. I am floored at not being able to find my scooter and fall into a fitful sleep—and get chased by scooters with big eye lights all night!

I hire a bicycle when I get to Gaios and ride down the little lane amongst the shops. The first lane to the right is a small lane, and there are a handful of scooters parked there. I see the number plate and can't believe my eyes—this is my scooter, and I must have walked past it 100 times last night. The high table and chairs are ahead of me, and to the right is the jewellery store, which I now do recall, as I had made a mental note of it when I parked the scooter as we had been inside; I recall it well! However, that mental note was so fleeting that my detail on the location went out the window!

I work out that my smug sense of knowing exactly where I was is the mistake I made. The other thing is that in another place there is the exact same table and chairs, and it was that area that I had focused on. Two exact same site landmarks in different locations! Perhaps there was a bigger scooter obscuring the view. I race back to the bicycle store and excitedly tell them I have found my scooter. They kindly refund me as I had used the bicycle for all of ten minutes. I can't believe that I have just saved myself R180.

I find a gorgeous little apartment just up the road from Lakka, and its heaven as my Airbnb was just for two nights to enable me to find something more suitable! It belongs to the Greek restaurant owner's sister, who speaks no English. It's a typical local house, and I love it. The lounge is small with a kitchen. The sofa is a dark blue with multicoloured patchwork throws draped over the back. A number of different cushions in all shapes and sizes are scattered around. There is a quirky oblong coffee table that looks out of place because of its very tall legs. The windows have lace curtains, and a small window sits above the sink in the kitchen. The fridge dates back to my youth, and the big, cumbersome door swings open heavily.

My single person's fridge items are lost on the shelves. I don't bother to look at the stove, as I have no intention of cooking. The bed is comfortable with a few pillows and a sheet. No other covering is necessary in this heat. There is no aircon but the doors and windows are well positioned to create a breeze, and there is a fan in the room that swings uncomfortably when on, but does the trick. Nothing matches, and I get the feeling that they furnished the place with whatever they could find, and nobody worried about the décor. There is a faded Persian rug on the lounge floor, and the cement floors have been glazed and remind me of marble and limestone mixed together. The floor is always nice and cool. The shower is just big enough to move around in, and the toilet is very close by! There is only room for one person in this tiny space.

I love being in the heart of the community with proper Greek neighbours who are always friendly and wave. I see no other tourists on the small road. Everywhere I go, there are dogs, and they follow me on walks, each choosing to walk a little way with me when encouraged. They are all pavement specials and a breed of their own. Some are scruffy-looking, others are short-haired, and they all have a mix of every kind of conceivable dog you ever saw in them, some more than others, some less, but mixed they all are!

My love affair with the olive trees continues, and I spend nearly every afternoon either reading under the trees, or writing, seated on my sarong with my back against a different tree each time, or lying flat on the ground with my head on my backpack. I feel the creaking tree limbs as they bend and bow during the course of each day. I think back to how many years old they are, and I conjure up images of life on the island during this time. These trees go back to around 1386 up to 1797 when they were first planted—back to King John 1 of Portugal and King Richard ll of England.

The history that runs through the veins of these branches, trunks, and leaves is just too much to comprehend. I am not surprised by the deep lines, frowns, bends, furrows, and hairlike bark fibres that form part of each and every tree. I talk to them as I go, and I divide them into a family. I find a section of trees that are the grandparents—big, gnarled, and bent; they tower above the other trees. Then there are the offspring of these big trees—smaller but equally full of character, just less overwhelming. Next come the "children" trees, who are more youthful-looking and fresh. They are a lot thinner and greener than the others. I give them all names and greet them on certain days. I take endless pictures, and I write poetry— tree poetry.

On the day I leave, I drive through my olive grove and weep. I am sad to say good-bye to love of a different kind. A lasting love, and one that will always be alive no matter what. I touch the trunks; I trail my fingers on the furrows, dents, crevices, leaves, branches, and limbs. I close my eyes, breathe, and feel loved and held. I stay like this for the longest while, hugged and adored by my olive grove in Paxos. On my last day in Paxos, it's not my favourite coffee spot, restaurants, or beaches that I will miss; it's my beloved olive trees.

CHAPTER 18
MR DELICIOUS

My phone beeps. It's a message from a group of people who live in our southern suburbs and all ride Harley-Davidson motor cycles. We are also all members of the greater club in Cape Town known as the Harley Davidson Club of Cape Town. The subgroup of members is for those of us who live in close proximity to one another. "Come and support Colin Plitt, our member who is part of the well-known band, Rock Steady, this Friday, at the False Bay Rugby Club known as the Bay Club."

The latter amuses me, as this club is situated in the heart of an upmarket leafy suburb that, for all intents and purposes, is nowhere near the False Bay area or the ocean! I have heard a lot about it but have never been there. I have also heard the band in the past but never knew Colin then; when I google him, he impresses me. He is the bass guitarist, has played the guitar since he was twelve, and has been part of many different bands. He has managed some high-end bands in SA during his time who were signed to Gallo Records and also accompanied them to major international jazz festivals.

I confirm that I will join the group. It just so happens that my goddaughter Carlin and her father—who is a well-known musician in his own right, also with his own band—will be there, so this makes the evening more appealing. The venue is set on a big sports field surrounded by all sorts of sporting fields, as well as a well-known gym in Constantia. Casual, with a long bar and surrounding tables, it's a good music venue with a large stage and space to dance, for someone like me who is always first on the floor, regardless of whether I have a partner or not.

Large windows and doors let in a lot of light. Those who do want to watch the rugby event can sit outside or view the game from inside. Local club rugby is being played, so the general focus is on drinking and having a good time. The usual musty smell of old beer and wine permeates, and it occurs to me that it must have been absorbed by the long wooden bar counter over the years. Rows of alcohol bottles are perched on shelves behind the bar, and there is a great selection. I immediately order a Jack Daniels on ice and pour in a little water. It was a favourite drink of mine before my later dating life. My previous husband, who also rode a Harley back then, introduced me to Jack Daniels and Ginger Ale. It is a drink I always have when I am at Harley gatherings. It's not something I drink often. I sip the golden spirit; it hits my tastebuds exploding delicately and at the same time ignites many beautiful memories of another time and place—many years ago, but that story is for another time.

I find the Harley group who have placed us at a huge table right in front of the band. If you know the band, you get to sit in the best spot in the house. It's great to catch up with the people I have known for over fifteen years, some for longer than others. The band plays loud rock music, making it impossible to talk most of the time, so I move to the dance floor and other places to just stand and get some enjoyment from the music at a distance.

It is while leaning against a round pillar at the back of the venue that I see him. He is the most beautiful man I have ever laid eyes on, and my mouth literally hangs open for a second; my eyes are riveted. Dark curly hair that has been pulled back straight across his head, meeting in a curly ponytail at the base of his neck. It is tied up a few times, which tells me it is long but in need of taming. He has a perfectly chiselled, strong jawline with a wide, full, perfect mouth. His brown eyes are deep and smouldering. His olive skin complements his dark hair and eyes. He fits every description you will ever have read of the drop-dead gorgeous Italian lover.

I cannot believe that I have found the perfect "handsome" in my book. I have no idea if he is single, but for the moment, I am held in time; the moment is "paused," and I simply feast my eyes on him for the longest time. He cannot see me looking at him, but from where I now stand, I have a full view of him. During this long gaze that makes me breathless, my heart races, my heartbeat quickens, and my breathing is rapid.

I take in the surrounding space that he sits in. He has joined three girls at a table, but from what I can see, they are simply friends, and he is not attached to any one of them. I continue to stand and look, mesmerised, revelling in this sight before me, unable to move. Eventually, I take myself off to dance, and he has his back to me now so I can look across every now and again to see his movements.

My biggest fear is that he will get up and leave, and I won't get to somehow meet him in the flesh, which has now become my full focus for the night. I see someone I know from the Harley Davidson Club at the table next to him. He is not one of my favourite people, but for a close-up view, I go over and say hello and promptly sit down next to him, and my back is almost touching the arm of "Italian, Mr Delicious." I accidentally bump into him on purpose, but this does not have a positive outcome, and he seems a little offended, so I turn around and touch his arm—this way I get a close-up, face-to-face view—and apologise. He smiles and says, "It's okay." His voice is gentle yet strong and sexy.

I was slow on the uptake here; I should have said, "I know you from somewhere," but I was completely tongue-tied and useless. I leave the table and berate myself for being so slow. I spend the evening dancing, and on my second walk to the bar, a voice at the table right next to him says to me, "Hey, we know one another." So, I go over and say hello, and I sit next to this man who now has me sitting right opposite Mr Delicious, and I quietly congratulate myself on a second chance. At that moment, he moves to get up, and I am mortified, as I think he is now leaving. At this point, the very polished man next to me is touching my arm, telling me how gorgeous I am and that he remembers me walking down a flight of stairs, and that I took his breath away.

I quickly touch Mr Delicious' arm and say to him, "Before you go, may I just tell you something?" He smiles, and I find myself sweating and nervous, barely able to speak. But I manage to whisper, "It's not often that perfection crosses my path in life. You are the most beautiful man, and not to share this thought with you would be a waste. We too often have thoughts that could make someone feel good but don't voice them. Thank you for allowing me to see this beauty tonight and for showing up."

He smiles a slow, sexy smile and says, "Thank you." When I turn around to speak to the man next to me, I see that he has left, which comes as no surprise. I feel a little bad about this. It's not nice behaviour. I get up and walk outside to go home. My night is over, and it is late. I bump into my goddaughter outside, and we catch up, as she was with her friends and I was with mine, so we didn't have a chance to chat.

In the midst of our catch-up, I look up, and walking towards us is Mr Delicious. I stop talking mid-sentence and say, "Carlin, Carlin, oh my word, it's him, and he is coming towards us! I have to do something!" As he approaches, I smile and say, "Mr Delicious, can I introduce you to my goddaughter?" He starts laughing, and this makes for easier conversation. At the same time, a friend of hers arrives, giving me a chance to have a one-on-one conversation with him.

I know we made small talk of which I have no recollection, as I am spellbound by his beauty. He has a beautiful, strong, even voice and is calm and relaxing to be around. I sense this about him immediately, for as soon as we stand in the same place, the energy is relaxed. I invite him for a coffee date, and he agrees; we exchange numbers. I am so nervous that I ask him to save my number and to "miss call" me while we are talking, as I am terrified of writing the number down incorrectly.

Inside my car, I sit and breathe. I can't drive immediately as I need to calm down. I am almost hyperventilating, and my adrenals are on fire. Even my hands are shaking. *Get a grip on yourself, woman,* I tell myself quietly. *This is ridiculous and so shallow! Since when have you been so shallow and so low? You know nothing about him as a person, yet you are behaving like a lovesick teenager!* And it occurs to me that it is exactly what I am. Do we ever grow up?

I sleep fitfully and wake up early. Later that morning, I send him a very casual message, "Good morning, Mr D. I am not nearly as brave now as I felt last night! So, before I lose courage, it would be great to do that coffee sometime. I don't know what your agenda is like, so no rush, just as and when."

I don't expect to get a quick reply, but less than ten minutes later there is a message to say his day is full but he will be in the centre of the city that evening listening to a band he wants to hear play. I was welcome to join him. Wow, he wants to meet with me so soon! I dance around my room and grab Molly, my adorable miniature schnauzer, who, with her little black and grey head and her ever-trusting eyes, is looking at me like I am acting a little crazy, and I am! She looks at me adoringly. All moments of being held are a joy for her, even if she is held upside down on her back. Life just took on a whole new meaning!

I am also busy during the day and into early evening and tell him that I will join him, if possible, but not to expect me as I am not sure I will make it, but to send me the name of the place and if I can, I will be there. The day is a blur, and I am tired as well. Too much hype and all that dancing has made me fatigued. I cancel my early evening arrangement as it's an easy one to cancel. Just a small group of us watching a rugby match on TV at her home. I rest and take it easy, and it's just as well I do! The small restaurant in the heart of town, where it buzzes, is cute. It is cosy inside with a fire crackling. The yellow and orange flames dancing in unison, a welcome warmth as I enter from a very cold evening outside.

He is sitting close to the fire, not far from the door, so it is easy to find him. Once again, he takes my breath away, and I swallow hard. "Hi," my voice barely audible, "I am really nervous, so if I babble on too much, just make me breathe, okay?"

He smiles, "Why is this?" His dark eyes are looking straight at me, and he is smiling the most gorgeous, exquisite smile, and I am lost, right there and then.

"When I have had only two drinks, my confidence level soars, and, as I am not a regular drinker, I quickly respond to whatever I have consumed! We would not be sitting here if I had not had two drinks earlier, so at three drinks, when we finally met to chat, I was at my absolute limit, and it's how I managed to pluck up the courage to speak to you."

"How many drinks then this evening? Hopefully at least three," he says, laughing.

I swallow hard and struggle to speak without a nervous lilt to my voice. "Just a single Jack Daniels on the rocks with crushed ice, if possible, filled to the rim."

"Quite a girl you are." I smile meekly and wait while he goes to the bar and orders my drink. The band is an African jazz group, and the music is laid back and rather nice.

"I need to tell you something before we get to know each other," I say.

"Are we going to get to know each other?" he asks, and I blush.

"I hope so." I take a deep breath. "I have a friend I see on weekends who is away. He is an attorney that I have known for over thirty years, and recently our paths crossed and we are dating casually, with no intention of having a serious relationship, and that is a comfortable arrangement." My words stumble into one another, "Not that I need to tell you this, as we have only just met! I don't usually make a move on men, and it certainly was not on my agenda to meet anyone last night, but you were there, and I could not help but notice you, and as you know, I made it my business in every possible way to connect with you, inappropriately, clumsily, and to some degree blatantly as well, which, in hindsight, I have to say, is rather embarrassing." I ramble on, "It's silly to even have this discussion with you, as we have not said more than a few words to each other, so it seems unnecessary. What I am really saying for now is that let's be friends, as I am seeing someone. He is away at the moment, so I am not in a position to be more."

"I too am seeing someone," he says—a lot more eloquently than me. "And she is in a clinic at the moment. She is having some serious therapy, and we have only known each other for a month, so we are in the same boat." I sigh with relief. I am pleased we are on the same page. He says, "I noticed you immediately, as you have an air of confidence that is not hard to miss, and you are clearly outgoing, gregarious, and fun, but as I am seeing someone, I did not want to engage with you, tempting as it was. You, however, made this rather difficult and caught me off guard."

He is a musician and chairman of the Music Club, and this evening he is scouting for new talent. He plays in two bands that play a mix of genres—a word I only get to know later during our time together. He is a quiet man with a very grounded presence. He speaks quietly and slowly. I like this a lot, as it eases my frenetic pace and slows my ever-busy mind down a little. It's a welcome change for me.

We decide to have a light bite together, and, over supper, I learn that he has two children and that he has been divorced for three years; that his wife asked for a divorce, and this came as a big shock to him. She had made it clear that she had no interest in saving the marriage. They had been together for thirty-three years.

He had worked as a top-level property projects programmer at management level, running a big team for a well-known large corporate that ran several massive property portfolios. At the age of fifty, he decided to do what had always been his dream—to play, compose, sing, and record music full-time. He had set up his own recording studio and was doing exactly that. He has a good relationship with his son, but sadly, his relationship with his daughter has been challenging over the last five years. I found this hard to understand as he was such a gentle spirit, and it made no sense.

He was also in a relationship for three years on and off and had been single for eight months—bar a few dates—and is only recently in his current relationship. My relationship was only three months itself, at this stage, so neither one of us was firmly entrenched, so to speak.

"How did you meet the woman you were with for three years?" I ask.

He tells me that it was on a dating site, but that it happened before he left the marital home, and this did not go down well with his wife, his children, or the close friends who were part of their social circle.

"I had booked a cottage in Constantia that I was scheduled to move into on the 1st of February. We moved in together, two days after we met. This was a mistake, and in hindsight I realised she wanted my rental income to cover her own expenses, but I was blind to this at the time."

"What does she do?" I ask.

His reply tells me that I know her and that she is very beautiful. He was ripe for the picking as far as I was concerned, and he was vulnerable, I decide. Particularly when I learn that his wife was his first serious girlfriend, so he is really naive and 'green', as we say.

When the band stops playing for the night, he suggests we go to a late-night spot further down the road that has good live music. We go in his car, which is a white VW Caravelle—a large van-type vehicle big enough for carrying music instruments. We agree to come back later to fetch my car, as it isn't too far to walk and it's cold outside. It's also not safe to walk the streets in the centre of town late at night.

The place is small. I have paced myself with one drink and proceed to drink only sparkling water and a latte at the restaurant. I figure it's safe to have another drink now after dinner, and we are not flirting or doing anything other than just talking and getting to know one another more. We are tightly packed in the small space and stand together at the back, listening to the music. It's at this point that I become aware of my body starting to come alive as he ignites a fire within me, and the heat is intense. It creeps up from my toes to my head, and the glow is magnetic.

As I stand just a few centimetres away from him and turn to face him to say something, our eyes lock. The stare is so intensely magnetic that I am lost for words; the sentence I wanted to utter is lost, and I can't breathe as I look deep into his brown eyes that take me all the way down into his soul. Desire oozes from both of our bodies and pours out into the open with an explosive connection that makes me feel giddy. It is at this point that he cups my face in his hand and plants gentle, soft kisses all over my face. They move from my forehead, down the side of my face, to my cheeks, passing over my lips. They then move to the other side and up again, and I am transported to a place of unimaginable sexual need. I long for his lips to touch mine, but he gently passes his lips over mine gently and then draws back and looks at me again.

I am reminded of another time in my life when the great love of my life first kissed me. Many years ago. I can't help it; my eyes well up and tears run down my cheeks. I am so moved and so full of the intensity and depth of this moment that it overwhelms me. He looks at me with concern, and a question mark across his face, but I just smile a big smile and say, "Special moments do that to me, and for this one I am so deeply grateful that it makes me weep. It's joy and sadness all in one. Thank you for an unforgettable moment in time. Right now, my life is already so complete, and I have had so many incredible moments. I am so grateful to you for this one."

He holds me close to his chest, and I succumb to the warm glow that moves through my body. *This is love!* runs amok in my head. I give in to the moment, for we all know this is not possible. But for the moment, I dream and believe, and it is magical. At a later stage, he pulls me towards him and kisses me so gently that I become desperate for more, for a stronger kiss with more intensity. But he keeps them slow, sensual, and shifts the depth ever so slowly. I am lost in this moment, and he is my everything. We leave in the early hours of the morning, and I drive home with my head in the clouds. His day is busy, and I am committed to a dinner in the evening, so we only exchange text messages.

We arrange to meet on Monday afternoon, and I invite him to my home, as I want to introduce him to Molly. This is always important to me. I am so excited to see him again and spend the morning putting everything into place and giving Molly a quick wash. She has to be perfect for this handsome man who is about to fill our home with his presence. He takes my breath away when I open the door. He is wearing a warm check shirt, jeans, and red sneakers. His grin is broad when I open the door, and he is holding a bunch of yellow roses in his hand. Molly is wagging her tail as she lays eyes on our visitor but holds back, unlike me, who throws my arms around him. I am so happy to see him. He bends down when I finally free myself from the overzealous hug, and Molly smells his hand.

He has big hands and thick fingers, I notice, and for a guitarist, this must be quite a challenge. He stays on his knees, giving Molly time to feel safer, and then he pats her head, rubs her ears, and speaks to her gently. She warms to him immediately, and this is "music to my ears," and I laugh at the pun as it goes through my head. He gives me a look that says, "And now, what's so funny?" and I tell him it's a private joke. I give him a tour of my home, albeit only two bedrooms, but the spaces are big. I leave out the guest suites that are income generators, as well as the one-bedroom flatlet, as these are all located well before entering my front door, by design.

I make us coffee, and we sit in front of the fire that warms the room in a heartbeat. Molly parks herself on the couch between us, making her presence felt in no uncertain terms, as she conveys a strong message of possession: "This is my human, so you need to know this!"

"She is a very possessive dog," I say.

"So would I be if you were my owner," he says, his eyes twinkling.

"Molly approves of you, so I know this is a good start. I want to tell you that I have been thinking... and I am no longer going to be dating my friend who is in America. Not after Saturday night. I don't kiss other men when I am in a relationship, albeit a casual one. This does not mean I expect anything to come from it."

"Susan, you have been on my mind since we saw each other, and I really like you. I don't kiss other women either, and I have already spoken to the woman I was seeing and explained to her what happened when I saw her yesterday. I felt really awful considering her fragile state, but to be dishonest would be more damaging."

"Neil is back tomorrow afternoon, and I will see him either Tuesday or Wednesday and will also let him know that our time together has come to an end," I say.

The afternoon passes in no time, and soon he has to go. I walk with him to the door. Soon his face is moments away from mine, and those delicious kisses from Saturday night happen again, and I know immediately that I am in trouble and that I never want him to stop. He finally kisses my lips, and at this moment I tug on his shirt and start to undo his buttons. We somehow work our way down the passage and fall onto the bed. The lovemaking is slow, purposeful, gentle, and deeply connected in every sense. I am transported to a place of bliss, of heightened pleasure that I had long forgotten about, and again weep with deep gratitude when we lie together afterwards. He is gentle, caring, and loving. Holds me, and we fall asleep momentarily. I don't feel the need to tell him that this is not my norm; inherently, I know it is not his either.

Molly has stayed by the fireplace but eventually comes to the bedroom. He picks her up and puts her on the bed with us. She is delighted. Bed sleep is a treat for her, so he is quickly earning her love at this rate. I am expecting my goddaughter to come home, so he dresses. I grab a gown as I would like to shower, and as we walk towards the door, I hear the front door open. Sheepishly, I open our door, and we come face to face with my goddaughter. A broad grin spreads across her face; her eyes open wide, and she smiles. "Hello, Mr Delicious," she says and winks at me. We both laugh. As soon as he has left, she comes to me in my room and gives me a big hug. "Mama S, you look radiant and are glowing. I am so happy for you!"

Renaldo and I spend a lot of time together, and our relationship quickly shifts into a serious, committed one. He spends most nights at my home. His presence is so calming, which I love. My home is designed to be tranquil, overlooking mountains and water with floor-to-ceiling windows and doors that bring the outside in. The colours are neutral, creating an uncluttered, minimalistic space. I encourage him to bring his guitar, and he laughs, saying, "Do you have any idea how many guitars and musical instruments I have?"

During this time, I do not get to see where he is staying, as he is in a temporary small apartment that he rents from one of the musicians in the band. He plans to move soon and will be looking for a place. I suggest that he looks close to my area, as it is not far from the beach and he is a surfer. He finds a place nearby, and then unexpectedly, my tenant, who lives in my one-bedroom apartment, gives me notice. We agree that it makes sense for him to rent the space, as it is the perfect music studio and study space for him, with a lounge, small dining area, a good-sized bedroom, and a nice courtyard too. It is unfurnished, so he can make it his own with his furniture.

We decide on a formal lease arrangement since we have just met and will be living together within two months of meeting. This arrangement works well; if things go wrong, he has a place to go to, a music studio to play in, and we can have separate spaces during the day.

My friends are shocked at how quickly this has all happened, but when they meet him, they approve, as he is a gentle man, very loving, and looks at me adoringly often, which makes my heart melt, and I fall more and more in love with him each day. I know instinctively that this will be the other great love of my life, and I am so grateful to have this opportunity at this stage in my life. I worship the ground he walks on, and we are happy together. His presence continues to calm me, and I love that it does.

We settle into a routine of walking Molly down our road either together or separately, and she adores him. She loves this male presence in my life, and my goddaughter gets along well with him too. She only spends some of her time with us, but when she does, he is really good at parenting and gives great advice.

I meet his friend Mike, who lives in Johannesburg. On the third day we spend with Mike, he mentions his daughter and the school she goes to. I ask her age, and then the penny drops. My stepdaughter was friendly with his daughter, and we have, in fact, met in the past but very fleetingly. Mike is a lovely man, and I like him a lot. He is also gentle and psychologically astute, and this fascinates me, as I am always in awe of those who have high emotional intelligence and not just high IQ.

They are very close and go back to their school days. It is one of those well-known Cape Town schools where the friendships are forever, and often these men work together later in life. Strongly bonded, they support one another a lot.

Before I know it, we have been together for a year, and I am so happy. I am deeply in love, and he remains loving, adoring, thoughtful, and gentle.

We head off to Namibia six months into our relationship, and it is spectacular. He is from this part of the world, so he knows it well. It is my first trip, and the days driving are long and exquisite. We go in my car because it is a proper 4x4, and he packs the car full of "things we might need" plus two spare wheels, which means we hardly have space for our suitcases. He is meticulous and prepares the packing for three days.

I love everything I see and am in awe of the varied landscapes that change over the course of a driving day. The wide-open spaces and spectacular sunsets are just magical. We often stop to take pictures but seldom venture out of the car as the heat is intense and January is one of the hottest months of the year. We listen to his selection of songs; mostly it is guitar music, which, to be honest, is not my favourite music, but I love this man and make it my business to enjoy it. On day 18 of the trip, we had been driving all day when I asked if we could perhaps listen to something else, and he looked at me harshly.

"What genre would you want me to play?"

My brain races, genre, genre—it's a new word, but I don't want to say so, and eventually I murmur, "Just something soft and gentle?"

"Well, I have 4000 plus songs on here, so tell me and I am sure to find it!" spoken ungently and with a mild bit of irritation.

At this point, I can't think, mostly because I am reeling a little from his reaction, which is severe and very unlike the gentle man I know and love so much.

I forget this incident, and we continue to live happily and comfortably together. He is an introvert, so we often sit in silence at dinner, which I find a little unsettling, and I always seem to be the one making conversation. None of this is a big deal; I love him and firmly believe that we will be together forever.

Covid has meant that in the last six months of our year together, we have been in lockdown. This has not changed the dynamics of our relationship much. We spend loads more time indoors, and we both keep busy in our respective spaces. It fascinates me how much one can get done when you can't go out or run errands. I also decide to take over the administration of my properties and am busier than usual. Some of my tenants give notice, and I need to find new ones.

I do an online writing course and learn a lot. Little did I know that this would lead me to write my first book—this one—a few years later! I love the writing course, as I have always enjoyed writing but never really had the time. I write all kinds of things: poems, essays, travel journals, diaries of events and occasions, and emotional pieces trying to make sense of mixed feelings that I don't understand.

I do an interior design course too, but it gets way more involved than I wish to be with CAD drawings, so I stop at the drawing point. It makes total sense to be able to know exact sizes and where they will and won't fit, especially large pieces of furniture. I tidy my house properly from head to toe and get rid of anything that is surplus or not necessary. I cook often and enjoy it as Renaldo does not cook, but we do often barbecue, so this is when he does his thing. I read a lot more than usual. We watch series and get hooked on one called Money Heist.

My life takes on a normality and routine that is foreign to me. We split everything 50/50 down to the last cent, and I open up a separate banking account, as I find the process of downloading and identifying household expenditure, even if in comma-separated values from the bank, too tedious, plus Excel and I have never been friends. My brain just won't switch gear!

He has also made it clear that he does not fix things around the house, that he has done his time, and that this is my investment, not his. I am a little stung by this—which he told me at the onset of our deciding to live together—but figure I have been doing it all myself anyway for the last eight years, and he has a point? The detailed splitting of expenses is also a little uncomfortable, but I choose to see it as him just being a structured and precise person, not as someone who is tight or mean.

Our second Christmas together, we are in lockdown, unable to venture out as my physiotherapist got Covid, and I saw her the day she got ill. We cannot go to lunch now with my close friend, nor can we spend Christmas Eve with anyone. So, we have this cute supper outside in our little courtyard, as the main house is let for the holidays, and we are sharing the flatlet that he rents. He benefits from not paying any rent to share my house, so I do not contribute to his rental, even though he is scoring because there is a substantial difference in rates for the spaces. I put a small Christmas hat on Molly and a red and white necklace that looks beautiful against her pepper coat of fur, and we take pictures. She loves all the attention, and I even put her on a chair to sit with us. It's a special time.

I am very keen to take our pedal boat out on the water that surrounds our estate and attend the Christmas Carols that take place on the other side of the canal at "Marina," where we live. They have live music, Father Christmas comes and hands out gifts to the children, and, because we are on the water in our pedal boat, we are not a risk to anyone. It is one of the best Christmas experiences that I have had, and I am super keen to show Renaldo just how special it is, and we can take Molly! Also, it is a lovely opportunity to get out in the open and enjoy a sunset as well. The weather is superb at this time of the year. Covid has eased, and we are allowed out.

He is not keen and says he does not want to go. I am a bit gutted, as I don't understand why he would not want to come. I tell him that it's really special and that I really would like to go, and would he please come for me, as it would mean so much? He reluctantly agrees, and I pack a lovely bottle of champagne, and we set out.

It's a magical experience. There are many boats out on the water and many dogs in boats too. We find a lovely spot, and I am thrilled to be there. Families are picnicking on the grass, and the band is set up in the foreground. There are bagpipes and a saxophone; a lovely singer; and other band members. The atmosphere is jolly; everyone is happy and in good spirits. People are talking to one another across the boats, and I am overjoyed. I thank him and tell him how much it means to me. He remains tight-lipped and does not get into the swing of the occasion, nor does his mood lift. I am taken aback and disappointed. This is my first real encounter with a different Renaldo than the one I have loved for so long.

Not long after this, he reacts angrily one night at dinner and gets very vocal, loud, and says some pretty hurtful things. I am again shocked and simply retreat. I don't like to argue, and my defence is simply to shut down and remove myself. I believe we can land up saying things in anger that we later regret, and I avoid this happening at all costs.

In April, on my birthday, I wake up crying, deeply sad. Our relationship is now 18 months old. He is very upset with me and has not wanted to engage with me for a few days. I have avoided any discussion and instead have emailed him. When he had an angry outburst and shouted loudly, I was shocked into silence. This man was so contrary to the man I knew. He explained that as an Italian, he can be fiery and quite vocal, but this was on a different level to what I expected, and his communication was unkind. I can't even remember what it was about. I blocked this out subconsciously.

My own issues make me shut down, and if there is a raised voice or criticism of any kind, I can't speak because I am too scared to do so. I clam up so badly that I lose focus. However, I can recall enough to email him the next day. In all our time together, I have apologised if I have upset him. I have acknowledged my shortcomings. He has never once said sorry and always believes he is right. I know that most of these small issues are centred around him not feeling important and validated enough. I am also aware that he gives 100% and that he does not have other pressing responsibilities, like friends or family, that he has to see or spend time with.

He is a loner and happy to spend days indoors in his studio, only venturing out to take Molly for a walk, or for us to sometimes do a longer walk than normal. I tell him that I can deal with most things, but days of silent treatment with an atmosphere in the air is not where I see myself to be long-term. There is now a very big chink in what was previously perfect armour. He apologises. This is the only time he ever said sorry.

After this incident, I become more aware of his levels of unhappiness, which mainly centres around my busyness and varied interests. I always have projects. Some are long, some are short. My properties constantly require attention, which means there is always work to be done, and more so in our current home, which must generate income. This means we sometimes move to his apartment for a few months.

I always do the bulk of these moves, and he only ever has to bring his clothes across. However, over time and due to my constant busyness, this has become something he does not like or want to be a part of. On a few occasions, when he got involved with a worker or a team on-site, he would be very unhappy. This would happen when I have something else to do. I tell him that he is not required to assist, nor do I particularly expect it, as he made that clear from the word go. I explain that in the past, before he was around, they either waited until I returned or got on with other work.

The straw that breaks the camel's back is when I embark on a project to revamp an overgrown mole heap of land down our road, transforming it into a 2,000 square metre garden. I love this project, and it's a huge success. We plant from scratch using cuttings from residents' gardens, and I put together a small group who plan and plant this space. We get an old rowing boat, a lovely big wooden bench, a wrought iron bench, and a 'rough 'n ready' bench that we put in various strategic spots in the garden, plus we get donated loads of pavers and pots.

The project is all-consuming, and I spend days planning and planting. He refuses to get involved in any way, saying he doesn't want anything to do with my project. This makes me aware that we have trouble in paradise. However, he does not share with me why and gets more and more withdrawn.

By now we have formed a handful of friends—also couples— and meet up with someone I once knew, and her husband takes a big liking to Renaldo. One evening we are all at dinner, and, as they knew the last great love of my life, I share with them that Renaldo is my other great love, that we will grow old together, and that I love him so much. Renaldo does not respond to this, but I don't think anything of it, other than he is just being his usual introverted self. I remain head over heels; my knight in shining armour is real, and all mine.

In June, we head to Durban for a two-week trip and visit his friends. We have five days at the coast, and they are people I like and get along with. We stay in one of his friend's parents apartments. It is a spacious three-bedroom unit, and we are given the master suite. It is an interesting dynamic with a couple who seemingly got married more for convenience than love, at a later stage in life. The other person is a friend of Renaldo's—a pilot who is single and has come alone.

It is clear that the wife of the other couple—let's call her Carol—is head over heels in love with the single pilot. She tells me how she feels and that the only reason she would never leave her husband is because he is her best friend, plus he provides the roof over their heads. The pilot has no money, and his friends are helping him survive. I don't believe it takes rocket science to work this one out. The pilot is clearly enjoying the puppy dog adoration and love, and it was actually rather sad to watch this dynamic at play. He loves the attention and probably unconsciously encouraged it due to his own shortcomings and traumas. They wake up every morning in the early hours and talk and spend time together. Physically, she is not Pilot's type, and he says as much. He also says that he has made it clear he does not love her. He does, however, encourage the relationship, and they are a friendly trio!

From there, we head up to the Midlands and meet friends of mine. I had spent time with them when my previous business partner passed away unexpectedly, at the age of eighty. Renaldo was incredible during this time, working alongside me, packing up the home. The family loved him for this. They had given us the Honeymoon suite at their lodge, and it was incredibly special.

I loved this holiday, but I did feel a change—subtle and barely noticeable. Every now and again he would "gaslight" me when I did not know where a place was on our travels. He did geography at school, whereas I am not always sure where South is. But logically, if you can see the sun before midday or after, it's an obvious assessment.

I found myself being more uneasy around him, and I started to watch my words. I developed 'restless legs' syndrome. This had never happened before and has not happened since. He would get very cross with me when it disturbed him, waking me roughly and harshly. I resented cooking so often, as it was not something I enjoyed, and lockdown was now over. But he didn't want to eat out or go anywhere. All suggestions came from me.

In hindsight, I was the "driver," and while I don't mind, I do like my partner to make suggestions or surprise me. I took him on a surprise pre-birthday weekend for his birthday and organised a meeting with his friends in a little town. I paid for a full birthday lunch for eight of us. He was not crazy about the surprise and did not really thank me either. In fact, in hindsight, he was not big on gratitude, like I am. He also is not big on tipping car guards, which I find unacceptable, especially at night, and was not kind to beggars or others in need.

On a particularly demanding day, I leave home early for the busy garden project and leave my faithful right-hand man to do some handyman work over and above his garden duties. I had some bricks laid earlier, and the dried residue of the cement needed to be removed. I return home later in the morning, and he is instructing my gardener to use the scouring pad attachment on my drill to clean the bricks.

He does not look happy to see me. In addition to all of this, the plumber was doing some last-minute work outside, plus the lady who cleans my home is there, and she lets the plumber in who knows what to do. His face is like thunder when he sees me, and I am completely taken aback, but by now I know it's to do with him overseeing the work.

Much later that evening, he tells me that I am irrational and disorganized. That he is tired of picking up my dropped balls and that either I change and become more organised and structured, or our relationship is at risk. Furthermore, how dare I not inform him about everything that was happening that day? It took him away from important work he needed to do for himself, and he is hugely upset.

I explain that usually a Friday is his practice day, and he leaves before anyone arrives. That the previous evening, when he got home, he informed me that he did not have band practice the following day. I thought that he would venture into his studio anyway, like he did every day. I had not wanted to go into any detailed activity "rundowns" or schedule, as I knew it would upset him. I reasoned that a discussion with him was unnecessary since my staff were on hand to either do the work or let workers in to do what was required.

Silence ensued for a few days; this was happening more frequently. I was trying to find a happy medium that would allow me to let him vent and to also better understand this manner of expression. He sits me down a few days later and gives me an ultimatum. Either I change or our relationship is over. I struggle to comprehend this kind of expectation and tell him that this is who I am; that when curved balls present themselves, there is always a solution, and I suggest we find it.

I ask him if we can try to come to an understanding that our home is a business for me and should be left entirely in my hands. It was clear to me that he did not want involvement of any kind, and I explain that I did not expect him, or need him, to assist. I tell him that, although it was not easy for me, I have taken note of his clear statement when he moved in that he was not interested, nor inclined, to do any work involved in my investment.

He is not open to considering a compromise. I am gutted and feel completely broken. I ask him to give me some time to think about this and that I would try, because I love him so much. His demeanour takes on a stone-like stance, devoid of any emotion, and I am shocked to see such silent anger manifest in his face and body. His beautiful, gentle face is hard and expressionless. His brown eyes are cold, and his warm and full mouth is tightly closed and thin.

A few days pass and we are together, continuing to exist as a couple, but all warmth has gone. I take myself on a Harley ride with a girlfriend and travel up front with just the big, wide-open spaces and beauty around me. We pass the ocean and then head through open lands and tree-lined roads. It is here that my head clears. It is here that my heart sinks and I find my answer. I do not talk about this to my friend, whom I ride with. I don't need to get any outside advice. I have made some of my best decisions in life while riding, and it is my go-to place for clarity.

The sun is setting when I get home. I ask Renaldo to join me in the lounge and tell him that I cannot change my DNA. I can pay lip service to make him happy, but I would be lying to him and myself. That I simply could not reduce a relationship that was built on such trust and honesty to an inferior one. That it was important to honour him and myself.

He looks at me expressionless. Slowly, he gets up and says, "The relationship and I are clearly not important enough to you. As you are not prepared to change, we are over." He walks out of the room and heads to his studio. I am inconsolable and cry so deeply that Molly comes to sit next to me. I walk around in a daze and can't do anything. At 8 p.m., I take Molly for a walk, feed her, and crawl up into a ball on the bed.

I sleep fitfully and wake up exhausted. I cannot get up. I am broken into a million pieces. I am so deeply sad that I cannot get up, but I do ensure Molly has a brief walk and her morning food, and I lie in bed all day. Emotionally, I am drained. My anxiety level skyrockets, and I struggle to function. I walk around in a daze. I can't eat, I avoid my phone, and eventually I go to see my doctor, who is more like a friend than a doctor. She knows me well and has seen me through many medical incidents, procedures, and illnesses. She prescribes a medication to stabilise my emotions. She tells me that I will function better and that my deep sadness will be held at bay.

Five weeks go by. Renaldo has moved into his studio bedroom, and we only see each other in the driveway. In the fifth week, I ask to see him.

I beg him to give me, us, another chance. I have never done this before, as I am too proud, but the heartache is too much for me. He is guarded and asks me why I have now decided that I can change, or, better still, in his own words, "What makes you think that you now know how to behave around me?"

I see all the warning signs in this kind of response but refuse to see the reality, and instead I say, "I am willing to try anything to make it work."

"I can try, but I do not hold much hope in this reconciliation," he says.

Unusually, we go out for supper. I am exhausted from the emotional strain. He is tender and loving and later that evening, massages my sore back and shoulders. The lovemaking is gentle and sweet and urgent in my case. My adrenals are peaked, and I pour five weeks of pain into lovemaking, and I am spent afterwards. Molly is so happy to have her "Dada" back at home.

A week drags by. He is due to move in a few days, and we have agreed to date each other rather than live together. During this week I am on high alert not to trigger any anger or upset from him. It's stressful, but I am blinded by love. He is not convinced this will work—I can tell by the way he looks at me. His face holds little real warmth when he smiles; he does not touch me much and is quiet and withdrawn. There is no spontaneity, and I feel it deeply.

I have a busy Saturday with guests vacating the main house, and I join a friend for lunch. She has been a great support to me during this time. My energy levels are low, and I have lost weight. I return in the afternoon for a nap. I have made the home comfortable and changed the sheets, except for the duvet cover, which is clean. There has been a sheet underneath, so removing this means one is under a clean duvet. We have a quiet dinner and watch a movie together. I always leave the movie choice to him, as he reminded me on several occasions that in his previous very turbulent relationship, he watched too many romcoms with "HER." This is not a big deal for me, as I seldom watch TV or movies. I prefer to be busy with something more meaningful, so I have never had a problem. He always checks whether I would like to see what he has chosen. I tire easily, and we go to bed earlier than normal. I tell him we will sleep in the main house, not his apartment bedroom, as it's a lovely big room. We can wake up to a view of mountains, blue skies, and lake water when we open our eyes.

As we enter the room, he looks at the duvet and says, "This is the same bedding the guests had!" I try to explain that, in fact, it's only the duvet that is the same, and two pillows were never used either.

But he is furious. "How on earth can you expect me to sleep in a bed that other people have slept in without changing the linen? They have done who knows what in there and exchanged bodily fluids as well! It's totally unhygienic, and if you did physiology at school, you would know this!"

He turns on his heels, and as he walks off, he says the following words, "If you are too fucking lazy to change the sheets, then don't make such irrational decisions. I am so tired of teaching you how to behave around me!"

The anger in his voice and the tone shock me rigid, and I say to him, "You don't understand. The bedding is clean. Sleep in your own bed, as I am not going to sleep with a hostile person who loses it over nothing." I am aware, however, that there is so much more to this statement than meets the eye and that the relationship is over.

I take coffee to him in the morning. He is still furious, angry, and sullen. I leave him alone for the day, and that evening we agree to speak. He says, "I no longer want to be with you. You are too irrational, too all over the place, and I can't deal with it. You don't spend enough time thinking before you do anything, and I am always picking up your dropped balls!"

My mind goes back to the time when we were leaving for Namibia together. He took three days to pack. The car was so full we had little room for our luggage as we took a car fridge, two huge spare wheels, sleeping bags, chairs, etc. The only thing we really used on the entire three-week journey was the one wheel when we got a flat tyre.

The overthinker and the underthinker were not a match. The old adage "opposites attract" came to mind, and I always believed this created a healthy match. I would often have to wait and pace myself to accommodate his thoroughness but chose to see this as positive and a good level of balance between us.

He leaves in a few days, and I am still unable to shake the overwhelming sadness. I am lost and devastated. I believed in "forever" with this beautiful man. I am a huge realist, so for me to have gone down the road of thinking "forever" was big. Very big. I am too sceptical of anything lasting, and this goes way back to my childhood filled with change, impermanence, and loss, often. I was so sure. He was in my Will, he was my life going forward.

A year later I am writing in Nantes, France, looking back on all the encounters, and this one still makes my heart ache deeply. I sit and wonder if I will ever get over this heartache and pain of a love lost, a love far-fetched and unsustainable. I have deleted his number from my phone and his email address as well. I unfriended anyone on Facebook who knows him. I heard a few weeks after we broke up that he was out with someone else at a morning market not far from where I live. That hurt deeply, but I was not surprised.

He was never alone for long in the three years he had been divorced. When I met him, his pattern was to go out and find someone new soon. This does not make him a fickle or bad person, but rather a romantic where "love" is important and necessary in his life. He falls in love quickly and deeply. He chooses to get right in, as we did, and their world becomes his world. This ultimately can only lead to disappointment and heartache. He does not have enough alone time to be "Renaldo solo"; he is Renaldo combined with another, mostly. We discussed this when we were together. I said to him that he gives 100% in a relationship and that this is difficult for another person to do in return. I believed he would always be disappointed long-term as a result.

In the ebb and flow of relationships in my book, there has to be room for other things emotionally that fill our souls and hearts. He was and is one of the most giving, caring, loving, and thoughtful human beings when it comes to the early stages of the relationship. Less so as he got more disappointed and disillusioned, but still way more inclined than any other individuals I have met. But that goes for most things in life.

He is the man who brings you flowers from the grocery store, even if it is your shared grocery bill. He is the man who will make you coffee every morning. Who will walk the dog when you are busy or tired. Who will always do the dishes when you cook—which he does not. I always found this odd, as most Latin men I have met love to cook, but then he is half Latin! He is tidy and easy to be around, albeit a little too quiet for me and too in his head, and conversation is limited as a result. He has a quiet presence, and this is what attracted me most. I loved the calm serenity he brought to my home and my life. I made a point of referring to everything as ours and was happy to share my home, my safe place, generously.

I asked him to display some of his beautiful musical instruments in the lounge, but he declined, saying they had to be covered. But occasionally, he would leave a guitar in the lounge for a while. He never played much when we were together, and only if I asked. He sang gently and sweetly and had been for singing lessons. He was not a great singer, but with more practice, he was pleasant to listen to. He spent every day in his studio but never shared what he really did. He was bogged down with a lot of administration as he was the executor of his father's estate and also kept books for the family of the funds and how they were distributed. His attention to detail would often mean that he would double-check what he was doing, and this was very time-consuming. He was a perfectionist, so this took a lot of his energy and focus.

Twice during the time we were apart, and in a moment of weakness, I tried to encourage him to spend some time with Molly, as he loved her a lot, but he declined, rightly so. I dread the day I walk into a venue or restaurant where he may be. I will be adversely affected, for sure. Just typing this thought makes my heart rate go up, my pulse race, and I feel a massive sense of panic spread throughout my body.

Do I wish that I had never met him? I can't honestly answer that question, as I don't know. I could do without the heartache and after effects, but would I want to forget the euphoria and love I experienced? No. The high was so incredible, and the love so intense for me. He was my knight in shining armour. I choose the positive from this, and I instead believe that maybe, just maybe, love like that will find me again.

My goal in the world of dating, be it on-site or offline, has always been to find love. However, due to my past history, I've always been fully aware that the chances of "everlasting" were slim and far-fetched for me. My world is too big, my life too full, and my mind too busy. I don't have room for much else.

I know that lockdown made a relationship possible as it took me off my ever-busy roller coaster life, and this is why Renaldo and I worked. However, when lockdown ended, I reverted to my true, adrenalin bunny self! For a quiet, always-in-his-head man, this was very unsettling. His serene space and organised life were constantly disrupted. Hindsight is an exact science!

I also know now that my restless energy escalates as I get older, so perhaps I need someone who already has one foot in the grave!! "Oh, dear Susan, you are impossible!" Tongue in cheek, but true! I could never trade my life as it is for love if it required me to change. I have had many encounters—some longer-term relationships and some very short ones. It's what works for my personality, and writing about them has given me this insight.

CHAPTER 19
KEVIN AND JOSH
- MY PERFECT FRIENDS

Since meeting up with my fabulous friend, Kobus. I have been online intermittently, but have been too busy at work to give the site much attention. I have a few male friends who fulfil the male company role when necessary. I have known my friend Kevin for about five years. We met at a friend's extravagant, elegant dinner one evening when I was still married to my ex-husband and we were both working in property.

Kevin has short, thick, white hair, a perfect jaw, well-defined dark eyebrows, a sensual, broad smile, and beautiful teeth. Chiselled and muscular, he has a strong physique and wears well-cut clothes, which makes him very appealing. A pink golf shirt, jeans, and a leather jacket depict a strong man who is confident and wears what looks good. The choice of colours offsets his colouring well. He is a well-off property developer who also worked for some big names in his time but went solo about ten years ago. He also owns a Harley. I liked him immediately. I wonder to myself, *Why is this man single?*

My friend enlightens me, however, as we work in the same office, and she says he was, in fact, married to her husband's daughter, but that they are now divorced. She thinks the world of him, and we both agree that he is definitely a catch for a single woman. So, when I bump into him at a Harley Club meeting one evening, I am thrilled to see him.

The club venue is a work of art, and there is even half a Harley mounted on the wall above the bar. There are all sorts of shining metal Harley memorabilia around: on the walls, the floor, the bar, and outside. It is frequented by Harley owners who are existing members or newcomers who are attending in order to become members. Some people have been members for 15 years. The club, by this stage, boasts some 400 members. It's a great place to make friends and to meet up with members you have ridden with, been away with, partied with, and had fun with. It is the kind of place I could happily go to alone. In fact, I preferred to do so as it was fun to talk to a lot of different people and catch up on all their news and life stories. I was not a regular and went on average four times a year, at most. I was at the very first ever Harley meeting some 15 years earlier, when there were exactly six of us, so I knew a lot of the members even though I did not often attend meetings. I was never going to be one of those members who hung with a clique year in and year out!

I chat with Kevin for quite some time and then mingle, as I have so many people I want to talk to. Later on in the evening, we catch up a bit more. He is single and will be doing the Sunday ride, and he asks if I am going. At this point I don't know, as my job often interferes with my weekend time, and I explain this to him. Buyers want to visit houses on a weekend, so this always takes priority. He asks for my number and says, "Well, if you don't make it, let's ride together on a day that you can. My time is totally flexible as I am the boss, so I work when I choose to! Besides, you need a male chaperone to assist in the event of a flat tyre or other mishap, and I am able to fix most things, so I am useful to have around, you know!"

I hug him and leave shortly afterwards. He smells fabulous—a musty, sensuous, yet subtle smell with a hint of lemongrass. His body is solid and rock hard. I am impressed, as he is in seriously good shape and a lot older than me.

Once home, I shower and flop into my lovely big bed under my high ceiling, pull up the big fluffy duvet, and snuggle up into a ball. I hear my phone, pick it up, and there is a message from him, "Trust you are home safe, Gorgeous." My heart does a little skip, and I feel warm and fuzzy all over. I text him back, "Not so gorgeous now, but thanks for the compliment, Mr. HS."

I switch off my phone to make sure I sleep; I don't want to get all distracted and excited.

The next morning, I see he sent another message, this time a "mojo" hug, and I respond, saying I will be in touch if I can make Sunday.

As it turns out, I am free on Sunday, so we schedule to all meet at the Clubhouse at 10 a.m. The ride is to a wine farm in Franschhoek, via the N2 and the R44, as this is a beautiful ride through the Helshoogte Pass, which is a well-loved biker's route, as it has some good corners and curves in the road, making it challenging.

There are over 20 bikes at the Sunday ride, and it's a perfect day. There is something to be said for the sound of 20 Harleys starting up all at once. The roar of so many engines is mind-blowing! The difference between Harleys and other bikes is that Harley engines give a deep throaty throb, whereas ordinary bikes have a high-pitched whine.

We sit together at lunch. I can feel the chemistry, but I keep my distance, avoiding any body contact or touching, as the Club can be a bit incestuous with various members dating one another, and once that relationship ends, they date another member. At some point at lunch, I feel his leg touch mine, and I like it. I like it a lot.

I get up as soon as lunch is over and go talk to some other members to socialise and take the focus off Kevin and me. Every now and again, I become aware that he is looking at me, and I feel hot and glance his way too. It's not rocket science that there is something going on, and we are not doing too well at hiding it!

The ride home is mixed, as some people leave earlier than others, and he and I land up riding home together. He invites me in for coffee at his house, and I agree to pop in to meet his dog, Josh, a miniature Schnauzer. His home is in a classy suburb and is elevated. Situated at the top of a road, it is surrounded by lush greenery and vegetation. He has a beautiful view over the suburb and, off in the distance, the majestic Hottentots Holland Mountain range.

A masculine ambience permeates the entire home. Josh is sitting on the couch, pitch black and adorable. He is docile and super chilled, and I fall in love with him instantly! That is how it works: love me, love my dog, except in this case, I love your dog more! Josh continues to sit and stares me down with his big brown, soft, gentle eyes. I have never met a dog who does this. He holds my stare, and he does not mind when I bring my face to his nose, and we sit looking at one another a mere 20cm apart. I am now infatuated and smitten. Kevin is looking at us from the kitchen where he is making coffee and says, "I can tell you two approve of one another."

"Approve," I say, "I am totally in love with your dog!"

We have coffee in the lounge, and Kevin puts on some great music. It's 70's music, and I love it. I snuggle up to Josh, cupping my coffee in my hand. Kevin and I chat easily and comfortably. An eclectic dark leather lounge suite with not much colour other than some faint orange in a few brown and beige fluffy Afghan scatter cushions that have been around for quite some time, with edges that seem to have lost some tassels. The room has a strong male presence that resonates in the décor.

I get up to go to the bathroom, and he directs me down the passage. The bathroom has black marble and grey tiles and walls. This, too, is very masculine, but it is, after all, a man's house. I have never been in such a dominantly male home before, and I have sold many properties in my time, so this home is an eye-opener in terms of male dominance.

On my return, he is standing and asks me to come and see the sunset. The sight is beautiful, and he puts his arm around me, pulling me close. "This sunset is almost as glorious as you, but not quite." Then he kisses me all over my face, avoiding my lips. His breath is hot and smells of coffee. He then draws away and looks at me for a long time. "I thought you were beautiful the day we met at Rachel's, but you are even more beautiful now. I like you, Susan, and I intend to see more of you if you will let me take you out?"

It's a quick ride home, and my mind is replaying the day's events and conversations. I think to myself, *Just when you least expect it, someone special comes along. Life is full of surprises, and I am ready for this one!*

CHAPTER 20
KEVIN - THE NIGHT

Two weeks go by, and I am meeting Kevin for a date night. We head to my all-time favourite spot, La Perla. A traditional trattoria that oozes Italy from every pore. Traditional crisp white tablecloths, waiters in short white jackets, black bowties, and matching pants are the order of the day here. It is a place I have been coming to for the last 25 years, and nothing has changed. The décor, wooden carved chairs, and colourful wall murals of Italian scenes are exactly as they were way back when.

The table booked does not disappoint, and it's nicely tucked away in a cosy part of the restaurant. Soft music— guitar and piano, mixed intermittently with cello, violin, and saxophone—wafts throughout. Dinner is superb: champagne and oysters to start with, a superb Italian pasta, and tiramisu. The waiters are part of the furniture, with a good 60% who have served me at some point or another during my various dinners and luncheons here. It is the only restaurant in my book, throughout the whole of South Africa, that can boast this kind of tradition, legacy of staff, and perfection when it comes to traditional Italian food.

We have so much in common, and I am amazed at how quickly the evening passes. We hold hands, flirt, and kiss every now and then. It's a perfect evening. It feels like I know him really well and that this has been a lifetime of knowing, rather than just a few weeks.

I don't invite him in for coffee when we get home; instead, I allow a long, lingering embrace and another one of those beautifully sensual, hot all-over kisses. Inside, I sit on my couch and am engrossed with thoughts of the evening and I just allow myself to absorb the chemistry, coffee in hand.

My phone vibrates: "Good night, Gorgeous. So glad that your ex let you go!"

I send a "mojo" hug and say, "Me too!" The next day I head off to Johannesburg on business, and I am away for two weeks. We agree to meet at Clifton Beach to watch a sunset and set the time for about 5p.m. as the summer sunsets are at 8p.m.

Clifton rates among the world's most beautiful beaches. There are four exclusive beaches that sit at the bottom of the mountainside, all with the most perfect blue ocean and the purest of white sand, and they are completely wind-free. The weather is playing ball, and it's a warm summer's day. With no wind, it's hot, and I decide to take my swimsuit along.

When I get there, I spot him immediately. Golden tan and a visible, well-defined torso. Wow! My stomach gets butterflies, and suddenly, I feel self-conscious, and I don't want to get out of my full-length, soft-flowing summer dress. The sweat is however dripping down my shoulders, and my dress is sticking to my back! Horrors! He has laid out a large picnic blanket. There is even an ice bucket with a bottle of bubbly and two glasses.

He walks towards me, and I quickly fan my dress a little, trying to get it off my back! *I so hope he does not hug me today!* I lean forward and kiss his cheek quickly, then run ahead and sit down! "A perfect set up here, Mr HS," I say.

"So, what exactly does Mr HS stand for?" He asks, with a broad grin on his face.

"Try and guess," I tease. This banter goes back and forth and eventually I say, "Mr Hot Stuff, and appropriately so!"

He turns around to face the sea, and I see a carpet of dark hair intermingled with black and grey on his back. I feel my mouth go dry, and I blink to make sure I am not seeing this, willing not to see it, and pull my sunglasses closer to my eyes. Oh, my Word, this is for real, and I am mortified! I have visions of running a comb over his back and the thought mortifies me!

All chemistry flies like the wind from my body, and I feel terrible. How is it possible that such a small detail can have such a huge effect on how I feel? It occurs to me that I am fickle, a "lookist"—a word I made up for being a person who is only concerned with the exterior. That I am shallow, unkind, and plain fussy. But I simply cannot imagine running my hands down that back! Not a chance!

The sunset, while gorgeous, can't happen quickly enough for me now. I decide to swim after all; the water is freezing, and I feel my feet turn into ice blocks. They turn blue, and I can hardly walk, but I push on, determined to get wet and sandy to avoid physical contact. It works, and we hold hands instead, but I am deeply sad. I think, *Surely he can have it removed? I lasered my legs and other parts of my body successfully. All good and well, Susan, but how on earth do you broach this without hurting his feelings, and at 65, if he had wanted to do so, he would have, right?* I have heard plenty of stories where men venture off to a salon to have some waxing done and they have never returned! Men are such sissies, don't you think?

I can't wait to get home and tell him that I have to leave at 8:30 p.m., as I have an early morning secret sunrise event. Then I realise how ridiculous this sounds, considering I have just watched the sunset! Awkward moment indeed, and I push my glasses tighter into my face to hide my guilty eyes. I know he is confused about the mixed signals, and I feel awful. I do not get a message from him that evening, and relief rushes over me.

After a sleepless night, with nightmares of wax attempts of hair removal and foam spray that turns into huge clouds of white that cover his whole body, I send him a voice note. I try my level best to say what I need to in a kind way. I can't tell him the real reason, so I say something else. I have forgotten what it was. I get no reply. He is hurt. This is not fun. It occurs to me that it is way easier to be dumped than to have to do the dumping!

CHAPTER 21
DURBAN DELIGHT MIKE

While writing this narrative, I have to refer to all my WhatsApp contacts for various communications, and it's hilarious. I have to save the various encounters in different ways so they are either DS Simon, ZK Mike, or SS Joe, but eventually they migrate to their proper names if they get past the dating tests and a proper connection is made. When I scroll through the various lists, I am a bit mortified to find there are some names I don't recollect, and I have to search WhatsApp to find communication to jog my memory. I am totally screwed, if there is none!

Having said that, I have been known to have some memory "freeze" moments, even with people I know well or have met in the past. I am convinced that it's due to stress rather than getting older, as I will often go into panic mode when I see these faces and anticipate the "freeze," and then it happens! It's purely panic that freezes my brain! Yes panic! Now I feel a whole lot better.

He is short, so this is a little off-putting, as I have done my time with men my own height! He is also not that great-looking, but he has character in his face and an ever-so-naughty look about him. I "like" his profile, and he "likes" mine, and we soon chat on WhatsApp. When he first calls, I can't answer as I am in the dentist's waiting room with several other people. I message him to apologise and explain my dilemma.

"Don't let them take too many teeth," he texts. I laugh loudly and get the odd look from others in the room. I mention that I will be here for a few hours as I need major work done, but then kick myself after sending this! He probably thinks he is about to meet a high-maintenance senior, and it occurs to me: that is exactly what I am getting to be! Yes, horror of horrors, but true!

My mind wanders... My medical history presents itself loud and clear: *Near frozen shoulder earlier in the year. Two months of physio that cost an arm and a leg! Later on, yes, still in the same year, my neck also plays up once more after behaving for over a year. More physio and a neck collar for a while!! Later on, my lower back also played up too, and it is only April!* This is a depressing thought process, and I decide to block it from my mind. Instead, I decide, *He does not need to know all this, plus I have a high pain threshold, so I generally fare well where most others would not! He will only know what I let on! Safe! Thank goodness he is far away.*

We connect much later that afternoon, as I have a crisis on my hands with a deep freezer fridge that broke down at my friend's house. I get there, and when I open the door, I am greeted by the foul smell of rotten prawns and seafood. I send him a message as he has tried to call a few times and we leave voice notes. We speak on the phone a few times and exchange pictures. I send him one of Molly, and he says he loves Schnauzers. I head off to Knysna for a week's break and send pics. I really like the sound of his voice; he has a great sense of humour and is funny.

He is due to come to Cape Town to pick up a Jeep. Not just any Jeep; he is a collector of old Jeeps, so this is a rare find. He times it with my return. We meet at my favourite meeting spot described earlier, and it's a beautiful, unusually warm autumn evening. I am seated when he arrives, and he confidently comes over. He is short, but just my height. He is also lean, which makes him look smaller than I would like. We converse easily, and I tell him that I have not been honest about my age on the site; that I am, in fact, three years older than him. He tells me that I look great and he would never have guessed, but at the same time he is honest too and says that he generally shops in a pool of women who are ten years younger than him.

He runs a family business and lives on a farm. He is semi-retired, as his son now runs the business that specialises in tool and machinery hire. It's indeed a good business and well known. It's a well-established business too, as it has been around since his father was young, so he effectively fell with his bum in the butter, so to speak, by taking over an already very successful business. This does not align well with my take on success. I prefer to be with people who create their own success, but I am not going to judge someone I don't know.

He has been on his own for the last two years, and his ex-girlfriend is ten years younger than he is. I ask him to tell me more about her and their relationship. She is a local woman, and they met at a pub a few years back. She is very pretty and petite, and she is well groomed. She works as a receptionist, so she is not a big earner. She is a lot of fun, and they only saw each other at weekends.

I gather from our discussion that she is a "bimbo" type—as I call them—and that he clearly is big on "eye candy" and not too concerned about intellect or independence. Initially, they had a very good sexual relationship, but in the last year they were together, she would want to read her book on a Friday night and was not interested in intimacy. He found this unacceptable, as they did not live together. He was generous: he bought her beautiful clothes and took her on some amazing holidays. He likes to spoil his woman. He starts laughing when he explains that she would disappear on a Saturday evening and come downstairs dressed up. Sometimes it was a nurse's outfit, other times a waitress, or other fantasy costumes that men love to imagine.

"Gosh, she is every man's dream," I say.

"I felt strange about this," he says. "I got the feeling that she was playing at caring about me. I felt that she did not really love me and that she was simply using this as a way to disengage from true intimacy with me."

"You have a point." I am impressed that he has this insight, but at the same time I wonder why he has not moved on from "eye candy" to something more meaningful.

"Look, I will be frank with you," I say. "If you are looking for love, then you need to shop in the right department. A girl who does not match you intellectually and who is not able to pay her way—at least some of the time—will invariably be in it for what you can offer. Also, if she is a lot younger than you, then take your blinkers off!"

"That you are so generous is something you need to curb at the onset of any new relationship until you can establish that she is in it for the right reasons. I sound like an older sister giving her younger brother advice! I also know that I am not a match for you and hope you will forgive me for not being honest about my age."

This is the first time I have realised how important it is to reveal my actual age. So, this encounter has benefited me, and I have learnt something.

"Thank you, Mike." I say.

"I am grateful to you, Susan, as you make a load of sense. I can't do older, but I will for sure call on you when I do meet someone I like!"

"Absolutely," I say.

We talk motorbikes as he rides a lot and tells me about some beautiful road trips he has done. I insist we go Dutch for dinner, but he won't hear of it. I think to myself, *It's going to be hard for this kind and generous leopard to change his spots.*

Over the next couple of months, he remains on the dating site, so I gather he has perhaps taken note of our chat. I know that he is active, as he comes up as busy online some of the time. So, this is another way of knowing whether someone is still looking and available. Either way, it is always a process, and we learn as we go along!

CHAPTER 22
DR FIX IT, A GREAT FIND

I have just stopped at a place called Camel Rock, a small, character-filled, rustic coffee spot and restaurant in Scarborough. The front is reminiscent of a hacienda with a short veranda that has some rickety brown, aged furniture outside. I am in a great mood. I am on a two-wheel ride doing a solo Sunday meander as it's a bit colder now in April and early mornings are no longer appealing. I want to ride while it is warm, to feel the sun on my face, to see the rays reflect off my handlebars, and to experience the warmth of the afternoon sun, which is up high and permeates through my body as I ride. I like it here because it's a hillbilly place, and most of the people who frequent this spot are locals who walk in with dreadlocks and bare feet and look like they are still living in the sixties. An eclectic mix of all sorts of creatives and professionals alike. You will definitely find a few surfers here.

I decide to sit inside for a change, in the courtyard, as it has a forest feel, even though there are no big trees. The décor is rustic, with benches and tables, lots of wood, and plants. It's hippie country here! It's the sort of place where anything goes, and you can bring your dog as well. It is completely laid back, and the staff fit the mood. A waiter finally saunters over, and I order my usual, a café latte. This is my "oh so happy" place, and the world is perfect. I feel very at home here, as I have done some spiritual journeys and other practices that fit into this space comfortably.

While I wait, I decide to check the dating app to see what's on offer. I find this amusing when I realise that, like this restaurant, dating is like a food menu! I decide that, at some point, I will give each encounter a name that one would find right here on what to eat! Appetizer comes to mind, and this is very apt because each picture and profile are pretty much exactly that! I spend a few minutes scrolling and start to feel bored. There are some of the usual old faces from way back—people move around on sites—so when this newly listed male pops up, it piques my interest. The app lists this as a new person, although I have my doubts about this generally. I am not sure if this is to lure old app users to continue to stay on the site, or if they are genuinely new? I have a suspicion that if you change your profile picture, you are deemed new!

Widowed, and an orthopaedic surgeon by profession. I figure he is genuinely new, as a more experienced dater would not put this sort of profession up. Particularly a male, as there are so many women who will want to date a doctor, especially a specialist! I don't know how many of you grew up in the era when marrying a doctor or lawyer was considered first prize! I certainly did. I do, however, stop momentarily when reading this, as it occurs to me that sawing bones and replacing knees and hips is rather butcher-like. His day must be rather stressful and labour-intensive, and I wonder if he would need to be fit in order to heave and shove bones and saw and hammer things together! It occurs to me that he would not be the gentlest man I have ever met.

His photo shows a nice, open face. Big smile and light-coloured eyes, either grey or pale green. He looks like a happy person. On the three apps I have subscribed to in the past, you are given an opportunity to send someone a message to say you like their profile, or you can send a 'Hi' mojo or a smile. This is a more subtle approach for those who are fearful of rejection. I don't like to waste time, so I send a message. At my age, it short-circuits things and gets things moving a little quicker. I don't see the point of playing it slow, and besides, there is a lot of competition! I send a message to say he has a great profile and ask if he does full skeletal replacements, and my mind wonders to a more suggestive message that would include the words, "between the sheets"! But I don't say anything like that!

He sends a message back saying thanks and that he is very busy. Fortunately, I don't see this as a brush-off, and I log out. Nothing ventured, nothing gained is my motto. The ride home is magnificent, as the sun is starting to drop slowly towards the ocean. The road has little traffic, which is why I love to ride it. The ocean crashes and rolls next to me, and the road winds ahead. My bike hugs the road, I lean into the corners, and it's a perfect day.

Two weeks go by; I log on and send a message to Dr Fix It, as I now call him. "Are you still on that hamster wheel? Are you up for air yet?" Not, "I am dying to be injected by you, now!" I wonder what on earth is going on with my mind that this keeps happening when I send him messages?

He replies, "Indeed, I am. I am overseas in Canada with my children on a week's skiing holiday." He's honest and says, "It's because my sister is a ski instructor here, not our usual hangout." I like that. No pretence. I reply and say how fabulous, wish him a wonderful holiday, and tell him I will be going away when he gets back. We agree to exchange WhatsApp numbers.

CHAPTER 23
DR FIX IT CHATS

I was riding the breeze with my best friend on our Harleys. We had six glorious days ahead of us with just the wide-open spaces and the throb of our beasts between our legs. There is nothing quite like it. I learnt to ride when I was forty and had never ridden a bike before then. The reasons are stories for another day, but from the day I got onto a motorbike, I was hooked.

The sense of freedom is breathtakingly overpowering. The road, so hugely wide; the sky, so visible. The scenery is enhanced, as nothing covers your peripheral vision. You are alone, and you have all the time you need and want to be exclusively in your head. There are no distractions, only visual beauty and scenery as you ride, and I am in my element. The weather has played ball, and the sun is shining. A few whisps of clouds are in the sky, and there is no chance of any rain. Rain, when you are riding a motorbike, is no fun! It can destroy a ride in two minutes flat!

It is a warm day. Clad in my black, 24-year-old, well-worn leather jacket with the traditional Harley emblem and orange lining, I am hot at the onset of the ride. Boots are non-negotiable when riding a motorbike and thick socks are preferable. It's all about protection. Jeans or leather pants are necessary, and I wear a new pair of thick, strong jeans. My last pair eventually split at the knee after twenty years. I had them fixed and dyed them a darker blue, as they were looking extremely old and tatty, but alas, the dye shrank them. I am not crazy about these new pants as they have a different cut, but when I bought them, I figured they would be better than the previous pair as they had a bit more room so I could wear thermal underwear and a few tops tucked in if necessary. They billow a bit, and I feel more like a ranch cowboy on a horse than a sexy, hot woman on a Harley.

We have decided to do a coastal route this year and are headed for Agulhas, which is quite far, and we haven't ridden for a while. By normal biker standards, it's easy, but we are a little older now! One has to be 'riding fit', believe it or not, to do long distances. The wind and the elements play a role in testing muscles you never use, plus there is 350 kilos of machinery to lift off the stand to get the motorcycle upright.

We take the coastal road, which is longer, but it is one of the most beautiful roads to ride in the Western Cape and worth the extra time. The ocean, cliffs, and winding mountain pass are nothing short of magnificent. The turquoise blue sea is calm today, slowly rolling in and dancing alongside us. This particular road runs from Gordons Bay to Arabella Golf Estate and is 50% coastal and 50% fynbos and mountainside. It is a favourite route for bikers, because it has little traffic.

We decide to stop in Kleinmond, which has eateries along a harbour area. It is quaint and picturesque. I check my phone and see that there is a message from Dr Fix It, Andrew. I am not sure whether he is English or Afrikaans, so in my responses, I alternate between the two languages. During a previous brief communication, he shared with me that his wife had died of cancer the previous year, after a four-year-long battle. He is now elaborating, and I like it that he does so. It shows that this was a big, tough event. He exposes his vulnerability at the onset. This is unusual in my various experiences with men over the years.

We exchange a few more brief messages, and I leave a voice note, as it's quicker and easier. My experience has been that voice notes tell me a lot about that person. How they speak, the tone of their voice, the sound, use of vocabulary, and ease of conversation. This is important, as I can decide very quickly whether I wish to engage further or not, purely from talking or a voice note.

I decide to speak to Dr Fix It, and we chat easily and comfortably. He has three children, aged 26, 28, and 19. He lives in Somerset West and works in a large practice of orthopaedic surgeons. He was happily married and is new to online dating. I pat myself on the back for being so astute.

We talk a lot. We discover that we both went on the Rovos Rail for the same reasons. Me, with my terminally ill friend who died a month later, and he with his wife. We share pictures, stories, and more. We agree to meet when I am back at the weekend. I like him from the chats we have. He is open, honest, easy to talk to, and a good human being. He is family-orientated and speaks highly of his late wife. She flows easily into our conversations, and I learn a lot about him from her inclusion.

He has only ever had one girlfriend, and she became his wife. This makes him unique in my book, as I have never met a man who has never dated another woman. It's fascinating. He is interesting, and interested. I learn that being an orthopaedic surgeon is very rewarding, as you get to change the mobility of a person overnight! I love hearing about all the different procedures and stories of what happens, how people get to the emergency, and what kinds of operations are performed.

CHAPTER 24
THE DATE WITH DR FIX IT

We chat often during the course of my trip and we agree to meet in Franschhoek when I get back. He chooses the venue, and it's nothing short of spectacular. It's a private boutique estate that belongs to Richard Branson, and it's in a perfect position. Rows of vineyards hug the mountainside, and greenery unfolds as far as the eye can see. I am very excited and take time to get ready. I wear a long, flowing, feminine, blue, gold, and white dress that has a slightly sexy touch. My best feature, my turquoise eyes, are accentuated by these colours. I feel confident and at ease.

The ride is longer than I would have liked, so I arrive about ten minutes late. I walk into the foyer that leads me to the bar area that has open doors that bring the beautiful view inside. I see him immediately, and he stands up to greet me. I hug him hello, and he offers me a seat and a glass of champagne. He is better in real life than his pictures, but looks older. He is also thinner than I imagined but wears clever clothes that disguise this well. He is dressed smart casual. We chat for a while, and I warm to him immediately. I find him attractive, and warmth spreads through my body, which tells me my hormones are alive and well.

He has beautiful manners and is well-spoken. We chat easily and decide to take a short walk. He is tall and towers above me despite the high shoes I am wearing! We are comfortable, and I feel like we have known each other for a long time. We find another spot to sit, and I pull my chair closer to his and sit beside him. I want to be closer to him. I want to feel his energy and heat. I kick my shoes off, and I tuck my feet underneath me. I lean forward and touch his arm, gently and softly, and just keep my hand there. It feels normal and comfortable. He reaches for my arm and strokes it gently in return. I sense that this man is gentle, sensual, and vulnerable. I just know it instinctively, and this draws me closer in to his space and warmth.

We talk about many things, and, before I know it, I have to leave too soon, as I have a lunch commitment. Neither one of us wants this encounter to end, but it must, and he walks me to my car. He kisses me gently on the lips and hugs me for a long time. He pulls away, looks at me, and says, "Do you think we could get a room here?" I am flattered, but at the same time I know that he is astonished that he just said that. He apologises immediately, saying "Oh my word, that is so inappropriate!" And I fall for him right there and then. So vulnerable, so needy, and so desperate for touch and connection.

When I arrive at the lunch everyone says, "Oh Susan, you look incredible!" And I feel it too. I have taken an enormous amount of time over my appearance for my earlier meeting, and my blonde hair is full and curly. It frames my long face well and gives it width. I have very thin hair, so it takes a fair amount of work to make it look full and naturally curly. I float towards them, still wearing my blue long dress. The soft fabric moves in rhythm as I walk, and I feel like a princess. My Harley friend is already there, seated with a gay male couple we befriended on a previous Harley trip we did. It's a birthday celebration for John, and their two long-time friends have joined us as well.

The venue is picturesque, and we sit out in the open on a deck overlooking the valley and vines. Golden sun rays bounce off the leaves and trees. There is not a breath of wind. Our newly acquired friends are a good-looking, successful couple, and we bonded with them both over a dinner in Swellendam when we asked them to join us as we ate dinner.

I love spending time with gay men, as they are always so real and so open. What you see is what you get. They are a little younger than us, mid-50s, and have been in their partnership for over 20 years. This intrigues me, and I am quick to ask for their recipe for success.

This answer is often the same, whether it's same-sex or heterosexual marriages. In essence, it's taking the view that they are in it for the long haul. They are committed and realistic. They know that temptation is always out there and that it's a choice to be committed and true. They are aware that things change over time and that a relationship requires work.

They are funny and entertaining. Schalk is dark-haired, shorter than his blonde partner, and more fashionably dressed. A strong character, he speaks freely, openly, and is engaging. Kobus is blonde, much quieter, and seems to be the more feminine of the two. I say 'seems' because, over the years, I have learnt through various friendships with gay people that what you perceive is not always correct. I notice that they respect each other and are mindful of who speaks, giving each other time to finish sentences, which makes for great conversation. Their friends are engaging and easy to be with, making this an extremely interesting and fun afternoon with much laughter.

It is Kobus's birthday, and we are the honoured guests, as this is a friendship that has spanned many years, and we are part of their inner circle, and it is very special. The food is superb and delicious. Fine dining at its best. Champagne is the order of the day, and it flows generously and often. I am dying to share my online encounter with them, but hold back. There are many reasons, and the main one is that my friend, whom I travelled with, and share all my innermost secrets with, is not party to this "new encounter."

She disapproves of the dating site and cannot understand why I bother. To her, life is over in the love department to a large degree, and it's completely silly to waste time 'shopping' or looking. It is not her bag, and she cannot understand why a successful independent woman still seeks a partner in her life. She is happy living alone in her home, with her cat, her Harley, and her friends. She likes her own company and finds huge joy in being at home. In her book, I am too old, and because I have been on a few dates recently, she is disinclined to listen to another "met a fabulous guy" story.

I will admit that I have spent more time online than ever before and have gone on more dates in the last three months than in the last four years.

I have my reasons for seeking a partner, and the main reason is that I was heartbroken when my boyfriend and I split up after two years of living together in lockdown. I was head over heels in love with my Latin lover, and he was everything I ever wanted and dreamed of. He was my knight in shining armour, and he took my breath away. I had loved like that only once before in my life. I was devastated when this last love told me, in no uncertain terms, that he no longer wanted to be in a relationship with me, that he pitied me, and that there was no ounce of love left for me.

Pretty harsh considering we had never had a huge row or argument of any kind. It hurt deeply, and I cried for five solid weeks. I could not stop. The mornings were the worst, and I would wake up bereft and broken. Not even my beautiful Molly, my beloved Schnauzer, could lift me from my pain and deep sense of loss. I eventually went to see my doctor to ask her for help to take the edge off. In addition to this loss of my "great love," my best friend was dying of cancer, and we had just found that she had, at best, six months to live. My brave lady warrior, who gave so generously of her love, her deep gratitude, and her time. She was a great teacher, and at this time, our friendship took on a deeper and more meaningful journey, but it was also a deeply sad time. This was effectively a double loss that not even the bravest part of me was able to bear.

The medication helped keep me on an even keel. I made a conscious effort late in January to put myself out there in an attempt to move on and find a distraction. I was not looking for a replacement, as that was highly unlikely and, in my book, near impossible. Despite my wisdom, I was using the age-old method of dulling pain with distraction.

The people who judged me had no firsthand experience with dating sites, so they had a jaundiced view from the start with no understanding of what happens. I have always found this judgement a little harsh and unfair, as it's not based on firsthand information or experience.

I have met and made some good friends when being part of online dating over the years, and I will always value these experiences that have made my life interesting, made me laugh, entertained me, taught me, and allowed me sexual freedom when I chose. Essentially, my online dating remained private for several reasons. I date because, despite loving time with my girlfriends, I enjoy male company, and no one man is anything like another. Each is unique. The concept of "looking for love" is overused. It is my firm belief that while most of us still want the fairytale instilled in us at a young age, we are way more advanced. It is a curiosity of men that drives me more than anything else, and a need to find a comfortable, vulnerable place with sexual engagement that has eluded me most of my life.

I am looking for an opportunity to unlock a closed door, and so far, I have had little success. Nobody would believe me if they knew the latter, as I am attractive, successful, outgoing, confident, and considered very sexy. Little do they know how flawed I am, but we can hide a lot with control and dominance in the bedroom, where the focus is not on self but pleasure for another!

Soon the day ends, and I am homeward bound. As soon as I am in my car, I check my phone, and there is a message from Dr Fix It. He apologises again for what he said, and I blush, feeling flattered that he was so attracted to me and could not contain his desire. I am a very physical person, so I am never insulted when a man shows a strong sexual attraction. He says he loved meeting me and would love to see me again soon! We make a date to meet on the Tuesday evening, and he will come through to Marina da Gama, where I live. He asks me where I would like to go, and I tell him that I will give it some thought.

I eventually decide on a popular, quirky little restaurant that has six tables and serves Mozambican prawns or chicken. It's a very casual place with plastic tablecloths. The owner is a waif-like Portuguese woman who has only one other person helping her. As it's so popular, one must book. We sit at a small table close to each other. I like feeling his body heat in my space and seeing the small furrow lines in his face when he smiles or laughs. He is gentle when he touches me, and I melt. I have longed for a gentle touch since my boyfriend and I broke up. He was an extremely gentle man physically, and his touch was like fire to me. I find this same energy with this wonderful human being with each encounter, and my broken heart begins to slowly heal on its own.

We head home and sit on the couch, and I light a fire. It's a perfect excuse to huddle close together. When he kisses me properly for the first time in the privacy of my home, my senses are on high alert and ignite explosively with the delicate kisses he places all over my face, my lips, my eyes, my hair, and my neck. He takes his time, and a warmth spreads throughout my body, exquisitely and beautifully. I am so comfortable with this man, and I kiss him back. He is hugely responsive and moans softly and deeply. This man is hungry and needy. I sense it in the gentleness, despite the fireball ignited underneath. He is tremendously controlled, and this turns me on a lot.

I had told him that I am in a sensitive place and will not be getting into any physical relationship too soon, as I had done this with my previous boyfriend, and I was not going to make the same mistake again. I needed time to get to know him and find out more about him before we embarked on a sexual relationship. He now says he will wait and that there is no pressure, and I know he means it. I adore and love him instantly for that!

CHAPTER 25
DR FIX IT
– WEEKEND MAGIC

Two weeks later, we are heading off on a weekend away to a cottage at Belvedere Estate, in Knysna. It is cold, as we are in the middle of winter. The house is adorable and nestles at the foot of the lagoon. It is private and secure. It has three bedrooms and bathrooms, and the lounge, dining room, and kitchen are all open-plan. The rooms are double-volume, with high ceilings and beautiful rafters running across the roof. Tastefully furnished, it is welcoming and homely.

I have a nagging thought, however, that I find hard to ignore, *This home has been frequented and used by his family for many years and must hold some special memories.* I feel like I am invading someone else's space and story, which makes me feel a little uncomfortable as his wife has only been gone for about ten months. I tell myself to stop overthinking and to let it go as it is, after all, new for me!

My Dr Fix It makes a roaring fire, and soon the place is warm and comfortable. He has brought music along with a boom box, so we have the rhythm and flow of a host of various songs, all of which I resonate with and like. It certainly makes a difference when one is of the same era! He has brought snacks and opens a bottle of champagne. It is our first two-day sleepover together, so it's a telling time. Night comes soon, and we have a wonderful evening of discovery as we openly communicate our likes and dislikes in the bedroom. He is a polite and gentle lover, and I am relaxed. We are perfectly in sync.

I am aware that he has only ever had one other sexual encounter: that of his wife. This is a first for me. He was open and honest about this from the onset, and I found it endearing and special. I had asked him whether he ever wondered what it would be like to make love to someone else, and he said that he certainly had. He was keen to experience variety, now that he has the opportunity to do so.

I store this in my memory bank and find myself wondering whether he is thinking about another encounter while with me. *This is, after all, something new for him, and he is unlikely to stick with only one more experience!* This thought unsettles me, as despite my real and deep connection with this man, I cannot consider us being "everlasting".

The next morning, we head out to ride bicycles together. He is a keen cyclist, accustomed to early morning rides that are about two hours long. I have informed him that my attempt at biking will be of the motorized kind and that my fitness on a bicycle is non-existent. He kindly tells me we are going on a gentle ride to a little spot up the road. It goes well as we cycle along the little straight path, but then we turn a corner and a hill looms. At this moment, panic sets in, and I stand, making my best attempt to master the smallest of climbs. Once at the top, I am huffing and puffing, and the sweat is pouring down my back and breasts. Unfit would be an understatement.

The road is flat now, thank goodness, and we arrive at the most adorable little place nestled among the trees. Lunch is fabulous, and we laugh a lot at my attempts to cycle. He says that the good news is that it is all downhill from here to the house. But I'm thinking "downhill" in other aspects too, *He needs a cycling-fit partner, and that is never going to be me!*

The weekend passes in a flash, and soon we are headed home. We have watched movies, read books, and relaxed. It has been fun and enjoyable. I am grateful to have met this untouched, unique, individual. I know that soon he will need to be set free to encounter others. I have convinced myself of this, and my brain will not allow me to think otherwise. I want this freedom for him more than anything.

Once home, I know that before long, he will be free, and I must be set to move on. Realistically, suburbia and normality don't fit well into my box. But I allow myself to put that to the back of my mind for a bit longer as I want to enjoy more time with this lovely human being.

CHAPTER 26
DR FIX IT – THE END

I have driven to Franschhoek to meet Dr Fix It who arrived there on the Friday evening. It is an annual event he attends with long time friends and this is the first time he will be going without his wife and will be alone. He mentioned this weekend shortly after we met and explained it would be difficult if I were to come along as they had already planned the trip as a group and were going to some of the same events. However, he decided that it would be acceptable to have me join him for the Saturday afternoon and we agree that we will attend the events that resonate with us and I am thrilled, for I have wanted to write a book since I completed my two writing courses in lockdown. I am excited to see authors, meet authors and hear about their books. It seems divinely ordained.

The festival is packed with a variety of events and authors and they vary hugely and are not all story line based. There are also self-publishing master classes, ways of adapting a novel for film or sound, some podcasts, documentaries, a course of what publishers really want, song writing and poetry.

I meet him in the morning and we have coffee and he heads off to the lecture he wants to attend and I head off to the two I wanted to attend. There is one event we both want to attend later in the morning so we meet again at noon. It's a new author who has written an autobiography about her experience when her husband is diagnosed with cancer in his early forties and his fight to survive at all costs and his alternative journey that sees him become a Shaman as he nears his death. It's a heart wrenching story that is candid, honest and real. There is no sugar coating. She juggles her own busy life during this time looking after their children, while he battles to live. Her story touches me and inspires me. I meet her after the talk and thank her. I tell her that she has inspired me to write my book. I tell Andrew that I am going to write my book and tell everyone so that I have to! I am so happy and I feel deeply fulfilled with this new project ahead.

We meet friends of his for a quick cup of coffee and for some reason I am completely intimated, feel extremely on edge and uncomfortable. They are good friends of Andrew and his wife who passed away. I feel like I am under a microscope and being judged. This is all in my head but it backfires and I feel tongue tied. It does not help that she looks 55, because she is and I am older! They have just come from a lecture on politics and they are well versed on the topic and about politics in general. I make the fatal mistake of saying that the problem with democracy is that the masses get to vote. The husband replies and says that one has to understand the history of politics and government in order to solve issues we have in South Africa. I reply by a saying I have no interest in politics. There is a long silence at this point and I blurt out a statement saying that I prefer to make a difference to humanity than try and understand world politics. The men start to engage and I tell her about the event I had just attended and that I am going to write my book soon. She says that she has written two books and both have been published. I ask her what the titles of her books are. She tells me that they are educational and to do with her role as a professor of politics at university. I don't talk anymore and instead let them chat and share as long-time friends do. I am very relieved when Andrew says we have to leave. I follow him to our spot for the night as we need to check in.

We stop at a beautiful cottage that is part of a small boutique hotel. This man knows how to impress and I am delighted. He has bought me roses and champagne is on ice. We step out onto the patio and drink champagne and look out over the vineyards. We kiss and soon we are making love on the bed and I feel deeply connected to this man's heart and soul. For a short while we rest and then I tell him that I am going home. We were scheduled to meet up with the friends of earlier and another couple, for dinner. I tell him that much as we are connected and have deep feelings, he needs freedom to date others and experience different sexual partners as I know that when we are making love his mind wonders what it must be like to be with someone else. He says I have got it all wrong but I insist. My real reasons have aspects of this truth in them but its way more. I am not comfortable with being so much older than his group of close friends. I don't see myself having a lot in common with any of them, and I could not and would not feel comfortable in visiting and sleeping over at his home where all his wife's things still were and where nothing had changed since her death. I also felt that he needed more time to get over her before he would be fully ready for another long-term relationship. I am not interested in cycling!

He does not try and convince me to stay and this tells me that despite how we feel about one another, I am right and he does not want to lead me on. We both cry and he tells me how much our time together has meant to him and how grateful he is we met. That I taught him so much and it will make our encounter one he will remember always. I drive home and cry all the way. He sends me a long emotional voice note. I only listen to it when I get home. It makes me sad but also helps me feel better. This was no ordinary encounter. Two people experienced genuine feeling and emotion but in the end logic and sense needed to prevail. I wish there was some way sense and logic could overrule emotion at the onset, but for me it has never done so.

CHAPTER 27
DR FIX IT – REAL SOON

Molly, my miniature Schnauzer, and I are sitting on the couch with the sun streaming into the patio, warming up the space from the cold winter chill outside. The recently installed glass panelling has made such a difference, and it captures the sun's rays and heat. Her little back legs are firmly tucked up next to my left thigh, and she snorts now and again as she falls asleep with her head slightly off the couch, making her ears, which are usually floppy, hang straight above her head. It's a funny sight that always makes me smile. She loves to lie in this awkward position, and I can never, for the life of me, imagine how this could possibly be comfortable, but she chooses it often.

My phone is on the coffee table in front of me, and I have my laptop on my knees, intending to do some writing. But then, my curiosity gets the better of me, and I look to see who is online on the dating app. I scroll down, nothing, then look a little further, and, yes, there he is! Online already! Exactly four days later. My whole mindset changes from being filled with gratitude and sunshine to a truly black one. My happy demeanour of earlier changes in an instant. Suddenly I am depressed and sad. Instead of writing, I find myself typing about Dr Fix It—my pseudonym for my last lover, the orthopaedic surgeon. The one that held promise when it came to feelings, connection, ease of conversation, and physical compatibility. He became, in a very short space of time, my best friend. He was so easy to be with and so untouched. We spoke endlessly, easily, and often, but it had ended.

I knew he would be shopping online soon. An opportunity he never had in his youth. I thought I was ready for it, but the reality is an entirely different ball game for me. It hits hard and deep. I sit staring at his profile, willing it to disappear from the page on my phone, but it holds fast.

My thoughts are racing: *Who was he connecting with? Is she more attractive, younger, more interesting, smarter, wittier, cuter, taller, thinner, sexier, or cleverer than me? What colour is her hair? Is it long or short? Blonde, or brunette? What might her interests be? Did they have more in common than we do? Does she have children? Is she sporty? Does she like cycling, as this would be a big plus.*

Eventually, after what feels like ages, I manage to scroll away and close the app. I berate myself for checking and opening up my "hurt door," as I call it. Why was I doing this to myself? What could I possibly gain from it? In the end, I settle on the word "closure." The word has a nice ring to it and helps me to feel better. Knowing that he moved so quickly also helps. It tells me that I was not that special, and that this man was so intent on getting his variety of encounters that he was going full tilt. In the end, I failed to tick all his boxes. It's really as simple as that!

I ask myself, *What boxes could they possibly have been?* I know from years of experience that this is not about what is wrong with me, but what does not work for him. I am in my critical head right now and clearly intent on staying there.

Was I too available? At my age, does that really matter? Surely not? I am convinced that when we are older, we know that time is valuable! Now I begin to wonder about that too.

Was I too complimentary and too giving? I say what I think and feel these days, particularly if it is positive or if it will make someone feel good! I can't see the point in holding back. People drop dead at my age, and, more recently, two people died. Life is just too short not to share positive thoughts and messages. Perhaps, when it comes to a matter of courting, I am still a novice?

Was my skin too flabby in some parts? Not that many I might add! I have a good body, thanks to my mother!

Were my voluptuous breasts too attracted to gravity? Were my sun-worship spots too obvious? My frown lines too furrowed; my energy levels too low?

What I do know is that my cooking skills fail all tests, but then I am upfront about this in my profile! I always say, "If you cook, I am interested! Very!"

Perhaps they think I am joking? Choking on my supper dish tells it like it is! There are many things that I am, but being a chef is not one of them!

Am I too independent? Too busy and all over the place? Is my dog obsession too much? My riding a Harley too alternative, perhaps, or embarrassing?

These endless questions permeate and run havoc in my head, until finally I say to myself, "For God's sake, Susan, it's enough! You have had countless successful relationships, so don't let this make you feel insecure." I have a moment of clarity and remind myself why it was never going to work and that I called it. I start to feel a whole lot better! I also realise that all the insecurities and thoughts in my head are not relevant and that none of those things were real. Just my insecure self who was not real nor did she have any ground to really stand on!

Let's face it, he's not exactly gorgeous. My last boyfriend was gorgeous, so I have a clear idea of what is perfect and what is not so perfect! Nice eyes and hair, and he still had it all! Plus, there is no grey it, and he's 59! His physique is thin— very thin. The only man I have ever dated who was thinner than him was actually very ill. He is also tall at 1,87 metres. Actually, a bit too tall for my liking, as I am only 1,67 metres tall. He is a professional who works fairly standard hours. He is a specialist, so he is clever and smart. He is certainly not Mr Adventurous by a long shot. My usual choice in men is the exact opposite. High energy, alternative, quirky, wacky, decidedly different, and not your average run-of-the-mill.

He rode bicycles! I rode a Harley, as in a proper, deep-throbbing, powerful beast, between my legs that made my pulse race and explode as I hit the highways and byways, leaving most of the road vehicles in the dust as I roared my way into the sunset! I am your alternative, whacky, successful female who has her own money and a full life. I am complete.

Logging onto the website app, however, changes this all. I know it is momentary, but right now, it feels like forever. It proceeds to dig up very old, buried insecurities in my life and is now waving them triumphantly in front of my face. Only for a while, however, before I feel the mature, self-assured me find her way back. I am okay, and I can deal with it.

I find gratitude as the day progresses, as the breakup opens up other things. I realise how much time, effort, and energy I spent on this six-week encounter, and it is a lot. We talked and messaged often, up to four times a day. A lot was just general chat about what we were up to and what each day held. Do I wish we had not met? No, for when we can assist a man to regain his power and make him comfortable, boost his ego, and convince him he is a perfect lover, then we do something worthwhile, and he was a worthy recipient. He is a very special human being.

CHAPTER 28
BAD BOY ROY

It has been two awful weeks for writing. I haven't written much—only a very rough guide, about a third of my book has been written. My enthusiasm remains. I sat browsing the date site, still licking my wounds from my "Dr Fix It," who only ever dated one woman whom he married, and in my book, one must have more encounters in order to lay to rest thoughts of, "I wonder what an encounter with someone else may be like?" This was based on my gut, which understands the gregarious male. At the onset of our first encounter, we chatted in depth about this. I had not met anyone before who had only ever had sex with one person. He admitted that he was very curious and keen to explore. I certainly would after being with only one person for 38 years!

He catches my eye, but it is not his look that attracts me, for he is very thin, plus he lives in another province. It's the colourful headband across his forehead, with longish wisps of red-brown hair escaping from the sides. He looks like Mick Jagger. I look at the worn features; he has clearly partied hard, and the furrows that crinkle across his face are telling their own story. He is wearing sunglasses in the photo and has a rather long nose that extends down to his lips. What catches my eye most is a big, broad, full, sexy mouth. Right there, I decide he is worth talking to! Nothing to lose, and he will be interesting if nothing else. Auburn hair and freckles are very sexy!

I know without seeing any other pictures that this man was a surfer in his youth. Probably a dope smoker and a wild party animal. Images of long hair, half-dressed in board shorts and bare feet with a tanned body, come to mind, and I ask myself, "Susan, what on earth are you doing considering this man?" I have a private conversation with myself and decide that if ever there is a time to get bad and naughty, it is now!

I have also always liked alternative men. The standard run-of-the-mill man and suburbia is seldom on my radar. Eight-to-five, movies, theatre, and dinner do fit, but I also like the "Biker in his leathers," the boy who likes to party and enjoy himself, the boy who is nuts about cars, likes to drive fast, who still challenges himself, who hangs with his kids and goes to Afrika Burn. The boy who is still a child in his outlook on life. Ideally, he has also managed to be successful and had a serious spell, and now he is back in "bad boy mode." Ready to live! It occurs to me that I am pretty much "that girl," and this awakening lights my fire, and I am excited!

I "like" his profile and send him a message, "This particular site is the third site I have subscribed to over the years. A relationship is not a must-have for me but would be nice to have! Independent, semi-retired, fun, easy-going, and youthful. My motto: "Live with gratitude." My purpose is "to make a difference to humanity!" Short and sweet, and I send a smile.

He sends a reply soon afterwards. "You're looking good, Susan! How's your sense of humour and your ability to see through the bullshit handed out on dating sites? I am not good at relationships but would like to chat to you, and maybe you can change my mind."

Somewhere during our communication, I tell him that I have started writing a book, and he replies, "You can practice your journalistic prowess on me, so living apart would not matter. You should consider writing the book overlooking a beautiful ocean here, as it is only two hours away by aeroplane!"

I reply, "I love the area you live in and know it well, but I have an equally gorgeous view here, and Molly, my miniature Schnauzer, would need to come with me. House or apartment?" I ask.

He replies, "Couple of businesses keep the wolves at bay. What is your career or profession?"

I reply, "Retired 10 years ago, small rental portfolio, and the odd bit of Airbnb. Varied careers before, very interesting life, and grateful for the many opportunities, relationships, trips, homes, holidays, business ventures, my Harley, and a life well lived. As always, I am three times my age! I pack a lot in! I am kind and caring, especially to those who deserve it. My greatest joy in life has been to give, but it has also taught me some tough lessons. If we can change one person's path in life, we have made a difference to humanity! No matter how big or small! Chat later."

He suggests we rather WhatsApp going forward, and I send my cell number and tell him that we can chat on WhatsApp, as I like what I see.

He replies later on WhatsApp, and a much bigger man on a silver two-wheel machine comes up on his profile picture. The only other acceptable alternative to a Harley in my book is a BMW RT1250, and I breathe a sigh of relief. Firstly, because he rides an acceptable bike, and secondly, because he still rides! We exchange loads of pictures, and I ask him for more recent pictures.

I learn that he has been very ill and lost a lot of weight—almost 45 kilos, or one-third of his total body weight, before he got sick. I ask for a more recent picture, as he says that in the dating site photos, he was still very ill.

A face full of freckles pops up on my screen with the most gorgeous dimple, with a hint of a crooked smile and almost closed eyes, as he squints in the sunlight while taking his selfie. His face looks less weathered and more youthful. This is getting better and better, as he also tells me he loves dogs and sends me huge smiley faces when he sees pictures of

Molly, my beautiful grey and white miniature schnauzer so full of character, and I would like to say "life," but she is the most docile creature you will ever meet, super chilled and laid back.

At times, Molly and I are both completely lazy together, seldom moving other than to eat, snuggle, and lie about when it's cold and raining outside. She is my perfect dog. She can be animated on the rare occasion, and this is a sight to behold as she charges up and down. It mostly happens at the sight of her boyfriend, Benji, who lives down the road from our home and joins us for a walk. When they are together, they are inseparable, and it's a love match made in heaven. They didn't need a dating site, just two older parents who met on the road four years ago when walking their respective four-legged children.

He sends me pictures of four cats snuggled together, and one is minus her ears. They are all feral rescues, and I thank the universe he lives in Durban, as Molly would have a field day with those four! She will for sure come off worse for wear, as they will win the contest of wills hands down. I decide that I am all for animals sorting out their own territory and rights, should it ever come to that! "You are drop dead gorgeous, and I love the picture of you with your uncle, Susan."

Eighty-seven years old with dementia, I had posted a profile picture of my uncle and me. It was taken at my last birthday, and it's a prized picture as he is still able to remember things and reminisce, but he is a shadow of the former man who was all-powerful, in every sense. It is a picture that touches me very deeply, for it will probably be the last picture of his "old self" still holding it together, only just. Tears well up in my eyes, and I am deeply sad, for he is no longer the powerful and wealthy good-looking man, full of life. I console myself with the comfort of knowing he can't see himself.

We talk easily—about pictures, pets, views, home, and adventures—and with each exchange, I like him more. We have not yet spoken on the phone, and this is unusual, as I always like to talk first. Voices tell us a lot about a person. I send pictures of my recent annual Harley trip with my girlfriend, and he does a double take! He asks, "You ride a Harley?"

"Yes, I learnt to ride at forty and to play the piano. But I liked the Harley more and have never looked back."

He says, "That's It! I am coming over. Where do you live?" I love the decisiveness of this reply, the cheeky aspect of it, and the sense of purpose. All this communication takes place in the space of a day. I let him know that I must sadly go as I have lots to do. We agree to chat again soon.

I am usually rather strict about lengthy WhatsApp messages, especially when I have not met someone or spoken to them yet, but he is fun, engaging and interesting.

I have my 15-year-old mentee Shakira with me, and we are spending quality time together here at home, and Martha is here too. She has come to spend the night, and we are "sisters" from another mother, as she is Xhosa, and I am a fair-skinned South African. We met by chance when I took two young children off the street one winter, and she became their foster mother. Our friendship spans 25 years, and she worked for me in my home for the last part of her life prior to retirement at 70. She has come from the Eastern Cape, and we are having some quality time together.

Martha is an incredible woman who fostered two children while she looked after another three of her own as a single mother. She is a legend, in my book. We watch a bit of television together, and Shakira joins us. We put the gas fireplace on, snuggle together, and have hot chocolate. It's the first of the cold nights to come as Cape Town settles into the onset of winter. I feel clothed in love and warmth. I feel incredibly blessed to have two amazing women in my life. One so young with the world at her feet, and the other, a wise mama who teaches me always, and I am grateful to the universe for these women who cross my path and who add enormous value and love to my life.

Much later, I head off to bed. Martha is snug in Shakira's room, and "Miss Muffet," as I call her, is sleeping with me. We read excerpts from the book I bought her, The Diary of a Teenager by Rachel Renee Russell from her series *Dork Diaries*. Shakira reads aloud to her "Umakhulu," which is the Xhosa word for "grandmother." I opt for this word in her mother tongue to honour her heritage. It's a well-written book, and we laugh at the antics that she reads with expression and feeling. I feel like I am in an audience and that I am watching a young, budding actress at play. She gets the French accent down to a T. "Bonjour, Madam, Welkom to ze beauty Pahlour of your aspiring "hairdrezzeer and chic make-up arhteest, Francoize".

What transpires is a disastrous haircut on the older sister; one half of her head is shorter than the other, and we laugh, rolling about as the story unfolds. "Zer is nothing wrong with ze new cut. Madahame, you are Booty-Ful; you zest have to close ze one eye!"

Both of us settle into quiet reading of our own after half an hour, and Shakira falls asleep around ten. Her elbows are sprawled on either side of her head, and her hands are under her skull at the back. This means I am a little squashed on my side, as she is off centre, so I am now on the edge of the bed. Molly is snuggled between us on the bed, and she is a dead weight too, as she is fast asleep and snoring lightly. I struggle for a few minutes, and eventually I get up to sort out the bed situation; otherwise, I am not going to sleep. I put Molly in her bed, and she simply lolls onto the edge of her basket, her head hanging off the small arm of the entrance and carries on snoring. This is an all-time favourite position of hers, and she reminds me of someone else I know who also has weird sleeping positions! Yep, our Shakira. Next is to move "Miss Muffet." My back is not going to be happy if I bend and pull, so I lean across the bed from my side and push as hard as I can. Nothing moves. I tickle her ear, and she stirs, so I push again. She rolls on to her side, and I push at the same time. I gain about 40 cm and quickly jump into bed, claiming my lost territory.

My phone pings, and it's a message from "Bad Boy." I feel all excited and then discover that I now need to get rid of the wine I drank earlier and go to the bathroom! This has me momentarily panicked, but I quickly put the fattest pillow behind Shakira's back and another two more, with a small empty spot on my side next to the edge of the bed. For now, my space is reserved!

Back in bed, I have put my hot blanket on for a while; it's cold out there, and snug and warm is not where I find myself. My feet are frozen now from my trip to the bathroom, my arms are cold, and my nose is like a block of ice. This bed business of sharing and getting up and down is not for the fainthearted, I decide. Keen to read my message I lean over to find my glasses, and they are not next to my bed. All good, my spare is in the drawer. Firmly placed on my nose, the letters swim around, and I grumpily remove them to clean the lenses, only to find one lens missing. It fell out the other day, and I completely forgot to find another pair to put in the drawer amongst the constant supply I always have on tap as they find homes elsewhere often, and it is never in my house. Sigh! For a couple of minutes, I just lie in bed, covered up to my nose, to warm up. But soon enough I am perspiring as menopause, despite the help of oestrogen, takes over, and for the moment I fear I will sweat and fog up my one-eyed glasses!

Roy tells me that he thinks we have a few things in common. I know that we do, instinctively, even though we have only been chatting for a day at this stage. I mention that I am impatient and that I am very much a spur of the moment girl, that I have done some crazy and outrageous stuff in my time, and that I am always up for a challenge and to try something new. We share likes and dislikes, amongst which are long text messages vs. actual chatting. I am averse to this at the onset of any new encounter.

I tell him my deal breakers; anger, or loud arguments. I am also unimpressed by anyone who does not tip a car guard properly or who is stingy. If you split the bill down to the last cent, if you're a hoarder, don't wash regularly, and are totally sloppy, these things put you on my "this boy has to go fast list!" He laughs and says he can happily report that he is none of the things on my list; in fact, he errs on being too generous and is super clean. He is a social animal, gregarious, outgoing, and adventurous, and he needs a speed bump between his mouth and his brain.

During the evening, we converse a lot, and I learn that he lost a son 8 years ago and became very ill as a result. His son was 21 at the time, and it affected him terribly. He lost his mojo and has only just found himself again. His story endears me to him in a big way, as I lost my older sister when I was ten, and she was 18 at the time, and then my father when I was 17 years of age.

Neither one of us had great parents, and I am further connected to him because — as mentioned earlier — of losing my best friend to cancer.

Both of us are self-made. We both have enough to live on and are adventure seekers, with still a whole lot of living to do.

At some late hour we stop talking, neither one of us wanting to, but sleep eventually forces the conversation to rest! We talk in the morning, and this time it is a voice call. We talk for ages, and he is even better on a voice call, as the strength of his character comes through vibrantly, so much so that it's almost as if the phone vibrates when he speaks.

He is animated and has a good command of the English language, despite his heavy Durban accent that throws me a little to start with, but I warm to it soon. It's not Colonial by a long shot! He is every bit the surfer type on the accent front. I can see him rolling a joint in the days when it was completely illegal and doing all sorts of other illegal things too! In fact, it crosses my mind that he probably has stretched the limits on all accounts when it comes to living on the edge.

He is forthright and honest, a quality I always admire, and he tells me he is still married but that she lives in another province and that they are no longer together. That his daughters would find it hard to accept him dating anyone. I am not too fazed by this as he lives far away; I potentially never have to meet his daughters and certainly don't intend ever getting married again, and it doesn't take a rocket scientist to work out why he is not divorced.

He was put on the dating site by a friend, who is in fact a

tenant; he rents out rooms on his property, so we are on the same page when it comes to "an empty room is rent!" I run a small rental portfolio of my own, and he does something to do with cars and decals of all sorts and shapes and supplies tape. By the end of day two, he tells me after endless messages to one another that I have captured his full attention and that he intends coming to meet me. We quickly decide on a tentative date in two weeks' time.

It sounds crazy, but at this point we are both pretty smitten, and I am constantly chatting to myself and saying, "This is crazy; you don't even know this man; he could be the exact opposite of what he says he is." But I instinctively know he is not. We exchange countless songs, and both like the same music. He adds me to his WhatsApp music group, and I feel honoured. This is inner circle stuff. It's big. I let him know I am off to France for a month at the end of July, as I detest Cape Town in August when it rains nonstop and storms and gusts relentlessly. He cheekily says his part of the world in Kwa Zulu Natal, in August, is fabulous weather, but I already know this. I lived there once; plus, I was on holiday there three years ago to escape a Cape Town winter at the tail end of the first lockdown!

It occurred to me in the early stages of our communication that much as long distance has its challenges, I would be more than happy spending three months a year in that neck of the woods vs. cold, wet Cape Town. He tells me that, in this case, he will get here sooner rather than later. He is scheduled to spend a week in Knysna with his girls and will come to me beforehand and drive down. He says he will do some low flying, and I know this means a sportscar of some sort, but I don't ask any questions as I am always more interested in the driver than I am in the car. But it confirms that he is a "boy" who likes fast cars and fast things and who likes to be challenged. We talk about the Tour de France, which I will just have missed when I get there, and I learn it is a lifelong dream of his to see this race, so I suggest we do so sometime on a motorbike. We tell one another how much we like each other.

By the 21st of the month, my Bad Boy tells me he is overwhelmed by me and dazzled to have made my acquaintance. During the course of our messaging, a deep, poetic man emerges who shares poems, quotes, and excerpts that are truly inspiring, beautiful, romantic, and sweet. Every day that goes by endears me more to him, and I am falling fast.

I continue to have these chats with "self," and I am mindful. I berate myself and say, "This is not possible. You are connecting with make-believe. With what you want to see and not with what is!" But instinctively, in this short time, based on deeper stories we have shared about ourselves, I know this is no frivolous encounter, and it feels deeply ordained, like it was meant to be, as if our two souls are somehow connected despite having not yet met. We have chatted at length about this and agreed that in the event of no chemistry, we would be lifelong close friends, always connected. We agree that it would be wonderful to meet the next weekend.

He books a truly special boutique guest house not far from where I live. He tells me that he had done this because he wants to remember our meeting for the rest of his life, and I totally get what he is saying. It will be exactly two weeks since we first started chatting on the dating site. It feels like I have known him my whole life. There is nothing we do not talk about, and there is nothing he does not tell me. He shares everything, and I love it that he does.

He has made me laugh more in two weeks than I have laughed in the entire year. He is so expressive and excitable. He talks fast, he thinks even faster, and he is "on fire" always. He tells me this is a far cry from the man he became once his son died and that after being so ill himself and nearly dying, he never thought he would find himself so energized. Like me, he expresses gratitude often, and this is what binds us like glue, never to be apart again. We both are deeply grateful daily for small things. For the things that money cannot buy and for all positive experiences that come our way.

There is a great saying: "If you seek happiness, find gratitude," and I live by this mantra, for it is so true! I am acutely aware of how behind I am in my writing, which was started a month earlier with a vengeance, and this constantly bothers me. However, I am writing a different kind of story here, so allow myself the distraction, as in the end, this too could form part of the book I am writing and may well be the last chapter. I like this idea a lot and relax. I listen to romantic music all day.

Bad Boy and I continue to swop endless songs, and I dance at the gym in between my training sessions. I go into the studio and dance around solo, happy and elated. Who would not be in my shoes?

Last year in July, my world crashed when the second great love of my life demanded I change, or else the relationship was at risk. Needless to say, the relationship went south, as at my age, or any age for that matter, we can't change who we inherently are, but we can change how we deal with a specific problem in a mature way. This, however, was not a solution in his book. I was devastated, broken, and cried for six weeks, inconsolable and heartsore. It took a long time for me to move on, and even now, I struggle a little, but it's a different kind of struggle now. I am sad that I did not see the wood for the trees and that I did not see the warning signs fully. I was aware of them, but too blinded by love.

In retrospect, he and I were not a good match, completely unsuited; he was too much of an introvert for me. As a musician, he lived a lot of his life in his head, and conversation was virtually non-existent. His quiet presence did, however, calm my very busy and unpredictable life that ever changed and grew in different ways. A man who liked routine, who seldom wanted to go out, and who surfed and cycled occasionally, which are not my pastimes of choice! I do not surf!

CHAPTER 29
BAD BOY ROY – WE MEET

It has to be French; I decide. A bottle of champagne to share for our first night together. I have not been this extravagant in a long time. I am relieved that Moët & Chandon is only R600 a bottle, as I had visions of it being R1000 plus! I am lucky enough to find it at a local bottle store and have left it very last minute, as we are meeting later that evening.

I do all the necessary usual prepping: nails, pedicure, and self-tan all over, which leaves my hand a bright deep orange, but a good scrub relieves me of this momentary crisis! I use an eyebrow shaver to remove a handful of grey hairs from under my arms, which the laser did not manage to remove all those years ago. Thank goodness I do not need to shave my leg hairs or a full underarm, which the laser did sort out. This is one of the best investments I ever made in myself! I even have the landing strip, but decide it needs to be a little shorter than usual and find some male shaving foam left by a previous guest and silently thank him!

We agreed before my arrival that we did not want to go out. We would spend time in the suite he had booked and chat. It has the perfect lounge corner with two big comfy chairs and a round table. A small bar fridge and coffee area as well, so this presents a cosy, snug environment. The room temperature is warm. The lighting is subdued and soft. I am grateful for the latter, as the wrinkles will be less visible! We were both in agreement that the comfy large chairs be placed tightly together. Kicking off my shoes, I cross my legs and tuck my feet snuggly next to my body. Those daily stretches help, and I congratulate myself quietly for being consistent and dedicated. The glasses that I brought from home make a lovely, gentle sound as they touch. Nothing beats crystal filled with only the best bubbly.

We cannot stop touching each other, and we talk animatedly. Roy is strongly expressive and openly complimentary. I hold back a little, but my puppy dog look tells its own story, and I am completely smitten. I study each feature of his well-worn face. He looks a lot younger than he did in some of the pictures he sent me, and he makes me laugh as he recounts his weeks' lead-up before arrival. His daughter insisted he go for a haircut and pedicure and that he buys some classy clothes. She had helped him pack and even laid out the clothes he should wear. I instinctively know she is special and that she loves him very much.

We discuss in detail some "issues" on the intimacy front. This is a gift I received from a previous encounter, and I quietly thank him as it opens up such an honest and vulnerable sharing on both accounts. It somehow binds us, and we connect in a way that is different to any connection I have ever experienced before. I feel safe and relaxed. I know that when the time is right, we will have a beautiful physical encounter, and that it's going to be more than okay. We talk for three hours, and I learn a lot. He is very real and does not pretend to be anything other than who he is now and who he was.

He was your proverbial cool beach surfer dude, happy to ride waves, smoke endless amounts of dope, and try most things illegal on the recreation front. He worked as a salesman who won all the awards for being a top performer and perfected the art of being super successful while at the same time managing a daily afternoon surf. I tell him he is an operator!

His wife is a qualified architect and was a stay-at-home mother who looked after the three children—two girls and a boy, whom he idolised and who were conceived after the wafts of dope and everything else became unacceptable.

It turns out he woke up in his mid-thirties and decided it was time to get serious, so he started a company doing something similar to the product he was selling, but in a more specialised field. He has never looked back. He has given his still-thriving business to his youngest daughter to run.

She is doing a great job, and his chest increases in size as he boasts about her and how extremely lucky he is. I learn that he lost his 21-year-old son eight years earlier, and this was a massive setback for him. He was killed on a motorcycle. At the time, he was running the business and had big plans to expand.

He got gravely ill after this; his grief consumed him, and he nearly died. His intestines just kept getting badly infected, which can only be a result of the stress he was going through trying to navigate this loss. He never made a full recovery, and many surgeries later, he is compromised. This makes him vulnerable when it comes to any future relationships, and I am the first girl he actually meets. I am fully in the loop and explain to him that we are all compromised in some way or another. For some, it is external and therefore physical. For others, it is psychologically scarring and is all on the inside. I remind him often, and do so again when we meet, that nobody is perfect, that imperfection is the teacher of humility, and that we only get to be better, kinder, more understanding, and more real as we start to wear the scars of life in different ways.

He is grateful that I can be so accepting of his condition, and I have seen the change in him over the three weeks we chatted on WhatsApp. He looks better; he has put on a bit of weight, he has cut his hair, and he is more confident. He is a tall man, albeit thin now, but he has a really big personality, and his presence is very present! His physical conditions, which are tough due to his illness, make him truly beautiful to me. His scarring is his greatest attraction, for I see in them my own wounds, my own deepest sadness and suffering. Mine are not visible body scars but emotional scars that I carried for the best part of 17 years, telling no one. I tried various doctors and specialists, and not one could help me. It pretty much destroyed all attempts at intimacy for a long, long time, and still does.

We are both individuals who have taken these hard, debilitating knocks and used them to reinvent ourselves, making us kinder, more humble, more gracious, and more giving. I feel like I was born to love this man. I drive home on cloud nine and fall asleep with deep happiness and love in my heart.

I continue to have private conversations with myself, "It's infatuation; you hardly know him; it's foolish; be grown up and realistic," but none of this works.

I decide that at this stage of my life, I am going to ride this wave and ride it big! I have nothing to lose. I know what pain looks like; last year, this time, I spent six weeks crying every day because I had lost the "second great love of my life," and I was gutted. I vowed then that I would never love again, but here I am, exactly a year later, and my love space is wide open to receive.

Saturday has a slow start, and he fetches me at home. We take a beautiful drive along the coastline and go to a local pub to watch a rugby game that is an epic match between the two most unlikely teams in the final. There is no sound from the TV and, as a result, zero "gees," local slang for "spirit," so we head back to our suite and have some time together, and things happen naturally, beautifully, and easily, together. It's like we have been together for a million years or longer, and everything just works and fits. We head out to a small pub situated on a narrow little road. The doors are wide open, and it perches perfectly on the corner of the road, allowing for access on two sides. It is weather-beaten inside; your typical surfer spot: a wooden floor, a huge bar counter that dominates one half of a room, and a small fireplace on the other that warms the space, despite it being so small. It's an intimate place, and there are all "walks of life" here. Some are regulars who party here most weekends.

The age group of revellers is varied and eclectic. It's a favourite spot of mine called The Striped Horse, legendary for its incredible music, and tonight, a top DJ is playing. We arrive early, and, as few people are there, I choose to dance in the small dance space, with or without "BB"—my nickname for my Bad Boy.

He dances with me when he wants to and likes to move when it's his kind of music, and it's usually loud rock, and it's here that I realise he is hard of hearing. I am not surprised, as the music in his car is loud, and he is unaware that the decimals are way higher than normal. We dance until after midnight, and he drops me off at home. We spend the evening loving one another, adoring one another, smiling, and laughing a lot. He is extremely funny, and I love that about him. Humour is key in my book. He tells me that he adores me and is crazy about me, and I tell him the same. It sounds corny when I type it, but it is so very real and so incredibly fabulous. We feel "love," and it feels "big." Who gets to have this experience at our age?

Sunday is a lunch day with some of my friends. We also meet one of his friends—someone who belongs to a group with shared interests. I learn a lot from this interaction as I watch and listen. He tells a great story, and again, his accounts of his life are honest and factual. I like his honesty a lot and how he tells it like it is—painting a proper picture, not make-believe, or what he thinks he should say. He insists on paying the entire bill, and I am grateful to him for his generosity. I notice small things that tell me a lot about him: late at night he tips the car guard generously, and he speaks kindly to waiters and staff. He engages with all sorts, and there is no class distinction. He has a superb music mind, and we like a lot of the same music, the same genre and era, but he is way more knowledgeable than me. He has a Ph.D. in music, whereas I am a first-year student, by comparison. He listens to the words, and he knows some of them off by heart. He is passionate about music and likes both old and new.

He speaks highly of both his children and does not badmouth his ex. He loves the beauty of nature that surrounds him, takes photos, and will stop to appreciate a small wonder of nature, a certain tree or animal. He loves Molly and falls in love with my neighbour's "pavement special," Benji. Molly is thrilled that he approves of her boyfriend. I am a little concerned, as he raves about Benji but does not say much about my beloved child, but I laugh and joke about this at the same time, as she is a fussy dog and only warms to people over time. Benji, I have to admit, is very special. Molly knows quality when she sees it.

We have an early night, and we both sleep at our respective homes.

I like this arrangement as I have my mentee, Shahkira, visiting, and I want to set the right example for her, so I stay home at night. He is understanding about this, and I like him a lot as a result. He puts me under zero pressure and treats me with respect.

The beautiful red roses that he presented to me shortly after I arrived at the suite on our first night remind me that he is a man who understands how to treat a woman.

He sends me beautiful text messages when I get home and the next morning. "You transcend me to another level. One of confidence, gratitude, faith in humanity, kindness, and love."

I love that he "sees me."

He sends me a lovely quote: "'Absence Makes the Heart Grow Fonder', is nonsense! We don't have long together; let's make it count!" He is so on my page, as I live my life in summers. I remind myself daily that my life is valuable and that it needs to be lived to the fullest, every day. Especially as my mother died at 70. But I don't need this sort of talk right now, so enough of that! Time to live!

Our last day is another beautiful drive along a different coastline, and we get sidetracked, as we are actually on our way to an art gallery in town! It's a small place and dog-friendly, as Molly has come along, and she is loving her ride.

After leaving the gallery, my foot catches on an uneven paver, and I almost fall flat on my face! It happens so fast that I don't even have time to feel embarrassed, but thankfully I have two free arms and hands to stop my fall! My glasses and my bag with left-over food for the guard are strewn across the road. The knee area of my white and mostly beige pants is now a deep shade of brown. I lose my earring as well when it comes off in the car and is nowhere to be found. He is hugely concerned about me and kind. This is another plus for me.

"Night, beautiful human, the world is a much better place with you in it." He also quotes to me from the words of Judi Dench, which most of us know, about what to prioritise with age and what not. He refers to me as his "magnet," and I just love that he does. He makes me feel so incredibly special and unique. More importantly, I know that this man is deep, he is honest, and he speaks from the heart. This is not airy-fairy make-believe, but "real believe," and I feel it too.

We text one another two to three times a day. The longest ones are before bed and in the morning when we wake up. We speak too, but the beauty of texting is that you can express yourself properly; well, it is like that for me, and you can go back to something special and reread it. It's amusing, as we had both agreed we were not interested in a texting relationship. We are amazed at how our paths crossed, how quickly the relationship has developed, and how easy it has been. "I have found a companion who shares my dreams." These words resonate deeply with me, and I am grateful.

It is our last evening together as he leaves early in the morning to go up the coastline to meet with his daughters and a couple who are friends of the family. Although it is not far from where I live—a five-hour drive—I have commitments of my own, so I can't afford time away, and meeting his girls will require some sensitive planning. His daughter who lives in Kwa Zulu Natal, knows that he has met me, but his daughter in Knysna does not. I am happy with this and prefer to meet them when we are a bit further down the line and more solid. I am fully aware that friends will be sceptical and think that we have "lost the plot," and to be honest, if I were not in this myself, I would be just as sceptical and cynical!

I have invited a handful of close friends around for drinks, as I would like him to meet them. The weather during his stay has been spectacular, which is amazing considering we are moving into winter and Cape Town has wet, cold, and often stormy winters.

The evening is another one of those perfect nights. My patio is warm in the glass enclosure, and the moon and lights of nearby homes dance on the water.

Roy dominates the room and space with his height and personality.

My sister listens and observes.

My friend Dave met Roy the day before, and they talk bikes and boy things easily. Joshi is here too, and Molly is over the moon, although my friend's Maltese, Pokey, gets aggressive and snarls at Bengi, who, despite his size and stature, cowers in the corner and is not happy. His big brown eyes are soft and pleading, and he comes and sits at my feet, away from the small dog with the big personality. They settle down eventually, and Pokey watches Benji and any movement he makes closely. This is Joshi's second home in many ways, and I am pleased he finds his safe place, not just with his dad but with me as well. His father, on the other hand, is also sitting near Pokey, the "Piranha," as we now call him!

Roy is a bit loud, and this is because he is hard of hearing and an expressive to boot. I sit back and observe. I just love watching him interact and get to know those people who matter to me. By nine thirty, everyone is ready to go home. My 'larger than life' being is also going home soon, and we spend a few last, bittersweet moments together. Both happy, content, and complete. We have each other, and the world is now a perfect place.

We talk about his son who died, and how much this affected him. He rode motorcycles like his father and ran the business with zest and drive. He had big visions, and they were the best of friends. He raced cars and surfed. He asked his father for the keys to his Harley. That was the last time he ever saw his son. He died riding the motorcycle. This had a huge effect on Roy, and he just died too. He suffered massively for giving him the keys, and blames himself for his son's death.

While he is in Knysna, we do not speak on the phone. It's complicated, as his ex-wife, his children, his best friend, his wife, and their daughter, who is best friends with his eldest daughter, will all be staying together. I don't find this strange. My one ex and I shared his children with a 50/50 arrangement, and we went away together with the children as well, and they loved it.

When he tells me that we won't be able to speak to one another, I feel a little uncomfortable and wait for him to text me. He senses this and tells me that we are an item and there will never be another for him. I am his beginning and end now. He asks me to always be honest with him and tell him if anything changes for me. He is feeling unsure now as I am quieter.

I reassure him. He ticks all my boxes. I explain that I am being sensitive to his needs and giving him the space to do what he needs to. He tells me that in time, I will meet everyone, and when I go to Durban mid-month, I will meet his daughter, who lives there. I sense, and know, that if she approves and likes me, this will be his cue to tell his daughter in Knysna. I do not probe. I know that the story will unfold when it must. The longer we are apart, the more intense our relationship becomes. He is romantic, loving, and speaks from the heart. There is no holding back, and whatever he thinks, he writes with abandon. I love his bravery and openness. His no-holds-barred. It's refreshing and uplifting.

In one of his messages, he writes that one of the reasons he "loves" me is that it's a kind of uncomplicated attraction, possibly because of his past flirts and affairs. I love this blatant truth. He feels free even though committed. He agrees that we have become very deeply connected in a very short space of time, and, had anyone suggested it, he would have been cynical too. He tells me that he has never felt so comfortable with a human being before, and this resonates with me as I feel the same way. That he had resigned himself to a sedate old age, like a stallion in a pasture, and then, wham, all his senses have been stoked and blow his mind. He says that he is so grateful to me. We are like one split in two.

I am eternally grateful. This wonderful man with an adventurous spirit who lifts me every day, who is fun, who is up for most things at the drop of a hat, who lives life to the full, who loves life, who is generous in every way, who is romantic, who is dilly, who is outgoing, clever, savvy, and successful, is fully embedded in my life! All that he says resonates with me. At this stage of life, I don't care if this lasts a month or years; it's been one of the best experiences of my life, and I am on this ride at full tilt until my life either stops or what we have ends.

During this time, we set a date for me to fly to Durban to meet his "Crew." He is a rugby fan like me, and a big game is on that weekend! I share an evening with friends I have not seen in ages. I take my mentee, Shahkira, with me. These friends of mine had spent time living in the Far East, and we decide before we eat to give gratitude as opposed to grace. I practiced this extensively whilst I was in Bali, and it's a wonderful daily practice.

He writes the most beautiful messages to me daily. He is a talented writer with a deep soul. He is adventurous and eager to do most things, and I love this about him. We agree to go to AfrikaBurn the following year, and he commits to tickets, although there is no set date as yet.

This is an event I have always wanted to attend but have never had the opportunity. It is described on the website as a spectacular event that is a result of creative expression by a group of volunteers who gather in South Africa once a year in the Tankwa Karoo, which is an arid, dry, countryside. It becomes a temporary city of art, theme camps, costume, music, and performance. For those that have been, no explanation is necessary; for those that haven't, none is possible. Their mission statement is a participant-created movement, an experiment in inclusive community building, decommodification, creativity, self-reliance, and radical self-expression, a chance to invent the world anew. Nothing is for sale on the camping site of the event since nothing is for sale; if people need something, they either trade it with something else or simply ask for it, thereby employing a gift economy.

CHAPTER 30
ROAD TRIPPING WITH ROY

It's winter in Cape Town. Roy and I have agreed to try getting together every 4 to 5 weeks. We decide on a road trip, the Garden Route and the Karoo, and he will drive down. We will take Molly, my much-loved four-legged child, with us. She is five, travels well, and is the perfect, docile, travel companion once she has made herself comfortable.

Roy is due in Cape Town on Saturday, and we will start the road trip on Monday. My phone beeps at lunchtime. He has a burst tyre just outside of Bloemfontein, which is a city that emerges out of nowhere. This is a catastrophe, as everything closes at 1 p.m. and his tyre is a special kind made for sports cars and not readily available.

On top of this, he has a sore throat and is not feeling well. He stays over in this one-horse city, and we arrange to meet in the Karoo on Monday, as it is closer for him and a short, pleasant drive for me. I head for Barrydale, where we have booked a cute cottage for the night. I pull up outside a house, and on arrival, I know instinctively that this is not the right house—although the GPS tells me I have arrived!

A delightful character with his two Golden Retrievers comes walking straight towards me. I smile sheepishly as I notice that my car is firmly embedded in the gravel driveway. This tall, elegant man glides rather than walks. He is a kind, friendly chap who explains it's actually the house next door I want and that he often has guests at his house looking for the Airbnb accommodation next door! As I reverse, there is this almighty noise as one of my wheels churns up a section of his driveway! I feel awful and want to make up for the disturbance and mayhem I've caused him. I jump out and invite him to come and have dinner with us. He declines the invitation, saying he is already busy, and asks that we come to him for breakfast instead. I am reminded of how friendly and hospitable small-town folks are and decide to take a leaf out of his book!

The cottage is adorable; the interior has a Balinese, eastern flavour mixed with countryside touches. There is a rustic roofless shower outside that fascinates me, as it is open to the sky and stars. I reach for my phone and take endless pictures! The kitchen is housed upstairs; rather unusual, but then town folks are different to those in the city! It has a view of the whole town from the perfectly sized wooden balcony. Altogether unique. The French champagne is chilling on ice, and soon he is here! Molly is thrilled to see him. He is, however, very sick, and I insist he lies down and rests. We spend a quiet, short evening together. I finish almost all the champagne and am secretly delighted to be spoilt in this manner. I do love sharing, but French, all to myself, is indeed a special spoil!

Breakfast with Clive and his two dogs is delightful; we become friends instantly, and he gets along well with Roy. He lost his partner a few years earlier and is lonely. Well-educated, his home is a museum of beautiful antiques, books of yesteryear, and an interior that is stunning and tasteful as only a "creative" can be, for he is an architect by profession. We exchange numbers, and he promises to visit me in Cape Town. It is on this trip, while considering renting or buying a home in the countryside, that I notice a house across the road is up for rent! It's a lightbulb moment, and I spend the rest of the trip looking at properties to rent in the area. I previously owned a country house, and now my hunger for another is on a route march! I am possessed. I have longed for a farmhouse ever since selling the last one I owned with my previous husband, and now it seems possible!!

Roy is so easy to be with, and we love driving together, and we listen to his music all the way to Knysna and Leisure Isle, where we will be staying the night. Surrounded by water, it is an old, established area in the heart of nature, surrounded by milkwood trees. These magnificent coastal trees are remnants of yesteryear with curling branches and trunks that have their own unique way of growing. They are beautiful to look at and are often windswept and skew, as they struggle in the wind and grow crooked as a result. This simply adds to their beauty. We have lunch at a café I know well and laugh a lot. He is very funny. Not quite top drawer and a little unpolished, so this takes a bit of getting used to.

His headbands are often part of his dress code, and sometimes I really like them, and other days they simply don't do it for me! He loves caps, and not just any old cap, but always something different. One I hate is ugly, weather-beaten, and belongs in the bin, and of course, it's his favourite! His hair is wavy and unruly, and he likes it longer as it covers his newly acquired hearing aid, which I am thrilled about. Top of the range, but limited, in that he often forgets to charge it, and sometimes he doesn't wear it, so it's difficult to tell when they are in or not! I think he does this on purpose to test me and others, convinced that his hearing is fine!

Our accommodation is a super-modern, minimalistic BnB that we love, but we ask to see what else they have, as we want a two-bedroom or two separate beds. We are given an upgrade and have an entire house to ourselves. We watch a movie, but he finds it difficult to follow as the hearing aid picks up all other sounds, and it occurs to me that perhaps he has not learnt how to use it yet? He is kind, generous, and adoring, and I revel in this adoration.

During our stay at the house, I realise that I adore him more from a distance than when I'm with him! We are such kindred spirits but also, very different. He is a loud, expressive personality, and a dominant personality at that. He often speaks without thinking and, he also seems to feel the urge to talk constantly. I remind myself about all his wonderful qualities and when I move the negatives into the background, I feel more settled. I am taking it real slow, and he respects this.

We meet his delightful daughter that afternoon for lunch, and I like her enormously. In fact, both his daughters are lovely young women. He is a great dad and loves them very much. He also spoils them. This does not sit well with me, as I believe in teaching children to take care of themselves; that by spoiling them we disable them in the long run. I feel quite strongly about it, but he feels that this is a way to show them love.

Our next stop is the Karoo on our way home, and we visit the quaint and well-known little town of Prins Albert. Our cottage is a small semi-detached. I find myself in love with the countryside even more now, and my need to find a permanent place grows stronger. I search the web quite extensively, but no rentals come up in suitable areas.

Roy is supportive of my search efforts and loves the idea! This makes me keener, so my search intensifies. His daughter and her boyfriend decide to join us, and Roy books them a cottage. We meet for a coffee, and then it's a rugby World Cup final evening, so I decide to stay home and read my book while Roy goes off to watch it on TV with his daughter and future son-in-law at the cute little boutique hotel down the road. I also feel that he would welcome the chance to have some solo time with them. I also need some solo time, as his presence exhausts me. It tires me when we spend a lot of time together, as he speaks loudly, and I have to raise my voice all the time.

We meet the next morning and find a little home bakery that is also a coffee shop. It's full of things to buy, as so many of them are, and Roy buys us each a big white knitted woollen lamb with a big round ball of a stomach and a black face. The eyes all have big lashes, and each sheep has its own unique eye expression. "It will live in the countryside at the house when I find it," I say.

The shop is quiet as it is winter and cold outside. There are a handful of patrons, and a roaring fire in the corner warms the room. Roy has not put his "ears" in and speaks loudly about some fairly private matters. I am embarrassed and touch his hand after a while to indicate that all the patrons are now party to our table discussion.

His retort is rather childish. "Oh well, then I just won't talk at all!"

His daughter saves the day by explaining to him that he can't hear how loudly he speaks. He then admits that he forgot to charge his "ears," and this is why he can't hear!

I am super sensitive about loud talk, as I use an enormous amount of energy to still my own ever-busy mind and to keep conversations quiet and calm. It makes me agitated and irritated, and it shows. It just expends too much of my energy, and then with Roy's dominant persona and strong personality, I find that later in the day, I need two hours just to be in silence.

I am beginning to "see the light," and I again remind myself of our great friendship and all his good points. He is a deeply philosophical man with a beautiful mind and heart, but is, by his own admission, no Einstein. He is a farm boy in many respects, and finesse is not on his agenda, nor in his make-up. He is savvy and smart, but simple too. An interesting mix. His music is also more intentionally rock, and this is not my cup of tea!

Our drive back to Barrydale takes us via Oudtshoorn, where we will view a house in the countryside area known as Hopefield. The house itself is ideal and nestles on top of a hill with rolling valleys and mountain views. It's exactly what I'm looking for, especially as there is a separate large cottage on the property. The downside is that the access road to the house is in very poor condition, and a proper 4x4 vehicle would be needed to get to the house and back. Also, there are only a handful of houses in the area, making it unsafe for me to live there as a woman on my own.

At this point, I tell him that I have found another place during my search, located up the West Coast, actually the Northern Cape, and I intend to see it on my return, but I don't want to get my hopes up! It looks like it could be exactly what I am looking for! We pop in to see our new friend Clive, who invites us for lunch, but we decline his offer, as we still have a long way to travel. By the way, did I mention that Clive insisted on me leaving my car parked outside his property while we were away? Country folk are simply the best. I am happy to be heading home.

CHAPTER 31
BAD BOY ROY
– THE FARMHOUSE FIND

The road is more beautiful than I could ever have imagined. As far as the eye can see, there are vast open spaces with mountains, rocky hills, and valleys on either side, interspersed with a variety of farms that grow many kinds of fruit and vegetables. In some instances, it is pure wine territory: rows and rows of grapevines with vibrant leafy greenery, interspersed with gnarled vines that curve and swerve their way up hills and down valleys. At other times, long, grassy, young wheat is swaying, waiting for the onset of spring. All around, the sky stretches wide and open before me. I inhale long, deep breaths, and I feel calm, despite the excitement reeling inside my body. For the first time in ages, I feel that I can really breathe. Not the kind of breathing we do every day that goes unnoticed, but long, deep breaths that clear my mind; that remove all the drama of daily life and my ever-endless to-do list from my consciousness. I feel relaxed, I feel grounded, and I feel whole.

Today there are clouds that move and gather. At times they are clumped together, forming a few big blankets of fluff. At other times, thin, long lines of white smoky puffs along the ever blue and bright sky. I drive in silence for the surroundings sing to me, a deep soulful sound of "coming home." I had forgotten how entrenched small-town living is in my make-up—formed in the days when I attended a school in Paarl—where I had time and room to grow and learn about life with its peaks and valleys. The city was within reach, but not part of my life where innocence prevailed with the sound values and principles of country living.

The four-hour drive is quicker than I imagined but took an hour longer, as I could not resist stopping at a farmstall in the middle of nowhere. Molly, my ever-present four-legged companion, stirs from her slumber. She loves drives in the car and falls asleep within seconds. She jumps up, looks out the window, and wags her tail eagerly as she senses an adventure in the midst! Two big dogs welcome us, and I allow them to smell Molly, and when their tails begin to wag, she jumps out, and runs alongside them in glee. Glancing back fleetingly to check that I am coming too and that this play time is allowed.

There is one other car, and the stall nestles under a large tree, next to a house that is home to the owners. Inside, the shop is sparse but cool and a welcome respite from the heat outside. There is coffee, tea, and cool drinks, as well as locally made "roesterkook" and pancakes with different fillings. My tummy rumbles, so I order a mince and cheese pancake, coffee, and some cold water. It is cool under the covered patio, with a faint breeze dancing around me.

The owner's wife brings the food, and alongside her is the cutest little lamb imaginable, all of four weeks old. He is glued to her side and keeps tugging on her apron, bleating intermittently. The stall owners had rescued him with his umbilical cord still intact at the time, but with no mother in sight. None of the local farmers have laid claim to him, and it's also not lambing season! I feel a warm glow spreading through my body, and I breathe in the scent of his newness and innocence. We chat for a while and immediately become friends. I tell them that if I buy the farmhouse, I will stop and let them know, as it is a road I will travel often.

Further up the N7 are two passes, and the vegetation is now rows upon rows of citrus trees and rooibos tea shrubs as we near the huge Clanwilliam dam on the Olifants River. Man-made, it is a massive 122 million cubic metres, and was purpose-built to provide irrigation to the agricultural region downstream—a magnificent sight that stretches for miles. It also tells me that I have completed two-thirds of my journey, and my excitement levels rise. The scenery changes dramatically as I venture further towards my destination. There are no dams or water supply further up the road now, and the land becomes harsh and arid. The sun leaves a shimmer on the road and bounces off the tar with harsh silver strands of transparent fire. This area is not for the fainthearted. The landscape becomes interspersed with little, wiry, hard bushes, an occasional larger bush, and a tree or two. I pass a sign that says, "Moedverloor" which translated into English, in my own words means, "to lose enthusiasm." I can see why when I think back to those who named these towns. People on horseback and with wagons and carts who trekked for days through treacherous terrain. That they even came this far is a miracle.

Once past this point, I see in the distance the rising of a little "koppie", a hill, which erupts from the surrounding flat surface. I instinctively know that my Farmhouse is at the next turn. As I get closer, a small clump of houses comes into view. The words of a poem I write later come to mind: "In the blink of an eye, you will pass me by." The house is easy to spot with its green roof and towering blue gum tree at the entrance. The word "Home" sweeps into my heart and I am overjoyed. It's better than the pictures I saw on the website; even if the roof is half green and half silver, the extension has just never been painted. My biggest fear is that I will find a modern 1970s house instead of a thick-walled, clay brick structure.

The fence is low and rickety, and it strikes me that one could simply step over it into the yard. A long, narrow, covered veranda, filled with pot plants, comes into view, with more plants in pots hanging randomly from the beams. Some pots are broken, some stand askew, a few plastic ones have burst on the sides, and others are held together by wire. The pots are all different shapes and sizes. A big, broad smile lights up my face. The front door is old, weathered, and worn. Emotions start to get the better of me at this point, and I hold back my tears, try to calm down, and scold myself, *You have not even stepped inside yet!*

The entrance hall is huge, and the walls are thick with age and history. The roof is super high and clad with wood. The light fittings are old, and some are missing their outer glass covers. The space is cluttered with way too much furniture and stuff. It feels like a time warp. I am taken back years as I absorb as much as my mind can comprehend. It is at this point that I start to cry. Tears of joy roll down my cheeks, and I am overwhelmed. The agent is dumbfounded but smiles. The bedrooms, previously stables, are small and overfull; they are just big enough. Inside the kitchen is a big cast iron AGA stove with so many things hanging from the wooden beams; it's like a museum.

The owners are a lanky silver-haired man who I have to look up to when I greet him, as he is at least a head and a half taller than me! And a round-faced woman sitting on the other side of a table. She remains seated as she has difficulty walking. Her big brown eyes look up at me from under her thick, bushy eyebrows and her wild, grey hair that is unkempt. I bend down on my knees and look at her close up, my eyes brimming with tears, and say, "I am going to buy your house because I love it and it is everything I ever wanted."

She laughs and says, "I don't really want to sell it, but we must."

I wander around the house and can see the potential, although it is not easy, as the house is so cluttered and way too full. Her husband tells me that she is a hoarder and cannot part with anything. I nod my head and sympathise with him until I get to the garage, which is an extra-sized double garage. Here, chaos reigns supreme, and there is no space for a mouse, never mind a car. Across the way is a ramshackle carport, known as an "Afdak" in Afrikaans, and it is exactly that—a half excuse for a carport—but I love it. Old, corrugated pieces of roof sheeting—some painted, some not—have been slapped together. There is more stuff here, but there is space for a car.

The chicken coop nestles at the back, and here I find six little chicks, all black with a white mother hen. The only white hen amongst them, she has stolen them from a black mother hen. Her chicks were left out by accident one night and were sadly eaten by night creatures. There are wild cats in the area. The other chickens mill around, and there is one very tall, handsome cock who struts around, making his presence very much felt as he peers over his domain and harem of hens! I don't have much time to spend as I still need to drive all the way back to Cape Town, and by the time I get home, it will have been a ten-hour road trip. On the way home, I phone Roy and tell him that he will next see me at "The Farmhouse."

He is so encouraging and enthusiastic, and I love this about him. He is my perfect relationship from afar. We agree to set a date to see each other again once my offer has been accepted. I wrote a poem the next day as I am in love, more so with my farmhouse, than my man.

THE FARMHOUSE

With a blink of an eye
You will pass me by
As you travel afar
To the land of the scars
Of the rough
and the tough
for it was oh, so gruff

pebbles n stones aplenty
all so relentlessly
lie scattered around
with silence the sound
as you sit and are ground
in this place so remote
you won't need a boat

untouched, is your find
nothing taken, for mind
this house, very old,
is what you discover
as you arrive with your other
so full and so busy,
it will make you quite dizzy

don't expect to find, new
its seldom and few
and very out of place
in this special space
on the farm, oh so far
where the very old,
is all really, all gold

clean it will be
so don't fret but just see
how old can shine
and perform mime
of a time, that's gone by
so, give it a try
and look at the sky

the silent stance
makes the clouds dance
don't miss this chance
of endless and blue
yes, it, is, true
that creation is best
so far very far west!

CHAPTER 32
ROY - THE MOVE

The large entrance gate is open upon our arrival at around 1p.m. The first thing that catches my eye is that the lounge area looks like the house has been ransacked. I feared that the day of moving would be a disaster based on the age and the state of mind of the sellers, an elderly couple, in addition to which they are hoarders, incapable of throwing anything away. The sight before my eyes, however, is a nightmare of the worst kind! Some furniture has been left behind, which we agreed was part of the sale. There is stuff lying around all over the house. Cupboards are full of every possible thing you could imagine, and the place is dusty, dirty, and windswept. I am at a loss for words, and Roy is dumbstruck.

The items we have brought along are left in the car, bar some groceries and basics, and we are unable to unpack until we can get some order going in the chaos that surrounds us. It is at this point that I silently scold myself, *"What were you thinking? At your age, another home, more work, more property to manage, furnish, and fix!"* It is fleeting as I slowly begin to see the potential and my ever-busy decorative mind slips into gear. All the ideas I had already thought about come to mind, and I tackle the problem with energy and enthusiasm despite the mountain that lies ahead of me.

Roy is equally motivated, and we start systematically tackling one room at a time. Fortunately, two staff members worked for the owners and they are here to help. I send them both off to tackle the master bedroom, as this will at least ensure we have a clean room to sleep in. We make a small dent in the chaos, but we have our bed made up, and we are assured of at least a good night's rest. We had the wherewithal to bring some ready meals along so we could have a light supper. I jump into the shower all ready to get myself well and truly clean, but there is no hot water! This means a walk to the other bathroom that needs a good clean, but at this point, I simply close my eyes and focus on the hot water spurting from the shower. I avoid looking at the dark marks all over the white tiles that look like they have not been properly cleaned in decades!

We step outside just before bed and are greeted with a milky way of the most defined and detailed proportion. The layout of stars is incredibly bold and exquisite! There are no street lights here, nor any house lights to detract from the night sky above. I feel as if I can touch the stars, and we stand gazing in wonderment at the sight. Silence is ever present, and nothing stirs. I can hear us breathe. I can make out every star constellation I know. Neither of us wants to move inside; it's such a special moment, but the hard work we did during the day reminds us it's time to rest. Never has a bed felt so good. We snuggle up close and tight, and I am so deeply grateful to this man who is here and who has been a constant support, always enthusiastic, always willing, and who gets stuck in and helps!

The week goes by in a flash as we wash more curtains, bedding, cushions, carpets, rugs, walls, tiles, windows, doors, etc., than I have ever done in a lifetime. The washing machine works 24/7. The staff work tirelessly and relentlessly. They are exceptional and impressive, here in the Hardeveld (the hard countryside). By the end of five days, two guests from Cape Town come to visit, and I am relieved to stop working. My to-do list is still very long, but it now must go on the back burner, which is healthy for an individual like me, who has no "off" button once I start any project. Roy, I suspect, is just as pleased. The poor man had no idea what he was letting himself into when he responded to my message on the dating site that referred to his Mick Jagger looks with a headband that goes back to the sixties. An older Rocker who, as we know, is hard of hearing from listening to deafening music his whole life! He ticks all my boxes, yet I am not yet open to love and keep finding reasons why we won't work despite feeling love and adoration.

My friends love the house and are amazed at what has been achieved in five days; they don't see the messed up concrete floor covered by rugs and bed, the peeling paint on walls in one room where there is a handmade bed that is 100 years old! I am so ready to turn this old bed into firewood, but it must remain till I can find a replacement.

We have a huge half-cut barrel for a barbeque (known as a "braai" in SA), typical of any farming community. The night is still and warm. There is not a breath of wind, and clouds drift slowly in the dark expanse while a big, bright yellow moon rises over the proud hilltop in the distance. The moon lights up the garden, which is but a handful of bushes and shrubs. There is no grass in this part of the world.

The homeowners here sweep the dark orange earth and fill their gardens with ornaments, entire bathroom scenes, tractors, old farming utensils, and animals crafted of wood and steel—creating art where flowers are scarce, and greenery lost. The harsh, arid ground has a different kind of beauty, and it is here that one truly walks an earth untouched, left to its own devices, and seldom watered; it's not for the faint-hearted. But it has captured my heart, and I am smitten.

I am touched that these friends made the trip so soon after my moving here, as it is a 4-hour journey so not just up the road! We spend our evenings drinking wine and whisky on the long veranda in our loose summer clothes, for the night is warm. It is an idyllic setting, overlooking a backdrop of hills with a handful of houses in the foreground. On the west side is a long and inviting dusty stretch of road that, at the top, turns into the hills. It's one of my favourite views, where around a corner are open expansive farmlands stretching yonder and more. One feels truly alone in the universe as one travels south for miles and miles.

My chest expands, and I have this deep sense to breathe, and with each breath, a calmness sweeps over my entire mind and soul. I am at peace and in harmony with my surroundings. I am home. Roy is a superb braai master and completely at home here too. Headband to keep his hair out of his face, and we have enough meat to feed an army! In his element with a braai, which is part of a man's culture here in the South African countryside. You simply cannot own a farm and not have a braai!

Morning walks are the order of the day here, and Roy heads off on his e-bike with its big, fat tyres, designed for the harsh stoney roads in this part of the world. His cap and headband have become a talking point in town—the crazy newcomer! Our walk through the whole town takes about 20 minutes, and my friends cannot believe that such a small place exists. The town's erven are no less than 1000 square metres, and some are double the size. The Mall is a tiny shop with the bare essentials and is literally the size of a triple garage. The play on the words "The Mall" is clever and witty, and this is but a small insight into the creativity and survival instincts that are evident in small towns, as I spend more time here.

Sadly, it is time to head back to the city where life calls and demands need to be met. Roy has a much further road to travel than I do, so he heads out early. I continue to be amazed by this wonderful human being who is so full of life. He has some major personal challenges that he simply accepts and finds gratitude daily. One of my favourite quotes comes to mind: "If you want to find happiness, find gratitude!" His bear hug stays with me long after he leaves. Tall, at 1,088 metres, I always feel small in his presence, and I love that I do.

CHAPTER 33
BAD BOY ROY
NEW YEAR 2023

This Christmas is unlike any other I have had. I am alone. I am in Nuwerus, and I am happier than I have ever been! Being alone is of no concern to me, as unfortunately, I grew up in a broken home environment where it often felt just like any other day and nothing special. I don't recall any special Christmas lunches or dinners, bar one, which we had at my grandmother's in Grabouw when I was six, and we drove up from Durban. She sang and played the piano, and my twin brother and I ran off, doubled over with mirth, at her high-pitched, soprano voice. The ones I also do remember were later in life, when I was married to my ex-husband, who had two children, and there were often 30 of us on Christmas day, as there was a very large extended family with second marriages mixed in.

On Christmas Eve, I sit outside my lounge on the west side of my home instead of my usual spot on the patio. The view from here is my favourite. There is a long, dusty, distant road that stretches all the way up a hill, and the fields on either side are shades of brown. There is no lush green here, only hard veld, known as the "Hardeveld" in Afrikaans, that best describes this harsh, dry terrain. The sun is setting, and the sky is orange, yellow, and red. As the sun sets, the colours grow and move, creating a carpet of colour across the distant and massive skyline. It is hard to explain how harsh ground and an extensive, endless sky can be the best view ever experienced! I never tire of this picture and each time find more beauty and peace in this simple view.

I don't feel lonely. I am at peace, and I can breathe. It is a strange thing to say, as people don't really understand what I mean. Life is one big chase, more so in my case, as my ever-busy mind constantly looks and creates things to take up my time and energy. Here, my mind is forced to slow down. To be still and to sit in the quiet. It is heaven for an overactive mind like mine. This is what I mean by 'breathe'. Breathe in every sense. I breathe the dry, pure, unpolluted air; the silence; the vastness; the desolation; the stars; the moon; the sun; the quiet; the harshness; the untouched; and the beauty. I feel like creation has not yet begun, and we are at the foot of God's blank canvas all those thousands of years ago. It is here that I find Him most present. Still later, with a glass of wine in hand, I breathe more silence and stars as they appear twinkling, a rhythmic Christmas carol in my mind.

The garden has a handful of 25-year-old olive trees that are small for their age. Everything grows painstakingly slowly here, and sometimes, depending on what plant or tree it is, not at all. There are massive cactus plants too—the biggest I have ever seen in my life. Initially, I wanted to remove ugly plants, but once I had spent some time here, I realised that "ugly" has its own beauty and, in this instance, the size and years are legendary and to be cherished. Besides, a prickly pear is one of the most delicious fruits ever!

Molly, my miniature Schnauzer, and I go for a walk with the stars, and this is a "gift" in itself. She is the love of my life, my companion, my all, and we are never apart. She loves Nuwerus, and everyone loves this sweet, gentle dog. Her walks, without leash and therefore with abandon, are her happiest moments, and she is in heaven. She is so easy to please and always so grateful. Dogs can teach us an inordinate amount. Once we return, I head back to my chair and revel some more in the stars that stretch brightly above, vibrant and full.

Christmas morning dawns, and it is a perfect Hardeveld day. Hot, with a light breeze and gorgeous sunshine. Molly waits patiently for me to stir, as she knows that walk time will only happen when I put my shoes on. She lies next to me but soon stirs and positions herself on my chest for morning snuggles. She has this unique way of staring straight at me, and our eyes lock. She can outstare me any day, but today she wants to engage a little and taps me on my chest with her front paws.

The church bells ring when I am drinking my second cup of coffee, calling us to celebrate the life of Jesus. It so happens that Christmas falls on a Sunday this year, and I love this. Makes it somehow more special.

The church is the biggest building in the settlement. With only four streets in the centre that all interlink, it's no town by a long shot, but rather a small selection of 35 homes. Today, the church is fuller than usual—barely 30 people at most. Our small gathering is lost in the vast space with a triple-height roof, enormous stained-glass windows, and six entrances. Everyone knows everyone, so it's a warm, comfortable group who, in their own way, are a family, the town family.

I invite two of the residents in the town to lunch today. They are also newcomers like me and own a cute "dolls" house on a large open erf. They are struggling financially and battle to make ends meet. There is no work, and neither one of them is employed. They are, however, some of the nicest people. They are down to earth, call a spade a shovel, and have known a hard life. I am delighted to be able to do something charitable today. I am no traditionalist, so it's a braai on the gas barbecue on the long, covered veranda. I have a bottle of champagne, and we spend a lovely afternoon getting to know each other.

Tess is the go-getter of the two, older than her husband, and talkative. He is extremely quiet, seldom speaks, and carries an air of heaviness about him. He is not in a good space and struggling. I understand that. As the man of the house, he is accustomed to being in control, and now that they are living a hard life, he feels responsible. I don't know how to help him. We don't exchange gifts, as I know better than to embarrass them in this way. It's an unusual day for me, and I am reminded of how incredibly blessed and fortunate I am. Tess has a good sense of humour and makes me laugh a lot; I really enjoy her. She laughs when she speaks, and it's an infectious laugh, and I am soon laughing too! Her laugh is unique and quirky! It is remarkable that she is always jovial and upbeat considering the challenges they face daily. I remind myself to make a point of inviting them over often in the future for a meal, and I send them home with all the leftovers. Her attitude is always positive, and she expresses gratitude often. Another reminder of my motto: "If you want to find happiness, find gratitude!"

Three days later, my good friend Michelle arrives from Cape Town with her second time round online "meet" as I call this man. They met two years earlier, but she had decided he was not right for her then. At the time, she had split from her ex-boyfriend, so she was also not ready for a relationship. When she met up with him again online, she decided to give it another go. They are coming up for the New Year, and my bad boy Roy is coming up as well, after having spent Christmas with his two daughters and ex-wife. An unusual arrangement he made with his two daughters, who, he says, made it very clear that anyone he dates had to understand that he spends important holidays with them as a family and that a girlfriend would not be welcome! However, at this point, I am unaware that his ex was also with him and his two daughters, and I am taken aback when I accidentally discover that she was, in fact, with them!

When we first started dating, he went on a trip to Namibia with her a few months earlier, explaining it had been planned much earlier, before my time. I was going to France on a previously planned trip, so this worked perfectly, plus we had only just met! Upon learning this, I did not make a huge fuss about it. It was early days for us, and I was not your conventional individual either; in fact, far from it. However, some months on, it did strike me as an odd arrangement!

Michelle and Gavin arrive heavily laden with food. I like Gavin on sight and find him engaging, pleasant-looking, and kind. He and Roy hit it off immediately, and we have a lot of fun catching up and finding out more about one another.

There is a New Year dance being held in a small town 17 kilometres from Nuwerus. The town is called Bitterfontein, which in English translates to "Bitter Fountain." Funny name, as fountains do not exist in a town where water is scarce! It is a typical farmers' party that will ensure dancing and drinking in true Afrikaans fashion. Men in khaki shorts and shirts, leather "veldskoens," beards, tanned biceps, and legs with light—albeit big—footed grace that would no doubt twirl any partner around a floor with ease. These nimble feet are a far cry from the muscle-framed farmers who could probably pick up a cow, solo! The floor is covered with flour to ensure smooth and easy movement. I grew up in an Afrikaans-speaking town, and this, I don't want to miss! Americans have "Country Music," and in South Africa, we have "Boere Musiek."

Michelle and Gavin head off early in the day for a drive to the beach, despite it being an hour and a half drive away, on a long, dusty road of vast farmlands and open spaces. We have a loose arrangement to try the New Year's party. At 20:30, they are still out, so we head off to find the party venue. Despite the town being tiny, we battle to find anything that resembles a venue! We are convinced that if we don't see it, we will at least hear the music! After circling the town three times, we stop at the petrol station and get directions. It is off the national road, three kilometres out of town. So, we head out into the pitch-black night and follow the blackness. We see lights in the distance and hurry there with excitement and enthusiasm. This is going to be a great experience, if nothing else.

The large warehouse-type building sits in the middle of nowhere. Cars are parked in a makeshift car park of gravel and stone. People are naturally regimented, and invisible parking lines are the order of the night! Each car well-parked in rows, like soldiers on parade.

The building radiates with sound. Inside, tables are placed all along the sides of the building. Party revellers are already in a good mood. Large, tall, thin, round, and short figures are swirling around the dance floor. The DJ in his khaki suit shorts, and "veldskoens" is having a grand time swaying his head in time to the beat of the ever-popular Afrikaans music that gets people up on their feet, nimbly moving across the floor. Roy and I head straight for the floor and get into our own version of "Langarm," which directly translates into "Longarm"—a dance of a totally different kind—a waltz on steroids! We are definitely the odd ones out! We love this "small town" New Year celebration where anything goes; if you are moving, it doesn't matter how! Roy is very funny, and I spend a large part of the evening laughing as he does a Zulu impression of this dance. I love this part of his persona wild and free.

The venue's bar is a wrought iron counter with an overhang. Drinks are dirt cheap and flow abundantly. We were going to pace ourselves, however, so it's one tequila each. Roy insists that the owner, who organised the dance, join us, and he does! In one sip, his drink is all gone, sans lemon or salt; this is "Boere" (farmer) territory! Here in the countryside, the men are notorious for being able to drink most under the table! They are usually strapping strong, tall, big men who tower over others.

We dance together and separately, and I pinch myself. This is one of the best New Year parties I have ever been to. Here, where the land is rough, people are real and extremely down to earth. Their value system lies in their land, their stock, be it plant or animal, and their families. These are their prized assets. Here they make time for their neighbours, and they care about one another. Here the community is your family!

If you asked me to choose between a star-studded world cruise New Year's party and this event, hands down my countryside New Year party amongst real, special, down-to-earth revellers would be my choice, without question.

We step outside as the countdown starts and gaze up at a brilliant Milky Way from a parking lot where there are no other lights to see in the New Year. Every single star and star sign in the galaxy seems to be visible, and it's priceless. The stars are like lights that dance across the sky, twinkling and glistening. Some stars are faint pinpricks; others are bolder and stronger. Some are further apart, and others are packed more closely together. The night air is warm, and time stands still. I know I will remember this New Year for a long time to come. Roy holds me close in a warm, comfortable, and snug embrace. His tall, thin body towers above me. I am content, and I am happy. I want to feel a surge of love for this amazing human, but instead, I feel a very nice glow. It's not love, and it's not friendship; it sits somewhere in between. I want to feel more, and in hindsight, the need to feel interferes with the natural process.

The following morning, when he wakes up, he is not happy. He is frustrated as intimacy eludes us, and I am the reason for this. I love him so much when we are apart but am overwhelmed when we are together for many reasons. Some have validity, some do not. We are similar, but also very different. He does not want to pursue the relationship, as his primal needs are not being met. On the one hand, I am relieved that he has made the call, but on the other hand, I love him enormously as a friend and fear that we will lose our friendship as well. I don't put up any argument and simply agree that I am to blame and refrain from sharing the reasons.

The dust swirls and fades as he drives off into the distance. I am sad that he is leaving. I have no idea how sad I will become in the next few months. Had I known, I somehow would have packed an extra helping of more happiness into our time together. Molly shares in my sadness in her own way, as they have become very attached, and he adores her.

CHAPTER 34
ROY MY ROCK
- LOSS, HEARTBREAK
AND MOURNING

We do not engage much during the next few weeks; Roy is smarting and, by his own admission, is licking his wounds. I miss him but also feel relieved that there is no more pressure. Then, out of the blue, he lets me know that he has met up with an ex-girlfriend and they are dating. I am always surprised at how quickly men move on. A doctor that I once dated moved on in under three weeks and was back online the same week we parted ways. This news always makes me feel rejected and a bit of a failure, but I know this thinking is emotional, not logical. But we stay in touch, and I even tease him about his new girlfriend, who lives in another province. Our friendship shows its real worth, however, a few weeks after our parting, when it becomes one that will be ever-lasting and meaningful, but in a very unexpected way.

In February, five weeks since Roy and I agreed to be friends, my beloved Molly, who is only six years and four months old, dies unexpectedly. She falls ill in Nuwerus. She has a stroke, and I discover she has leukaemia, and I have to put her to sleep. I find it impossible to relive the moments that led up to this diagnosis. It is too painful. A raw, weeping wound that bleeds non-stop. It hurts all the time, and I have to stop and catch my breath to kill the tide of pain as it cuts into my heart and tears my soul to shreds. I have to hold my breath in order to freeze the rising grief as it claws away, threatening to consume me.

On the fateful day that my close friend and vet tells me there is no hope, time stands still. I become a figure who is on the outside, looking on. I simply cannot fully be in that moment. My friend has barely finished speaking when I dial Roy's number. He is my rock, and I am utterly broken and shattered when I share this devastating news as I stand in the vet's rooms holding my Molly in my arms. Roy is supportive and gentle and offers to fly down to Cape Town to be with me, but I decline. I realise that in my deepest hour of need, he is my safe place, my rock, and the person I can lean on.

I spend the whole day lying with my Molly at the vet, in the courtyard outside, with her resting on my tummy and chest. She sleeps, and it is hard to believe that she is dying; that I will have to leave her soon. I stroke her, hug her, and tell her how much I love her. I tell her what a joy she has been to me. Her coat is soft and silky. Her breathing, even and quiet. I kiss her nose and scratch her ears. The tears run uncontrollably down my face in salty rivers. I am in shock and find it all unreal. I simply cannot think of my life without her, so I focus on the precious minutes we have left. She is bloated, as her organs are shutting down, and she is unable to stand.

Time ticks by slowly, and I am grateful to spend the entire day loving her and holding her. This pain is like nothing I have ever experienced before. Nothing can be compared to the razor blade that cuts through my heart, stripping me of every iota of happiness, as I fall into the deep devastation and trauma of her dying.

I go onto autopilot, and I simply exist. At 16:15, I move to the comfort room and lie on the floor next to her as she sleeps on the big cushion they have on the floor. As he attaches the needle to her drip with the medication that puts her to sleep, I freeze and can't breathe. A deep sob emerges that I am forced to stifle, as I don't want Molly to feel my anxiousness or my pain. Molly flinches as the medication enters her system, and very soon, she is still. It looks like she is just deep in sleep. I lie with her and hold her for the last time. I get up in a daze and walk to my car. I feel that it is all surreal and that I am on the outside, observing this person who gets into her car. The disconnect is huge and is the only way I can deal with this loss right now.

My days are filled with intense mourning. I have had to come to Cape Town. Each day that passes, I dread the thought of returning to Nuwerus without her. This was her heaven on earth for four months of her precious 6-year life. I feel like I will never be happy again. My dear friend Dave drives me to Nuwerus, as I can't find the strength to go there on my own. Roy calls often to check in on how I am doing. He offers to fly me to Durban to spend time with him, but I decline, as it would not be fair to his new girlfriend, or to him, for that matter.

I know that my heart will mend, slowly but surely. I know that in time, I will look back with less hurt and pain. I know that I will be able to focus on the gratitude of her existence. Our animals are all on loan, and we are destined to outlive them. I just never imagined her life would be so short. Her three months in Nuwerus were the happiest moments of her life. She loved the freedom of leash-free walks and of bounding down the dusty town roads. She would greet all the other dogs and run up and down the fences, playing a make-believe game of catch. Everyone knew her name. The long, winding road up the hill was our morning walk, and these were our most carefree times. Often, she would run ahead, but always turned back after a while to check that I was following her. She would sniff often, and one day, she barked in amazement when we encountered a tortoise!

The gazillion smells were a dog's perfect dream, and she could take as long as she liked to smell and sniff in the quiet stillness of a road with virtually no traffic. I am able to find some aspect of happiness knowing that although she was only six, we packed a huge amount of adventure into our time together. She travelled everywhere with me. We were rarely apart.

I mourn, not the love of a human, but a dog. A totally different encounter, and my most valued to date. My best-ever relationship and my happiest. My Molly. My Moo. My companion. You are missed today, tomorrow, and all the days thereafter.

CHAPTER 35
ROY ROCKS MY BOAT

It is six months since Roy moved on, and his birthday is coming up in August, a couple of weeks away. We have become good friends and stayed in touch. I have been open and honest and tell him that I love him, even if he is with someone else. It is weird to me that I love him so much from a distance but back off when he is present and close up. It feels like he is just too much of everything. He is a very big presence, and this is daunting.

I have an outgoing personality coupled with a very quiet one, and I can't do either all the time, but too much noise affects my ability to calm my mind and be still. I figure, however, that we will succeed in a deeply connected friendship based on our shared traumas of life. Our offbeat interests, our love of life, our ability to be crazy, wacky yet deep, humble, and most of all, grateful for all the small things in life. He expresses gratitude often. He is appreciative and kind. He honours his girlfriend at this time and never oversteps the mark. I never get the feeling he is keeping me in the wings or boosting his ego. I like that he does this.

His girlfriend lives in another province and is a businesswoman. She is attractive and dresses well. Probably a bit too classy, but then the province she hails from is all about money and status. I don't see this working, but I leave it to run its own course and encourage him and tell him that I just want him to be happy. I write a small speech for his birthday party that I have been invited to but decline. I ask one of his good friends to please read it aloud at his party.

A mountain of a man with a voice that booms

You will know he is around, for silence is not the sound

A heart of gold with an ocean wide smile

So loyal and true and seldom ever blue

Incredibly generous of heart, kind, caring and arty
He will lift you when down and behave like a clown
You will smile ever so wide as you laugh oh so large
I am lucky to know this Mick Jagger of mine
Crazy, wacky, eccentric and also very smart
He writes like a dream, so talented and so supreme
A Matriarch man who embodies legacy and more
A friend you can lean on and one you can trust
Don't let us down, DO the Zulu war dance
Stomp your feet and move your body to party
As only you can!

I leave a voice note on the big day. It will be fabulous weather in KwaZulu Natal while those of us in Cape Town freeze. When a few days go by and he doesn't mention my speech, I feel a little sad. It is unusual for him. He will always say thank you. Two weeks go by, and then he calls. He is going to a 30-year school reunion and would love it if I came along as his friend. It is highveld territory, and I have not been to Gauteng, never mind the highveld, in forever. It reminds me of Zimbabwe, where I was born. I ask him if his girlfriend will mind, and he says, "Oh no, we broke up after my birthday." We actually only ever met twice, and she simply was not my type. I don't ask him to elaborate, as I will get all the details when I see him.

On the drive up—he drove up from Kwa Zulu Natal—I say to him jokingly, "So what are we going to introduce me as? Your GF (girlfriend) or your BF (best friend)?" We often talk in code and are always on the same page. He smiles, raises his eyebrows, and says nothing, but the look is one of love. and

ROY ROCKS MY BOAT

I say, "Listen, you should be so lucky to call me a GF again! I am your Best Friend and don't you forget it!"

We arrive as the sun is setting, casting long tree shadows and soft lighting. The Lodge is beautiful, nestling among large thorn trees; there is a river running through the grounds and rolling hills on either side. It occurs to me how good it is to be with him again, and we have not stopped smiling and laughing. He has been attending these events every ten years, and in the past his wife would accompany him. I love every minute of our time together and enjoy meeting all the people he was at school with. There is a lot to be said for history and friendships that have spanned in some instances since Junior School—42 years! Most of the couples have been married forever, and only one person there is doing marriage for the second time around. There are only about 50 people, so it's not a big group for a school that had 1000 matric pupils. It was a co-ed boarding school. But for those who had made the effort, it's a great occasion. There are old photos on display and some school albums. This makes for a great read, camaraderie, and connection. I am touched to be at this special occasion with so much history.

At dinner he refers to "The Vrou" (Afrikaans word for wife), and it is not me. I add to this by saying with the wave of a hand, "Oh, I am the ex-girlfriend!"

He laughs and says, "Only she broke up with me." I love him for saying that. He has no ego, and it's not even true!

By the end of the weekend, we have decided that we would like to move to an exclusive relationship without any titles. I understand that this will make life a lot easier for him, as he puts himself under a lot of pressure to be in touch, writing long messages, and it's all very consuming. It strikes me that this is precisely why our relationship fell apart. He was putting in way too much effort, and I felt overwhelmed by it all and burdened. Now that this was all out the way, we were both happy and content.

We fall into a rhythm; he visits me in Cape Town, and I visit him in Kwa Zulu Natal. We see each other about once every three months. Each time I see him, it is better and better. We get to know one another well. He spoils me, and we see Bryan Adams in Pretoria, and we attend the Straab concert in Mozambique. It is at this concert, on the last night, that he looks at me and says, "I love you, My Susan. Thank you for giving me another chance."

I look at him adoringly and say, "I loved you from day one, and that has never changed."

I have met my soul mate, and I am complete. I fit in well with his circle of friends, and we feel like we have been together for years. My friends adore him too. We are both conscious of time ticking and how special and lucky we are. We live for the moment. We see nothing more than having the most amazing time when we are together. It works for him, and it works for me.

CHAPTER 36
IN CONCLUSION

I am concluding this book with what I have learned. We are all unique, and this is not an attempt to give you answers or to guide you, as I have guided myself. Some women will have way more experience in this department than I do, and some will have way less. Each of us has our "own uniqueness" that makes us tick. If, however, you find some nuggets in the book that teach or enlighten you, then this will make the book worthwhile. If nothing else, I hope it is a fun read, as I enjoyed writing this, my first book, enormously.

Try to always be honest with yourself when you go online or when you date someone. Use current pictures. The biggest complaint from men whom I met is that a lot of the women do not look like their pictures; they are sometimes older and have let themselves go. The same can be said of men too!

If you're serious about meeting someone you would like to see long-term, then be the best version of yourself that you can be. Set that goal; lose some weight, get fitter, and look after yourself. You are your best investment. We owe it to ourselves to take care of us first. If we do this, we free up energy for others and do not get depleted!

Be realistic about yourself and "shop" in the same physical department. Don't shoot for the stars if you are not a star yourself. There is room in this dating world for ALL of us. Chemistry is often not about how attractive or good-looking someone is. Some of my pointers that I look for are: How generous and how kind are they? How do they treat beggars on the street? Are they funny, witty, unselfish, considerate, and prepared to listen to your guidance in the bedroom? Men can be egotistical—as can women—so, when they are sure they are superb lovers and they are not, guide them. Most men are open to this kind of guidance and want to hear what you like! Trust me, we are all very different. There is no standard manual out there for how it has to be done. I am amazed at how many men say they have never had open discussions or talks about sex or guidance of any kind.

Educate yourself and do research on Tantra—this is a great way of understanding both female and male anatomy, and there is a lot to learn—I was astounded at how many pleasure zones there are in the vagina alone! Stretch your boundaries!

If you are uncomfortable sexually, seek help. A love connection with amazing sex is priceless. I am not talking about mind-blowing sex, where you "act" out his fantasies or pleasure him like a pro. By all means, this can be a turn-on for men, but don't compromise your chance for a deeper connection that ticks all your emotional boxes. We are women, and our emotional boxes are number 1, by and large.

One of my dates proceeded to tell me how his ex would dress up and that this in fact was not a turn-on after a while. Ask your man what he likes, and if this is something he would enjoy, before you don the outfits to "perform," as this in essence undermines your connection without you realising it, and you are avoiding yourself in the process.

Watch out for the perfect profile photo that looks like it should be in a magazine or an advert, because that is exactly what it is! Usually only one photo, and if there are a few more, they are also perfect.

The best profiles are the ones with about five to six pics as this tells a lot. For example, he rides a bicycle, he loves his dog, he has different looks, he plays musical instruments, etc. This also sorts the rats from the mice for me!

I soon exchange phone numbers when I am suspicious, and I leave a voice note at the onset, asking them to do the same.

When they text and don't voice note, that's a glaring red flag! I also ask for more photos and if they are on Facebook or Instagram. If they say yes but supply no further information, you pretty much are onto them and can delete their numbers and block them without wasting time.

Time-wasting is another thing I am very conscious of. If you apply some of the things I have learnt, you will save yourself a lot of time and energy. Endless talking because they are away, on a business trip, or live elsewhere often ends because it gets too tedious, too time-consuming, and just too demanding. More importantly, I don't care what anyone says; you simply cannot experience chemistry without pheromones.

If you are a seasoned online dater, then chances are you are already savvy. However, we forget how many women become first-time daters due to a partner passing away, a divorce, or simply ending a journey that is no longer fulfilling. I am also aware that those who are savvy continue to learn, as I have.

Some of this is basic information; our younger counterparts are way savvier, switched on, and aware, than we are! I'm not sure that many women want to ask their children for guidance on this!

Use a paid-for site, and one that is a little pricier than others. This too sorts the men from the boys. Also, use sites that ask for a lot of information. It can be rather time-consuming when you load your profile, and you may feel inclined to skip some questions and say very little. However, my experience is that the more information you give, the better your match quality. Take your time, as this is your "best shot" and worth the time, effort, and energy. Go for that makeover if you are feeling nervous, anxious, and daunted by it all!

Accept that you are in a shop on a shelf, so to speak! It's hard to get one's head around that in the beginning, but the more realistic one is, the easier it is to move forward. Be aware that everyone is shopping—both you and him are! You will perhaps be picked up off the shelf, handled a bit, and then put back, and that is okay, because in essence, you will do the same as well. It's how this game works, and it's not a train smash if he prefers someone else, because you will too, at some point.

Know that most online daters are talking to more than one person at any given time. There is, sadly, always that thought lurking in the back of most minds: maybe there is someone nicer than them, or someone "likes" your profile and sends a cheeky message, and this piques your interest momentarily. This is okay. As you go along, you will learn about these things and navigate them as you see fit. You can reply thanking them and explain you have just met someone and will therefore not be chatting.

There are no hard and fast rules! Someone "liked" me, and I mentioned that as I had already met someone, I was not going to engage with him; I was not into shopping and was committed to this connection, encounter, friendship, attraction, or whatever you choose to call it. When my liaison sadly ended, I sent him a message to say it had not worked out and gave the reasons. I sent him my number to allow for WhatsApp communication. He seemed quite fun when I told him initially that I was seeing someone. He had said, "Leave him and come with me; let's FaceTime." I had read that response in the completely wrong vein!

He later sent me a message saying, "Hi, its Mike." I left him a voice note explaining what had happened, and his response was curt, "I don't believe your story, and now that you're no longer with him, you expect me to be interested. I am your second choice!" Needless to say, I simply deleted him after that and blocked any further contact. The word "issues" came across loud and clear.

Be aware that when you are online on most dating apps, anyone you may be talking to can see when you're online and may feel offended. You may feel the same! Being online does not necessarily mean the person is not keen on you; they may just be telling someone they were talking to that they are now talking seriously to another person, and therefore the conversation will cease. The rule of thumb is that once a couple is intimate, you both take yourself off the dating app. Have this discussion early so that the understanding is clear! Be aware that unsubscribing is always difficult, by design. Often you think you are unsubscribed only to find at the end of the month another payment has gone off. Make sure you are!

I am convinced that dating apps allow fraudsters, as this gives them income. Often a new profile appears, and it is glaringly obvious that the person is fake! If you have a slight feeling of fake, then trust your gut! A great pic, usually only one or two; or little information. A dead giveaway is their communication skills and spelling. Ask for a contact number and call them randomly! This is a sure way to cut the process dead! I mentioned this in one of the chapters. When they ask you to email, delete!

Sadly, I have to admit that when I discover that a man has no money and is not self-sufficient, it's a turn-off for me, and I am honest enough to admit this. I worked at age 14, during weekends and in school holidays, to earn money and support my needs. I am hugely afraid of having no money; it's my biggest insecurity. I spent my life working hard to ensure that I could take care of my financial needs and live out my last days with sufficient money. No matter how amazing that person is, I am just too damaged and insecure to take any chances. I wish that I could be like some of my friends or, for that matter, like my mother, who never owned anything, not even a car at age 70, but who firmly believed her ship would come in and managed to keep the wolf from the door, working till she died. I simply cannot. People may think I am shallow and that I love based on money. I am attracted to ambitious, career-orientated individuals who are driven, so the end result is usually a good income.

Know who you are; be clear on what you are looking for, and don't settle for less just because you are older. I have had three great loves in my life. Lastly, you are never too old to date online! Never! Being older is being wiser and smarter. Lastly, don't be hell-bent on finding The Great Love of your Life. You are the great love of your life! Dating online, or off line, is simply meeting different people, meeting a more varied kind of person, having a wider circle to choose from, and forming friendships that will often outlast love!

Go online; what you don't know, you simply cannot form an opinion on. Those who usually have a negative stance have not been online. Some women get scammed, but some women also have car accidents, fall, or hurt themselves physically. Nobody is 100% protected. At 30, my closing line when launching my own business was: "If you go with this concept, you have nothing to lose and everything to gain." It went on to be a hugely successful statistics business for the real estate industry that had been tried before, unsuccessfully! We succeeded.

NEVER PART WITH MONEY, EVER, no matter how real he sounds or how sad his story is, like how his ex has cleared their account. He will say all the right things. The quickest way to expose him is to say that you have just had the same thing happen and were hoping he could loan you some money. He will disappear from your screen in seconds!

Susan Harrison? Tragically, you died at 18.
At 10 years old, nothing could have prepared me for this loss.
It happened to other people.
Not to us. But it did.

Susan Harrison, my sister, my heroine.
My all, my everything. A mother, a best friend, my teacher, my joy,
my safe place, and the person I trusted most in the world.
So many years later, you are present once again, part of my life.
Giving my life a voice, a story, and a journey for others to share.

All names, including mine, have been changed, but every word in the
book is true with some minor poetic license to protect all who are
part of this story.

An autobiography about dating that started online and morphed into
so much more.

Susan Harrison, you tell the story perfectly. Just as I would have,
and have done, with you.

9 7 8 1 0 3 7 0 3 1 4 9 6